1, 2, 3, 8

BRITISH OPINION AND THE
AMERICAN REVOLUTION

BRITISH OPINION AND THE

AMERICAN REVOLUTION

By

DORA MAE CLARK, Ph.D.

NEW YORK / RUSSELL & RUSSELL

1966

CONTENTS

PREFACE

THE first suggestion that I investigate the subject of British opinion in its relation to the American Revolution came from Dr. Annie Héloise Abel who was at that time a member of the history department of Smith College. To her I owe not only assistance in preparing the first brief paper in this field, but also the encouragement to continue my graduate work at Yale University under the direction of Professor Charles McLean Andrews. While a student at Yale I acquired from lecture and seminar courses a broader background for my study of the revolutionary period, while continuing my research in the original sources of the period. For every step of the progress I owe a deep debt to Professor Andrews who has not only contributed generously from his wide knowledge of British and colonial history, but has also given invaluable assistance in shaping the material of this essay, which in its original form was a doctoral dissertation at Yale University, into final form for publication. To Dr. Allen Johnson, now editor of the *Dictionary of American Biography*, and to Professor Clive Day of Yale University I am also indebted for criticism of the original manuscript.

Without the friendly assistance of trained librarians the work of the student would be greatly increased. My experiences have led me to appreciate most fully the never failing courtesy of the members of the library staff at Yale University. I have reason to remember also with pleasure the opportunities for study opened to me at the Widener Library, Harvard University, the Boston Public Library, the New York Public Library, Columbia Univer-

sity Library, the British Museum, and the Public Record
Office in London.

In conclusion I wish to acknowledge also a debt of
gratitude to those who have helped me in preparing the
manuscript, and to those other loyal friends who in in-
numerable ways have contributed to this work more than
they perhaps realized.

D. M. C.

Wilson College,
   Chambersburg, Pa.,
     February 9, 1929.

CHAPTER I

THE STATE OF PUBLIC OPINION IN GREAT BRITAIN, 1765-1783.

"AMERICA furnishes matter for disputes in coffee-houses, sometimes warm, but without abuse or ill nature, and there it ends. It is unfashionable and even disreputable to look askew on one another for difference of opinion in political matters; the doctrine of toleration, if not better understood, is thank God, better practiced here than in America."[1] Thus, in 1775, spoke Samuel Curwen, exile from America, driven because of his Tory principles to take refuge in England.

The distance from which merchants in the London and Bristol coffee-houses viewed American affairs gave them a perspective which patriots congregating in the taverns of Boston, Massachusetts, obviously lacked. For that reason, as Samuel Curwen found, Englishmen were more tolerant of dissenting opinions in regard to America than were the colonists themselves. Furthermore, the American plantations were for Great Britain only one of many interests. In the eyes of British officials and the British public, difficult foreign relations and serious domestic unrest tended to dwarf the importance of colonial affairs. There was constant danger of war with France or Spain; and when, in 1778, France opened hostilities against Great Britain, the struggle with the colonies paled into insignificance. Ireland was restless under British rule, and threatened to take advantage of England's difficul-

---

[1] *The Journal and Letters of Samuel Curwen*, Boston, 1864, p. 39.

ties. For several years the case of John Wilkes obscured all other questions in home politics; but the government was aware only of a general discontent among the people. Officials failed to suppress the attacks of opposition writers; and in the period of the American Revolution the administration suffered from the liberty, not to say license, of the British press. An occasional bread riot called attention to economic grievances. Idle cotton spinners protested against the use of horse and water power, and in a frenzy of destruction made havoc with the new machines which cheated them of their employment. Ferment among the starving laborers and the political liberals, imminence of foreign war and an Irish revolt, although indirectly related to colonial conditions, distracted the attention of the British people from the immediate concerns of America.

Before 1765 the preoccupation of Englishmen with their own affairs had resulted in a general indifference to America and an ignorance of her problems. Colonial questions were left to politicians and merchants. Even officials, burdened with other business, knew too little about the provinces to make regulations entirely suited to provincial needs, or to appoint governors well fitted for their tasks. Comparatively few Englishmen ever visited America; few cared to travel in that distant land. Unless primarily interested in politics or trade, they were inclined to forget about the colonies until personal injuries brought America suddenly to their attention. This lack of interest in colonial affairs should not seem strange to us when we reflect that even Americans, who were naturally concerned in whatever happened to their country, were apathetic until Samuel Adams aroused them to revolt. In spite of Adams many Americans continued to ignore the philosophy of the Revolution, and to take no part in the campaigns. Backwoodsmen had

quite as many quarrels with their brother colonists of the
seacoast as with the British government, and hesitated
to neglect their harvests in the cause of independence.
The statement that a minority fought and won the Revolution has become a commonplace. In view of the fact
that many Americans were indifferent to their relations
with the mother country, the interest which the revolt
provoked in England is significant. After 1765 even Englishmen outside the official and mercantile classes were
obliged to recognize the existence of America, and to acknowledge the intimate relation between colonial contentment and British prosperity. In spite of other distractions,
the American revolt compelled the attention of the British
public; and almost in a night, the colonies became a subject of popular discussion.

Samuel Johnson's contemporaries, who had always
prided themselves on their general intelligence, now realized that they were more ignorant of America than of almost any other part of the world. A correspondent for
Lloyd's Evening Post and British Chronicle suggested
that the government ought to undertake a systematic investigation of the customs, history, and geography of the
interior of North America, for the sake of educating the
English people.[2] When the possibility of losing the colonies first presented itself, Englishmen began to consider
as never before the importance of those provinces. Books
about America found a ready sale.[3] Authors who knew
little of the new world presumed upon the ignorance of
their readers, and capitalized their own slight knowledge
and fertile imaginations. To meet the need for informa-

---

[2] Dec. 30, 1771—Jan. 1, 1772. This newspaper will hereafter be cited as
Lloyd's.

[3] *London Magazine,* June, 1771. Review of Wynne's *A General Survey of
the British Empire in America.* "The importance of the American colonies
to the British empire gives us a favorable impression of every work which
appears calculated to render them better known to the mother country."

tion, ex-governors, familiar with America, wrote learned
treatises. So popular were these works that repeated
editions scarcely supplied the demand.[4] Theorists found
in the relation of the colonies to the mother country a convenient field for speculation, and their writings appealed
to a surprisingly large number of readers.[5]

In the eighteenth century the pamphlet was the popular medium for the propagandist and the reformer. A
cause was indeed hopeless if it could not find a pamphleteer, for the world and his wife, if we ignore the illiterate
masses, were not only reading but writing pamphlets.
These small books had many advantages. They were in-
expensive and convenient to handle. They reached a
larger audience than the orator in the House of Commons. They were not necessarily the work of the man of
genius, as the temporary character of most of these writings testifies; but the greatest literary light of his age did
not scorn to appeal to the public through the pages of a
pamphlet. Observing the power of pamphleteering, government officials made use of Samuel Johnson, John Lind,
Adam Ferguson, John Shebbeare, and James Macpherson to defend administration policies.[6] Sometimes the
government paid for the printing of their works. More
often a pension to the author or to some member of his
family was the reward for loyal writings. Partisans in
the controversy between America and Great Britain
made the years of conflict more bitter with their publications. Even the laws concerning libel could not check the
pamphleteers, and no one may expect to find in the pam-

    [4] For example: Thomas Pownall, *The Administration of the Colonies*,
six editions.
    [5] For example: Richard Price, *Observations on the Nature of Civil
Liberty*, fifteen editions.
    [6] See articles in the *Dictionary of National Biography* under first four
names. *The Correspondence of King George the Third*, London, 1928, V, 414,
for Macpherson.

phlet literature of the eighteenth century an unbiassed statement of facts. The contemporary reader was happy to see his own views corroborated, or angry to see them refuted. For the modern historian the pamphlets of that period are a rather uncertain mirror of public opinion, because like the pier glass they are untrustworthy, flattering or distorting the object which they reflect. The reality of public opinion is hard to find, but fortunately the historian has other sources for the period of the American Revolution than the pamphlets.

Even the critical British public of that time refused to be satisfied with the ideas of men, who were perhaps as ignorant as themselves; they demanded facts from which they could draw their own conclusions. Booksellers proffered maps of North America, and sold copies of the colonial charters which led to disputes about the fundamental relationship between Great Britain and her colonies. Several magazines contained not only information about current literature, science, and commerce, but also political discussions and summaries of recent events. Controversies over colonial affairs enlivened the pages of the *Gentleman's Magazine,* the *London Magazine,* the *Monthly Review,* the *Universal Magazine,* and *Scots Magazine,* not to mention a number of other monthly publications of shorter duration. The literature of the eighteenth century had a distinctly political flavor, indicating the growing interest of the English people in affairs of government. Parliamentary debates were almost as popular as the races.

Before the American Revolution printers had begun to disregard, or to evade in one way or another, rules against printing accounts of parliamentary proceedings. Early in the eighteenth century the *Gentleman's Magazine* published reports of "Debates in the Senate of Great Lilliput," in which the "Hurgoes" represented the House of Lords, and the "Clinabs," the Commons. To avoid the penalty of the law, printers rearranged the letters in the names of the actual speakers without disguising their identity. Because outsiders were forbidden to take notes in either house, reporters wrote the debates from memory. William Woodfall, of the famous family of printers, was skilled in this art. After listening with concentration to a debate lasting several hours, he is said to have been able to return to his room and write down the speeches, in many instances word for word. A simpler method of picking up information was to wander about among the tables in the coffee-houses frequented by members of parliament, listening to the conversation. In this way John Almon, probably the best known publisher of his day, obtained material for the parliamentary debates which in 1771 appeared regularly in the *London Evening Post*.[7] Dr. Johnson probably composed his reports from the same sources. In 1771 the House of Commons tried to stop a practice which had proved most embarrassing to the government. The Commons decided to revive a resolution of 1728 declaring it a breach of privilege for any person to give to the newspapers an account of the proceedings of the house or of any committee. An order for the prosecution of eight London newspapers followed, for by that time, newspapers as well as magazines were keeping the public informed on parliamentary business. The order resulted in a conflict between the magistrates of the city of London and the officers of parliament as to their respective jurisdictions. Parliamentary officers were placed in such a ridiculous position in the course of this contest that the government was glad to use the prorogation of parliament as a pretext for discontinuing the

---

[7] A. Andrews, *History of British Journalism*, London, 1859; and H. R. Fox-Bourne, *English Newspapers*, London, 1887, contain accounts of these methods of reporting parliamentary debates.

case against the printers.[8] From that time on, newspapers and magazines were comparatively free to print accounts of parliamentary debates; and during the period of the American Revolution readers of the London papers could keep in fairly close touch with government policies. By 1774 the *London Magazine* was printing debates, using the real names of the speakers, without danger of prosecution. Although years passed before division lists were made public, electors had a chance to learn the opinions of their representatives through the publicity given to parliamentary debates. Constituents then made a serious attempt to instruct members of the House of Commons during sessions, and to hold them responsible to the electorate through pledges made before the election. Newspapers thus contributed one element to the growth of representative government.

The popular demand for information about current events gave rise to the publication of Burke's summaries in the *Annual Register;* to the collection of scattered documents concerning the American situation, as for example Almon's *Prior Documents;* and also to the rapid increase in the circulation of newspapers. Between 1760 and 1782 newspaper circulation increased from 9,464,790 to 15,272,519, annually. The excitement over the war must have been partly responsible for this growth, because by 1790 the circulation had dropped to 14,035,639.[9] But newspapers at the price of twopence or twopence halfpenny, were a luxury which the common man could scarcely afford. Taxes, both on the paper itself and on the advertisements which it carried, tended to discourage the publishers. High postage rates hindered the circulation of city papers in remote districts. Such provincial centers as Bristol, York, and Coventry had their own news sheets;

[8] *Journals of the House of Commons,* reprinted 1803-1804, XXXIII, 142.
[9] A. Andrews, *History of British Journalism,* I, 211 and 236.

but their editors copied freely from the London papers, contributing little original matter except items of purely local interest. In the period of the American Revolution seventeen papers were published in London, and seven of these were dailies. But in spite of the rapid increase of the circulation of these papers, the number did not begin to supply the public adequately. The estimated circulation for 1775 was 12,680,000, or a daily average of about 34,-730. These rough calculations are sufficiently accurate to show that many of the 7,000,000 inhabitants of England remained in ignorance of what was going on in the world, shared a newspaper with friend or neighbor, or depended upon some other means than the newspaper for their information.[10]

As a matter of fact, one news sheet could serve a remarkably large number of people, especially if it found its way into a tavern or coffee-house. Masters of the coffee-houses made a practice of subscribing to several newspapers for the convenience of their guests. Politics was a favorite topic of conversation. Although scorned by Samuel Curwen, the American loyalist, as the "resort of newsmongers and political dabblers," the coffee-house, nevertheless, performed a valuable service to the public in helping to circulate the news of the day.[11] In the villages the tavern was the common meeting place of the community. The tavern keeper was often the best informed man of his class in the village; and was considered an authority on politics. He had the advantage of constant contact with travellers. The post-boy stopped there to deliver letters for the villagers. From the tavern keeper or his guests the illiterate rustic first learned of Lexington or Bunker Hill, then carried the news home to

[10] *Journal of the Royal Statistical Society*, 1913, LXXV, 286, for estimate of population.
[11] *The Journal and Letters of Samuel Curwen*, p. 158.

his good wife for her to pass on to a neighbor. In the cities, at the taverns and coffee-houses, and in the clubs, the repeal of the Stamp Act was debated more hotly than in parliament itself. The haphazard method of distributing news through the coffee-house or the tavern had its disadvantages, for a tale was bound to gain or lose something in the telling. Accounts of the French alliance or the surrender at Yorktown, heard at Lloyd's or the King's Arms, were far from accurate, but since there was a dearth of reliable sources of information, even newspaper correspondents depended quite largely upon the conversation in the coffee-houses for their reports. A conscientious editor might introduce news of the tavern with some such phrase as " 'Twas rumored at the King's Arms" or "A ship's captain, lately arrived from New York, declares." The difficulty of finding facts was a serious one, complicated by the slowness of communication.

According to twentieth-century standards any news from America was already stale when received in England. The voyage from the colonies occupied from four to six weeks even in the best weather, and when storms drove sailing vessels from their course, several more weeks might be lost in the passage. Even the carrying of mail from one part of England to another was subject to serious delay. From the time of Charles II until 1784, when the introduction of mail coaches revolutionized the service, post-boys, sleepy old men on decrepit horses, carried letters and papers from one town to another at the rate of four miles an hour. Between London and Bristol light carts were utilized; but a letter from Bristol or Bath to London took fully two days.[12] Correspondents who had urgent business preferred to trust their communications to private messengers or to accommodating

[12] John Latimer, *Annals of Bristol in the Eighteenth Century*, printed for the author, 1893, pp. 457-458.

travellers, who could make the journey in somewhat shorter time. But slow as transport might be, news eventually penetrated to the far corners of the kingdom; and in comparison with previous ages, people of the eighteenth century were well informed about contemporary events. Even if the news was old and statements inaccurate, readers yet had the advantage over earlier generations of a press comparatively free from governmental influence, able to publish opinions of the opposition as fully as those of government sympathizers.

The *Public Advertiser,* for example, though favoring the opposition, opened its columns to friends as well as enemies of the administration. The appearance in this paper of the *Letters of Junius,* attacks upon the king and his ministers, made the *Public Advertiser* notorious. Report stated that this paper was read at court; and as a consequence, writers who wished to air their grievances before the king sought space in its columns. Although there were ministerial publications such as the *Royal Gazette,* labelled by its competitors, the ''Royal Lying Gazette,'' or the *Morning Post and Daily Advertiser,* controlled by a clergyman who proved his gratitude for a government pension, their prejudiced statements did not apparently deceive the public.[13] Several independent newspapers counteracted the effect of government publications. The *Middlesex Journal* under the proprietorship of Philip Thicknesse was the most extreme of the opposition papers, and knew no discretion in its attacks upon the government. *Lloyd's Evening Post,* one of the conservative journals, independent in its attitude toward government, but more restrained in its statements than were some of its competitors, emphasized matters of industry and commerce, and appealed to the great class of British merchants and traders. Editorial influence

---

13 *The Correspondence of King George the Third,* London, 1928, V, 471.

through these papers consisted in the choice and arrangement of facts, for there was no strictly editorial column.
Indeed the printer might be both editor and publisher.
A student could guard against the prejudice of one paper
by comparing accounts in other publications; but the
scarcity and price of news sheets tended to discourage
this scholarly practice. In spite of the publication of di-
verse opinions in the press, the ordinary individual found
it difficult to obtain an impartial statement of facts.

The reader of the daily paper had before him a harder
task than does the modern business man who takes his
morning news in one gulp, as he swallows his coffee. In
the first place, there were no headlines to furnish a short
cut to the news. The editor classified his items under only
two heads: foreign and domestic. With that one exception the printer threw everything together in a hodge-
podge of scandal, politics, crimes, commerce, religion,
executions, and lotteries. The treatment of every topic
except robberies, vices, and Tyburn hangings left much
to the imagination. Statements regarding trade, industry,
or politics were condensed into a couple of lines, or, at
most, a brief paragraph. The succinct sentence, however,
was often spicy with thinly veiled meaning; and the pi-
quancy of the briefly worded phrase was no mean rival
of the elaborate descriptions and expositions of modern
journalism. The newspapers commonly left to the magazines the fuller treatment of contemporary news; and the
magazines, like the newspapers, were generous in opening their pages impartially to colonial sympathizers and
government supporters. The pamphleteer, too, recognized no limit to his freedom of expression.

Because of the liberty of the British press in the period
of the American war, and because of the comparatively
well-informed public which existed then—a public well
qualified to form opinions—the historian can find in the

writings of the period a valuable source for the study of popular opinion.[14] The use of public expression of sentiments alone, however, may lead to unsound conclusions. Much of the contemporary writings was propaganda, and must be discounted as such. The student may correct public statements by reference to private views expressed in correspondence, memoirs, or other personal papers; but the surest guide to the views of the British public on the subject of the American colonies and the American Revolution is an account of the activities of the British people.

Men are more nearly true to their convictions in what they do than in what they say. For instance: as an expression of belief in the colonial cause, the refusal of a few army officers to bear arms against the colonies, especially if they lost the chance for advancement by so doing, carries more weight than the sentimental ravings of any number of British liberals on the subject of the natural rights of man. There is no better key to the activities, and hence to the interests, of the masses of the British people than the newspapers of the day.

By following the news reports in the spring of 1776, the twentieth-century reader can slip into the various coffee-houses, haunts of the merchants engaged in colonial trade, and can learn how British policy is affecting commerce. At the King's Arms Tavern the investigator comes upon an assembly of merchants planning a demonstration to convince the government that coercion of America will ruin British trade. A glance at another paragraph takes the reader down to the docks of London or Bristol where he sees whole fleets of merchant vessels idle, waiting, it may be, for the repeal of the Stamp Act.

[14] F. J. Hinkhouse, *Preliminaries of the American Revolution as Seen in the English Press, 1763-1775,* has considered this subject, but has omitted pamphlet material from his study.

With the next sentence the reader finds himself in Norwich, Birmingham, or Manchester, taking statistics on the number of unemployed laborers, out of work since colonial orders ceased. The reader takes up a news sheet of the year 1780, and enters a county meeting where the gentry are discussing the effect of the war upon their taxes and their rents. He finds that trouble with America is gradually affecting in one way or another an increasing number of the British people; and as he wanders about among these discontented groups, he picks up one expression here, another there, which tells him what Englishmen are thinking about the American Revolution. Growing curious about the London radicals, who constantly made trouble for the government, the reader steps into the Robinhood Society, while Burke is speaking on the subject of colonial policy, and notes the votes cast by the members on the question of the evening. One may even visit the Cocoa Tree and try to gauge public opinion by the way bets are being laid on the chance of conciliating the colonies. At a meeting of the Society for the Propagation of the Gospel in Foreign Parts, the secretary is reading reports of missionaries in America, urging the society to strengthen the church in the colonies by establishing a bishop there. The impartial reader must not ignore the attorney general who pores over his law books, seeking a precedent for some phase of colonial control; neither must he forget the chancellor of the exchequer who prepares a speech for the House of Commons, full of brilliant subterfuges, while he feels the tide of public opinion rising to engulf him and the ministry.

Public opinion was indeed a force with which the government was obliged to reckon. George III, who, in spite of his failures, was one of the cleverest politicians of his day, understood the value of popular support, or, lacking that, the importance of the semblance of public

approval. He begrudged neither money nor effort which
was spent in securing petitions favoring government
policy, or on pensions to pamphleteers who developed in
a convincing manner the arguments which his ministers
supplied, or to the newspaper editor who gave space only
to government sympathizers. If the opposition had been
able to agree on colonial measures, the government of
George III would have found it necessary to give still
more consideration to public opinion. Unfortunately,
policies that promised well for the merchants might cost
the country gentlemen dearly in taxation. Every man's
views about colonial matters were colored by the effect
of American measures upon his own affairs: upon his income from trade, from manufacturing, or from land rents.
The churchman cherished his pet project for America;
the politician, his. In attempting to humor first one group
and then another, officials gained the reproach of inconsistency in handling colonial problems, until they finally
determined to ignore particular business interests, and
considered only the political aspect of dependency. In the
meantime, members of the opposition were gradually
suppressing their differences, and finally concentrated on
their universal disapproval of the war. When public opinion crystallized on this point, the government that had
been prosecuting the war fell.

During the period of the American Revolution theories
about colonial control, the proper relationship between
America and the mother country, intrigued philosophers;
but abstract theory had little to do with the actual course
of events between 1765 and 1783. Merchants, country
gentlemen, and crown officials hoped to gain something
from the colonies; and their ideas about the passage of
the Stamp Act or the Boston Port Bill, or granting independence to America, were based respectively upon the
probable effect of those measures on commerce, the price

of land, and the power of the state. The personal interests of these various classes were often in open conflict; and disputes among them increased the difficulty of adjusting relations between Great Britain and her colonies.

CHAPTER II

INTERESTS, ACTIVITIES, AND OPINIONS OF THE MERCANTILE CLASSES.

I. PERIOD OF SUCCESS, 1763-1766.

In the colonial period America owed to the British merchant a debt embarrassingly large; and history cannot neglect him. Money loaned by London merchants launched the *Mayflower;* and traders as well as knights and gentlemen contributed to the stock of the Virginia Company. These heroes of finance made exploits in the new world possible.

Commercial expansion was the cry of the age. When Cartier and Roberval claimed the St. Lawrence in the name of Francis I, silver and gold from Mexico and Peru were already filling the royal coffers of Spain. Naturally James Stuart, king of England and Scotland, was inclined to welcome any suggestion for checking the power of his rivals. Practical men of business, hard-headed merchants, with long years of experience in trade with the East, convinced him that English settlements in America would be practical undertakings and advantageous to the crown.

Humiliating dependence upon the Baltic states for everything that made a navy possible seemed unnecessary when primeval forests were waiting for the woodsman's axe. Before the first English settlers had stepped on the shore of Virginia, lords of the admiralty were picturing proud fleets bearing from America pine for masts, oak planks, resin, tar, and other naval stores.

Harassed treasury officials dreamed of mines rich in the precious metals which nations of that day counted wealth. James himself doubtless let his imagination play with the idea of humiliating the haughty Spanish monarch. To plant an English colony on land which Philip III had claimed under the ancient bull of Alexander VI would cause consternation in the Spanish court. Meanwhile merchants, figuring their accounts, cheered themselves with the pleasant prospect of warehouses filled with colonial products or with merchandise ready for the American market. Long and disappointing years passed before many of these dreams came true. Some of the visions were phantasies rudely dispelled, but the merchants realized their dreams at last.

The colonies in America prospered as they grew in size and number, and because they were commercial as well as political dependencies British merchants shared in their prosperity. In fact, trade proved to be the strongest tie that bound America to the British Isles. The British navy became in time mistress of the seas, equal to the great task of protecting British commerce. No previous experience in England's history, however, prepared her to solve problems of colonial administration and control. Experiment followed experiment. If British merchants approved, if commerce thrived, government officials judged the experiment successful. Because England grew powerful as her trade expanded, officials gradually developed a mercantilist policy in colonial regulation—a policy framed for the protection and encouragement of commerce. Under the circumstances, British merchants became more influential in government than their slight representation in parliament would lead one to expect.[1] They ranked high in the unofficial councils of the realm, where they supported not only their own interests, but

---

[1] See *post*, chapter VII, for a discussion of representation in parliament.

also the interests of a silent multitude of industrial laborers and seamen.

According to Arthur Young's estimates, over one-third
of the population of England depended upon manufacturing and commerce for their livelihood.[2] Although America
was not the only market for British goods, the number of
people suffering from the ups and downs in American commerce was large enough to deserve attention. This great
trading population included merchants, manufacturers,
and the shipping interests. Of the three classes the merchants enjoyed the most peculiarly intimate relation to
the colonists, for the Americans were in their debt figura-
tively and literally. The enterprisers who sponsored the
infant settlements and advanced the capital which made
them possible continued to befriend the colonies when
politicians were too busy with intrigue to bother about
British subjects in America. The colonists received supplies of food which saved them from starvation, tools to
use in building homes, weapons to protect their lives from
the savage, whether they could pay for these things or
not. Even after one hundred years of colonial growth the
value of the manufactured goods which America imported from Great Britain was far greater than the value
of the raw materials which the colonists sent to the
mother country; and colonial trade with other parts of
the world failed to supply the Americans with sufficient
cash to discharge the remainder of their debts to British
merchants. Under these circumstances London and Bristol traders frequently accepted property in the colonies
as security for the payment of their debts, and became
consequently as concerned in American prosperity as
were the colonists themselves. Merchants studied the land

---

[2] Arthur Young, *Six Months Tour through the North of England,* London,
1770, IV, 569.

and the people; and they understood conditions in America better than most British officials.

Occasionally one member of a family or firm doing business in America would reside in the colonies, in order to keep in closer touch with the market. For instance, Henry Cruger, senior, lived in Rhode Island during the difficult period of the Revolution, while his son was the head of the firm in Bristol, England. In other cases British merchants hired factors or agents to represent them in American ports. The factors discovered new markets and developed the old. They took orders for British goods, received consignments from home, and delivered these to American retailers or consumers, taking in exchange colonial products or arranging for credit. Merchants in London, Bristol, and Liverpool usually accepted tobacco and other colonial products to sell on commission. Glasgow merchants, on the other hand, maintained stores or shops in the colonies, where their agents sold the goods sent out from the mother country.[3] In either case the British merchant was constantly in touch with colonial affairs. Frequent communications through long years of intercourse secured for him not only customers and debtors in the colonies, but friends as well.

Like the merchant, the manufacturer had a personal interest in the colonies; but his relation to America was indirect and less personal. Although by the time of the American revolt, the industrial era was under way in England, most of the manufacturing was still carried on in the home. Sometimes, however, a master workman owned a small shop where he employed a few journeymen and apprentices. Occasionally an enterpriser with a little accumulated capital furnished the wool or other raw material to the farmers or their wives in the dis-

---

[3] Public Record Office, Colonial Office Papers 5: 116, f. 107. (Henceforth cited as C.O.).

trict round about. He collected the finished goods, stockings or cloth as the case might be, and arranged for
their sale. It was impractical for even the enterpriser to
seek a market for his goods in America or other parts of
the world; and the British merchant was quick to discourage a practice which would have destroyed his own
business. Any manufacturer who tried to sell directly to
the colonies would have missed his usual orders when the
agents came down from London with commissions for
the spring fleet. British merchants were careful to keep
business in their own hands; and the manufacturers remained at work in the towns and signed formal contracts
for the delivery of their goods at a specified time. The day
had passed when the manufacturers from the small inland towns loaded their goods in wagons and rode or
walked beside them to London, to sell there to the highest
bidder.[4] The newer method was more efficient and eliminated a certain amount of risk. There was no chance,
however, for direct contact with America; and in the
absence of telegraph and cable, railroad, and swift trans-
marine service, there was a great gulf between the consumer in the colonies and the producer in England. The
manufacturer felt his dependence upon America, but
knew very little about that country.

The ships' captains and ordinary seamen were responsible for much of the American news which reached Great
Britain. Every merchant ship carried its bag of letters
and papers; and the officers often had business in England for their clients in America. They brought first-
hand information to eager listeners. They had personal
messages from friends, the latest gossip, news of politics
and business, which they mixed with wild tales of their
sea adventures, as they quaffed their ale in a favorite

[4] William Playfair, *The Commercial and Political Atlas,* London, 1786,
p. 14, note.

tavern. Many captains had spent their lives in the service; they realized the value of American trade. Even the ordinary seaman knew from personal experience when the colonial non-importation movement grew stronger. Sailors who were fortunate enough to find a ship ready to sail had to be satisfied with lowered wages; others rolled disconsolately along the streets of Liverpool or Bristol, missing the familiar planks beneath their feet.

When, on the other hand, relations between Great Britain and her colonies were normal, all branches of trade flourished. Merchants, manufacturers, and sailors were busy. The eighteenth century brought a greatly increased demand for British goods in America, for population grew by leaps and bounds. The trade with the American savage developed as the Indian trader pressed farther and farther into the interior of the country. This was especially true after 1763 when the French traders withdrew and left the field to the British. The manufacturing towns which supplied the colonies were scattered all over England, for every variety of British manufacture found a market in America.

Although the frontiersmen dressed in homespun and lived in log houses, using the rude furniture of their own construction, men in the seaboard towns were more dependent upon Great Britain. No picture of colonial days is complete without reference to British manufactures. Lace for the christening robe, silk and linen for the bride, black cloth for the mourner—these were imported. Nottingham hose in London slippers tripped lightly through the figures of old square dances; and ribbons woven in Spitalfields or Coventry fluttered in easy triumph at a governor's ball. On the Sabbath a London bonnet permitted only a modest glimpse of a pretty face, as the owner sat straight in a high-backed pew. Consciousness of broadcloth from Bradford or Melksham in Wilts added dignity to a courtly bow; and a gentleman carried himself with more assurance if he wore a hat from Newcastle. Even after 1773 colonial patriots took their Holland tea in cups from the potteries of Staffordshire. Guests were regaled with wine from English goblets; and colonial sideboards gleamed with plate which an English silversmith had fashioned.

Even in the more humble and prosaic walks of life the colonists were bound to their British brothers. The farmer sharpened his scythe and axe on an English grindstone. The painter imported his colors and lead; the glazier, his panes of glass. Carpenters' nails came from Dudley and Norwich. New England fishermen sailed out from Salem and Gloucester under canvas of English weave, equipped with nets and lines from Bridport in Dorset. Harvard and Yale filled their libraries with books of English print. Even the convict dangled at last from a length of English rope.[5]

In at least forty-seven different English towns from Newcastle-on-Tyne to Taunton in Somersetshire artisans were producing goods to meet the colonial demand. Wheels turned briskly at the bidding of spinners and potters. At Witney in Oxfordshire shuttles flashed in the looms, forming the woof of numberless blankets. At Manchester and Birmingham forges flamed and anvils rang. But months of unemployment followed the non-importation agreements, and hunger and misery dogged the footsteps of many humble workers. Merchants and manufacturers suffered, too; but the laboring poor were most keenly aware of the loss of colonial trade.

Exports to the colonies, however, included more than

[5] Public Record Office, State Papers Domestic, George III, 14, contain an interesting list of articles exported from Great Britain to America. Further information is found in the newspapers, and in the parliamentary journals in the many petitions from the manufacturing towns.

articles made by British workmen. Colonial housewives
prized the linens and laces from Flanders, Holland, and
Germany, as well as the products of Portugal, Spain, and
the East. British merchants made a double profit in exchanging English goods for foreign wares which found a
market in the colonies. Products of the East Indies coming through England to America often passed through
some process of manufacture, and so provided work for
the artisan as well as gain for the merchant. The American demand was varied; far more so than the products
which the colonies could give in exchange.

Ships from America brought to England a few raw
materials for manufacture: pig and bar iron for the steel
works, dye for English textiles, beaver for hats, and
whalebone for ladies' stays. Naval stores, tobacco, indigo,
and rice formed a large part of the cargoes moving east-
ward from the mainland colonies. These products were
so highly valued in Great Britain that parliament listed
them among the enumerated commodities which could be
sent only to England. Maine and New Hampshire exported timber and masts for the royal navy, indirectly
helping to clear the sea of pirates, and to make the ocean
highways safe for American as well as British commerce.
When there was a scarcity in Great Britain, merchants
imported American wheat flour, Indian corn, and salted
provisions. Furs, deer and other skins, train oil, beeswax, pot and pearl ashes, helped to make the balance of
trade more nearly even. To a certain extent, but never
quite completely, England achieved her ideal of a reciprocal relationship between the colonies and the mother
country, a state which modern writers have called "the
self-sufficing empire."

Colonial products never fully paid the American debt
to Great Britain. Bills of exchange on merchants trading
to the West Indies and other quarters of the world where

the Americans had credit covered a part of the remaining obligation; payments in cash discharged another fraction.[6] Although colonial seafarers brought back gold dust as well as slaves from their voyages to Africa, most of what little bullion the mainland colonies acquired came from their trade with the West Indies. New Englanders, who were the chief colonial traders, picked up a cargo wherever they could find one; but their best markets were among the Spanish and French of the Caribbean region. The British West Indies, however, needed fish from the Banks of Newfoundland, slaves from Africa, lumber, barrel staves, and provisions from the mainland colonies. The islands gave in exchange molasses, which the New Englanders turned into rum, bills of exchange, or bullion, for the balance of trade between New England and the southern colonies was always in favor of the north.

This trade with the British West Indies gained many friends for the colonists of the mainland. West Indian planters were dependent upon the other colonies for many necessaries, and they realized that their supplies might be cut off if friendly relations between Great Britain and America were broken. Samuel Estwick, assistant agent for the West Indies, declared: "Great Britain can neither support nor protect the West India Islands."[7] Because they relied upon supplies from America the landholders of the islands joined the British merchants in petitioning parliament and the crown for concessions to America and for the protection of American trade. In a complex commercial system injury to a single branch brings inconvenience, if not disaster, to the rest.[8] It is no wonder that the trading classes clamored at the doors of

6 British Museum, Additional Manuscripts, 33030, f. 215. (Henceforth cited as Add. MSS.)

7 *A Letter to the Reverend Josiah Tucker, D.D.*, London, 1776, p. 55.

8 Add. MSS., 33030, f. 146, report from Liverpool on injury to African trade.

parliament for the repeal of legislation which threatened to destroy their whole commercial system.

Yet even the mercantile classes had a suspicion that the colonies were not an unalloyed blessing, and the country gentry had long begrudged the favors which merchants demanded. The colonies were rapidly outgrowing the dependent, subordinate position they had occupied since their settlement. When Englishmen became aware of this fact they realized that British interests were in danger. Colonial success in fishing, American attempts at manufacturing and the resulting demand for British artisans, and perhaps most of all the increase in colonial commerce were causing uneasiness and even jealousy in Great Britain.

The New Englanders were the chief offenders, for they not only competed with Englishmen in the fisheries and in trade, but their seamen claimed exemption from impressment. Englishmen had fished off the Banks of Newfoundland before the American colonies existed, and British fishermen considered the New Englanders usurpers there. Even in 1706 the little fishing town of Poole in southern England complained that the New Englanders "much conduce to the ruin of the said fishery, by bringing rum, sugar, molasses, and tobacco, which is so closely coveted by the men employed in the fishery, and so closely followed that they neglect their business; the Americans also furnish them with provisions, shoes, hose, soap, nets, lines, etc., at an under rate than the English, who used to supply them therewith, can do, to their great prejudice, and at the end of the fishing season, carry away many fishermen, who would otherwise go for England and man the fleet."[9] Seventy years later another generation of English fisherfolk used the same reasons for approving

---

[9] *Commons Journals*, XV, 118. For further reference to colonial impressment, see chapter III, *post*, pp. 89 ff.

parliament's plan to punish New England. Colonies that
threatened to rival Great Britain in her own field had no
place in the mercantilist system. British merchants had
often proved their friendship for America, but they
frowned at the news that New Englanders were under-
bidding them in the Newfoundland market. When British officials learned how the colonists were cheating the
British navy, they shared the merchants' vexation. The
fisheries were a "school for seamen." Young sailors returning home with the fishing fleet were likely to find
themselves suddenly transferred to his Majesty's service,
but Americans claimed exemption from the press for
themselves and for all who took refuge with them. Even
the most loyal friends of America found it difficult to
defend New England against these accusations. Other
colonies suffered less from the attacks of English critics;
but certain charges rested heavily upon the whole American continent.

The colonists were guilty of luring to America the
youth and strength of England, the most valuable of all
resources—artisans to whom England owed commercial
power. Obscure workers in remote villages patiently,
day after day, spun and wove the cloth, forged and ham-
mered the steel, which made cargoes for British ships and
business for London merchants. But in months of idleness hungry men dreamed of Pennsylvania wheat fields
ripe for the harvest. A Welsh miner preferred to till the
soil in Pennsylvania rather than starve in Glamorgan.[10]
Linen weavers left the lowlands of Scotland to set up
their looms in the hills of North Carolina.[11] To Boston,
New York, and Philadelphia went craftsmen who were to
make the new world independent of the old—stocking
weavers from Nottingham, clothiers from Gloucester-

---

[10] *Middlesex Journal*, April 4, 1770.
[11] *Ibid.*, Feb. 13, 1770.

shire and Somersetshire, skilled watchmakers from London.[12] Cheap land and high wages were strong attractions; and when a Spitalfields weaver was starving in the shadow of a debtors' prison, he envied even the criminal who could secure free passage to America.[13]

The Americans were eager to welcome British laborers, and their crime was more than silent acquiescence as these workers deserted the homeland. An agent with an office near Cornhill offered advice and encouragement to prospective emigrants.[14] Even British newspapers connived at the ruin of British industry by printing advertisements for workers whose handicraft the colonists demanded.[15] American merchants offered passage money to secure the laborers who were most needed.[16] In vain British officials tried to stem the tide of migration. Laws passed in the reigns of the first two Hanoverians prohibiting the export of tools and instruments, and making it a crime to entice artisans from the country, were practically dead.[17] Suggestions for prosecuting the publisher of the *Daily Advertiser,* because he printed notices of opportunities in America, came to nothing.[18] The exodus went on unchecked. British officials even offered money for return passage, but without effect.[19] In the colonies infant industries threatened to mature and become competitors of the British.

More menacing than possibilities of future competition were the increasing debts of colonial importers. Most British merchants knew that the colonists would con-

12 *Ibid.,* Jan. 11-13, 1770; Dec. 14, 1769; April 11, 1770.
13 *Jopson's,* Aug. 24, 1767.
14 *Middlesex Journal,* April 11, 1770.
15 State Papers Domestic, George III, 12.
16 *Ibid.,* 11.
17 5 George I, c. 27; 23 George II, c. 13.
18 State Papers Domestic, George III, 12.
19 *Ibid.,* 11.

tinue to buy from England as long as their credit was good. In a new country where land was cheap and capital scarce, agriculture and other extractive industries were more profitable than manufacturing. In 1773 a bitterly sarcastic correspondent for the *York Chronicle* explained why the colonists would continue to buy British goods rather than make their own. "They [the colonists] can have as many goods as they need gratis, or at least paying for about one half of them. The truth of this extraordinary reasoning indeed, twenty great merchants on the 'Change of London have within these fifteen years fatally experienced, whose failures were for a sum not less than one million sterling; the estates of some of these unfortunate persons have never given a single farthing dividend; others have paid three fourths in the pound, some 7s. 6d., and some few 10s., all the remainder is so much clear gain or inheritance to the colonies; there can therefore not be the least reason to think that the Americans will ever be so stupid as to become manufacturers, they know their interest better, and will prefer giving their orders for goods to cloath themselves rather than be at the trouble to make them."[20] For years American buyers and British merchants were equally ready to abuse the credit system.

The distance between England and her American market furnished an excuse for extended credit and lax business methods. After the merchant had shipped goods to the colonies, months must pass before he could hope for a return from the sale. Although British exporters gave only six months' credit to Dutch and German traders, and even less to French, the colonists regularly demanded from one to three years'.[21] Barlow Trecothick, a London merchant with a large American business, was satisfied if

20 *York Chronicle*, Mar. 18-20, 1765.
21 *Lloyd's*, Feb. 10-12, 1766; Feb. 28-Mar. 3, Mar. 17-19, 1777.

he received his pay in eighteen months with six months' interest.[22] Many merchants waited longer—four or five years.[23] Merchants and manufacturers who shared the disadvantages of slow returns from America nursed a grievance against the colonies.

New England perhaps needed longer credit than the other colonies because she had fewer articles of her own to exchange for British imports. New England traders could procure bullion or bills of exchange to satisfy British creditors only by selling their own products in other parts of the world. Often the routes of New England trading ships were long and devious, extending from Newfoundland to Africa and back to the West Indies, perhaps even around the world. Southerners raised rice or tobacco for British markets; but they often yielded to the temptation of ordering from a commission merchant more than their own products were worth. Planters might be in doubt as to what their tobacco would bring months after their slaves had packed the last hogshead. The price of tobacco fluctuated widely. In the early years of the American Revolution profits on tobacco plantations were seldom large, and losses were often heavy. Under such circumstances American debts increased; and the colonists became dependent upon British capital.

In the middle of the eighteenth century the British share of responsibility for American financial dependence increased. Financiers were beginning to experiment with credit. Never before had capital been so easy to obtain; and bankers as well as independent money lenders grew reckless. A new generation of British merchants, doing business on borrowed capital, gave generous but unwise credit to colonial buyers. Young traders overemphasized the value of America as a market, and neg-

[22] Add. MSS., 33030, f. 93.
[23] *Ibid.*, f. 161.

lected the colonies as a source of raw material. Officials still tried to encourage production of naval stores, silk, flax, and other materials for manufacture; but British merchants disliked to bother with colonial products of uncertain value. They preferred to trust to future payments. Gradually land, houses, negroes and other chattels of colonial planters became British property; but there was no cash to satisfy the merchants' own creditors at home. During the American Revolution British merchants reaped a harvest of bankruptcies. American Sons of Liberty, celebrating the repeal of the Stamp Act, gave little thought to the plight of their British friends. While Americans rejoiced, the London merchant sat at his desk through the long hours of the night. Heedless of dead coals dropping in the grate, or the monotonous "All's well" of the watch, unmindful even of the scratching of his quill pen on the page, he added row after row of fateful figures, book debts against America. His attitude toward the colonies depended largely upon his own financial failure or success. Because neither American property nor book debts were worth much to the British merchant if the colonies revolted, successful traders tried to keep America contented under British rule. On the other hand, merchants whose American business had failed grew hostile toward the colonies. They chafed under the injustice of a situation which left them penniless while their debtors relaxed in comfort on some Virginia plantation. Merchants and manufacturers who feared colonial competition or were disgruntled by their own misfortunes hindered every effort to preserve harmony between Great Britain and her colonies.

Disunion in the ranks of the merchants was all the more disastrous to their interests because country gentlemen and government officials were beginning to have new ideas about the colonies—ideas that differed fundamen-

tally from mercantilist doctrine. Until 1763 Englishmen
had granted, though grudgingly, the preëminence of mercantile interests in colonial matters. Even in 1769 a pamphleteer wrote: "That the wealth and the power of Great
Britain depends upon its trade is a proposition, which it
would be equally absurd in these times to dispute or to
prove."[24] Representations of the Board of Trade and
laws of parliament show the influence of British merchants, who in return readily acknowledged their obligation to the government. Indeed the merchants realized so
keenly what they owed to parliament that many of them
could see no advantage in keeping colonies which were
independent of parliamentary legislation. In practical
ways, to say nothing of general policies, parliament
helped the merchant. An act of parliament passed in 1732
permitted British creditors to sue for the collection of
colonial debts in English courts, and to place an attachment upon the most valuable possession of a southern
planter, his slaves.[25] After parliament established in the
colonies a uniform rate of exchange for foreign coins,[26]
and prohibited the use of paper money,[27] British merchants were less likely to suffer from unstable money
values. Crown and parliament through the seventeenth
century and down to 1763 consistently subordinated all
other interests in America to the welfare of the British
merchant, for, in the words of the mercantilist, commercial strength made England great.

In 1763, however, a new era in colonial affairs opened.
After making the former French possessions hers, Great
Britain had almost undisputed sway in North America.

[24] Thomas Whately, attributed author, *Considerations on the Trade and Finances of the Kingdom*, London, 1769, p. 3.
[25] 5 George II, c. 7.
[26] 6 Anne, c. 30.
[27] 4 George III, c. 34.

She had paid well for the new territory by an expensive war. Men began to inquire what kind of bargain had been made; they asked what the older colonies were worth, and why new colonies were desirable. Faced by the necessity of governing provinces with a foreign population, British officials scrutinized more carefully than ever before the business of colonial administration. The public was critical and demanded that officials justify their actions. Country gentlemen were especially censorious, and urged their leaders in parliament to demand new measures of colonial control. In the new period merchants found that they were not always able to dictate colonial policy as they had done in the past. From their point of view, the years from 1763 to 1783 fell quite naturally into three distinct periods, each period marked by the lessening influence of the merchants. The first period closed with the repeal of the Stamp Act in 1766. Up to that time the merchants continued, though with great difficulty, to have their wish made law.

England came out of the Seven Years' War with new needs, new aims, and new policies. Imperialistic motives rather than mercantilism influenced the peace commissioners to choose Canada instead of the French islands in the Caribbean as part of the spoils of war.[28] The merchants had little interest in a new country which was costly to maintain and which promised no advantages to commerce; but they were losing their influence in shaping governmental policy, as the terms of the peace treaty show. In the territory acquired from France there were vast unsettled areas which presented peculiar difficulties of administration and defense, quite different from the problems of governing the old, established colonies. To organize the new territory large sums of money were necessary. As England was already burdened with a

[28] See *post*, chapter VII, for a discussion of the imperialistic motives of government.

heavy debt, the first task of the ministry was to increase
the revenue.

Country gentlemen, long jealous of the privileges which
merchants had enjoyed in the colonies, had no intention
of bearing a heavier land tax in order to pay American
expenses. The commercial classes were naturally opposed
to any increase in customs duties which might interfere
with trade. The safest resource seemed to be the excise,
but when Bute suggested the cider tax, he provoked a
miniature revolution in the cider counties. Parliament
abandoned the excise, Bute resigned from the ministry,
and Grenville began his fatal experiment of seeking revenue in America. To tax the colonies to pay for imperial
defense and development was logical enough from one
point of view, but the plan was in direct contradiction to
mercantilist doctrine and to long established custom. So
far the purpose of parliamentary regulation of colonial
trade had been to protect British merchants. Grenville
first followed the familiar path of commercial legislation,
but he had a new object—the collection of revenue.

As a preliminary to new measures Grenville planned
to enforce the navigation acts and other old commercial
regulations. Reorganization of the customs system and
the vice-admiralty courts was intended to make possible
the collection of duties under the acts of 1673 and 1733 and
to prevent smuggling. Parliament reduced from sixpence
to three, and later to one penny on the gallon, the duty on
molasses entering the colonies, thus lowering the impost
to a comparatively reasonable sum which really might be
collected.[29] In restricting American trade with the foreign
West Indies, however, parliament tended to cut down the
colonial supply of specie. At the same time the extension
to all the colonies of the act prohibiting the use of paper

[29] 6 George II, c. 13; 4 George III, c. 15; 6 George III, c. 52; G. L. Beer,
British Colonial Policy, 1754-1765, chapter XIII.

money increased financial difficulties.[30] British officials introduced new regulations at a time when they were least likely to succeed. In 1763 British merchants, taking advantage of the peace, increased their sales in America by one-third; but colonial exports to England remained the same.[31] Colonists who had never been able to pay cash for all their imports now found themselves more hopelessly in debt than ever. They were obliged to stop payment on old debts and to cut down new orders from Great Britain. As early as 1764 British merchants began to complain of the effects of the new colonial policy.[32] The Sugar Act may have benefited the West Indies, but New England business men and British merchants complained.[33]

The colonies were in no mood to submit kindly to new experiments in taxation; and the stamp tax was frankly an experiment. For the first time, parliament proposed to lay a direct tax on America, an impost for revenue only, with no pretext of commercial regulation. Yet apparently no one in England, merchant or statesman, dreamed of the storm which was brewing in America. Granted that England must raise funds in the colonies, even Henry McCulloh and William Knox, officials of long experience in America, could suggest no better method than the stamp duty.[34] The colonists, with a year to devise

[30] 4 George III, c. 34.

[31] Anderson, *Origin of Commerce*, Dublin, 1790, pp. 55-56, 78-79.

[32] *London Magazine*, Jan., 1766, p. 31. It is difficult to decide just when the effects were first felt. Statements of excellent trade conditions in the spring of 1764 may refer to actual exportation rather than to new orders. *Lloyd's*, Mar. 26-28, 1764.

[33] *Lloyd's*, April 9-11, 1764.

[34] McCulloh, *Miscellaneous Representations Relative to our Concerns in America*, edit. by W. A. Shaw, reprinted London, 1905, prefatory note. *Grenville Papers*, London, 1852, II, 373-374, note. McCulloh, *A Miscellaneous Essay concerning the Course pursued by Great Britain in the Affairs of her Colonies*, London, 1755 pp. 92-93. Knox, *The Claim of the Colonies to Exemption from Internal Taxes*, printed anonymously, London, 1765.

more satisfactory means, could only criticise the plan and
offer as a substitute a requisition on colonial assemblies,
a scheme with years of failure to its discredit. British
merchants, who should have known the colonial temper,
failed to understand American grievances. Possibly the
rumor that for the first five years Great Britain would
use the proceeds from the tax to build post roads and
bridges in the colonies "to facilitate an extensive trade"
allayed fear of trouble.[35] In March, 1765, the bill passed
through parliament with little opposition. When report
of its passage reached the colonies, a new America awoke.
Orators and statesmen—Patrick Henry, James Otis, and
Samuel Adams—roused colonial patriots to action; and
their voices woke answering echoes in the islands of the
West Indies. British statesmen heard and wondered. In
America angry mobs, a defiant rabble, seized official
papers, threatened the persons, and destroyed the property of tax collectors. More sober patriots met in solemn
conclave, and declared in haughty language their rights
and grievances. In New York, Boston, Philadelphia, and
Charleston, merchants and traders pledged themselves
to boycott British goods until parliament repealed the
hated acts.[36] On the question of the Stamp Act there was
neither north nor south, town nor country, frontier nor
tide-water. The Sugar Act had affected New England
alone; the stamp duty touched the pocket of every man
who bought land, gave bond, or read a newspaper. Business men objected to the act because it called for silver
and they had no silver to give.[37] Indignant patriots found

[35] *Lloyd's*, March 22-25, 1765.

[36] See A. M. Schlesinger, *The Colonial Merchants and the American Revolution, 1763-1776* [*Columbia University Studies*, vol. LXXVII] for a full
account of the situation in America.

[37] According to the general impression, the tax could be paid only in
specie, and the bill certainly specified specie. However the author of *Considerations on the Trade and Finances of the Kingdom*, London, 1769, p. 150,
declared that taxpayers could have given paper with security as strong as
that of bank notes.

at last a common cause for union and boldly planted their standard on the ground of "natural rights," with the rallying cry that "taxation without representation is tyranny." American merchants, however, had chosen the more effective way to compel attention from Great Britain. And the psychological consequences of non-importation were as pronounced as the material.

British merchants and manufacturers had already experienced more than a suggestion of misfortune since the passage of the Sugar Act in 1764. Imagination painted the future in deepest black. Parliamentary repeal of recent American measures was the only ray of hope. British traders had made a fetich of American commerce; they were bound in the toils of colonial trade by a century of tradition. Threatened with the loss of business, they waited with trepidation for January 1, when the colonial non-importation agreement was to become effective. Before December, 1765, popular report had fixed the value of countermanded American orders at £700,000.[38] All other commissions were conditional upon the repeal of the Stamp Act. Only an occasional British merchant assumed the risk of engaging manufacturers to fill his orders. For the most part, factors dallied in London during the long winter months, instead of travelling as usual through the clothing counties making contracts for goods to go out with the spring fleet. Few manufacturers could afford to fill conditional orders; and only the wealthiest and most optimistic enterprisers were willing to pile up a surplus stock for future demand. Pressed by their creditors, manufacturers were ready to sell at the buyers' own prices the goods which they had on hand; but they waited for better news from America before investing more capital in labor or raw materials. Neither merchants nor manufacturers could find immediate consolation in for-

[38] *Lloyd's*, Dec. 13-16, 1765.

eign markets. Time and study were necessary to develop new outlets for trade. Each market had its own peculiar demands, and goods produced for the colonies had little sale elsewhere.[39] Inevitably, then, work stopped, and the common laborer lost his job.

In those days of doubtful statistics, newspaper reporters talked vaguely of "thousands" out of work. Manufacturers in the iron works at Birmingham dismissed hundreds of laborers, but prophesied idleness for thousands, if a settlement with America failed.[40] In Sheffield only twenty per cent of the iron workers were employed.[41] From Norwich a manufacturer wrote up to London that since the Stamp Act there had been no work for his three hundred journeymen.[42] Similar reports came in from every town in England where British laborers had supplied American demands. Even the man with a job wondered how long his slender earnings would be able to feed his hungry family. Exorbitant prices of wheat raised the cost of the worker's loaf, and made more desperate the plight of the unemployed. A bounty on wheat of five shillings per quarter encouraged exportation, with the result that English wheat was cheaper in the French market than at home.[43] In Scotland and England rioters demanded food for British workers.

At such times America, the land of opportunity, beckoned most irresistibly to British laborers. An eighteenth-century Jeremiah lamented the exodus of five thousand manufacturers of nails from the neighborhood of Birmingham;[44] and bewailed the loss of Spitalfields weavers who had sailed for America because they could no longer

39 *London Magazine*, Jan. 1766, p. 31.
40 *Lloyd's*, Jan. 17-20, 1766; Jan. 6-8, 1766.
41 *Ibid.*, Mar. 19-21, 1766.
42 *Ibid.*, Mar. 5-7, 1766.
43 *Ibid.*, Dec. 30, 1765—Jan. 1, 1766.
44 *London Magazine*, Jan., 1766, p. 32, footnote.

earn their bread in England.[45] Another prophet, referring
to the colonies, had already warned the British people
that "necessity will teach men to become manufacturers."[46] When an anxious merchant, scanning the morning
paper, read of colonial plans for manufacturing cloth, paper, cordage, iron pots, and stationery,[47] and realized that
British artisans, recent emigrants from the mother
country, were helping to make those enterprises successful, he resolved that the Stamp Act must be repealed.
Shipowners, captains, and ordinary seamen offered a
ready second to the merchant's resolution.

After the first of January piers where American ships
docked were forsaken.[48] An unwonted, almost uncanny
stillness, hung over the waterfront of the western ports,
in place of the bustle and stir of other days. Vessels with
shrouded sails rose and fell with the tide, and pulled on
their hawsers in vain attempts to be free. Here and there
a solitary deck hand half hidden by the mist, crawled
about among the rigging, making a mooring more secure.
Ships returning from Philadelphia or Boston, laden with
hats which patriotic Americans had refused, only intensified the general gloom.[49] Dock laborers earned a few shillings, then returned to their mugs of ale at the tavern
where shipwrights and caulkers soused away their idle
hours.[50] Commerce with America had not been entirely
one-sided. America continued to send some products to
England when the colonial market was closed to British

[45] *Jopson's*, Feb. 10, 1766.

[46] *Gentleman's Magazine*, Apr., 1765: "The Mutual Interest of Great
Britain and the American Colonies Considered," reviewed, p. 190.

[47] *Lloyd's*, Feb. 10-12, 1766.

[48] *Jopson's*, Feb. 10, 1766.

[49] *Lloyd's*, Feb. 10-12, 1766.

[50] *Ibid.*, Jan. 6-8, 1766. Seamen's wages in Glasgow, for example, were
lowered to twenty shillings a month because of the decline in business.
Ibid., Feb. 3-5, 1766.

manufacturers; but because vessels could not afford to sail repeatedly in ballast, goods from the colonies were delayed and American products became scarce in England. The price of barrel-staves, which British merchants bought for re-export, rose five shillings a thousand; and Carolina rice, two shillings a hundred.[51] A British merchant could no longer sell to Europe at a profit.

While traders were losing money on current business, they found it impossible to collect old debts. Bills of exchange came back from America protested;[52] and, if one may believe the report, cash remittances from the colonies, in Spanish dollars only, lacked more than two millions of the usual annual payment.[53] According to British merchants, the insecurity of American investments was the result of the governmental policy and, more specifically, the stamp tax. Threatened with bankruptcy, the merchants wasted no time in futile theorizing on the rights of parliament. They did not choose to play the rôle of martyr in the cause of parliamentary supremacy. They demanded that parliament satisfy America, and repeal the Stamp Act.

Parliament, in the meantime, had been investigating conditions in a leisurely way. Grenville, *persona non grata* with the king for reasons which had no connection with America, resigned his position in July, 1765. The change in ministers aroused false hopes of an immediate reform in colonial policy. The Marquis of Rockingham had no special inclination to support his predecessor's measures; and General Conway, one of his Majesty's principal secretaries of state and leader of the House of Commons, was friendly toward the colonies. In October rumor was rife that parliament was about to consider

51 *Ibid.*, Feb. 12-14, 1766.
52 *Ibid.*, Jan. 13-15, 1766.
53 *Ibid.*, Dec. 30, 1765—Jan. 1, 1766.

American measures. Months, however, passed before ac-
cumulating evidence of financial loss and real suffering
forced parliament to repeal the Stamp Act. In the meantime British merchants worked together to impress
parliament with their needs.

Common interest had always united British merchants
in a more or less formal way, although in the eighteenth
century incorporated companies such as the Merchant
Venturers of Bristol were exceptional. In London merchants gathered at favorite coffee-houses to exchange
colonial news. Lloyd's was perhaps the most famous
rendezvous. There captains posted notices of ships about
to sail; and merchants found underwriters and brokers
who offered marine insurance.[54] Other coffee-houses attracted merchants whose trade lay in a particular province: the New York Coffee-house catered to merchants
who sold their goods in that most cosmopolitan of all
colonial ports; the Virginia Coffee-house offered hospi-
tality to traders who sought markets in the old dominion
and were consequently most interested in tobacco or
slaves. Whenever American disturbances threatened
their trade, London merchants dined together at frequent
intervals, and developed an *esprit de corps* over their
wine. Committees collected statistics of trade, conferred
with government officials, drew up resolutions and petitions, corresponded with merchants and manufacturers
in other towns, and with merchants' organizations in the

[54] This part of the eighteenth century was important in the history of
marine insurance. In 1760 the insurance agents at Lloyd's formed a company
which published the ''Register'' or ''Green Book.'' The publication of the
register, however, dated from about 1726. It contained lists of ships clearing
from London, indicating their class and condition. In 1769 the association of
more conservative insurance agents seceded from Old Lloyd's and moved to
Pope's Head Alley, and later to the Royal Exchange, where sailings were
then posted. Charles Wright and C. Ernest Fayle, *A History of Lloyd's*,
pp. 84, 87, 98, etc. *Annals of Lloyd's Register*, London, 1884, pp. 3-12.

colonies. In 1766 it was the merchants who secured the repeal of the Stamp Act.

Barlow Trecothick, prominent in business and in city government, was chairman of the general committee conducting the campaign. Early in December he had collected an imposing file of American letters countermanding orders for British goods. With other leaders he called upon the secretaries of state, the Duke of Grafton and General Conway, and presented this correspondence as proof that the colonists were serious and determined in their opposition.[55] A committee of correspondence wrote to the inland towns and outports, begging the merchants and manufacturers to let parliament know how the Stamp Act affected them. London merchants, however, refused to furnish a model petition, but urged each group "to speak from their own feelings."[56] Although London was strong in initiative, the ideas of unified action came spontaneously from other leading towns—from Bristol among the first.[57] On January 11 the merchants drew up a petition to parliament, and chose William Reeve, their master, Joseph Farrel, and Thomas Farr to carry the petition up to London. But any matter of trade affected the whole town; and the effects of American non-importation were far reaching. Not to be outdone by the merchants, other citizens of Bristol, led by their mayor and aldermen, met on the same evening, January 11, and used their ancient right of petition to lay before their representatives an account of their distresses. Two of the leading citizens, Samuel Sedgely and Henry Cruger, carried this petition to London and added their personal influence to that of the petitioners.[58]

[55] *Lloyd's*, Dec. 11-13, 1765.
[56] Add. MSS., 33030, f. 101, ff.
[57] *Ibid.*
[58] *Jopson's*, Jan. 20, 1766. Latimer, *Annals of Bristol in the Eighteenth Century*, printed for the author, 1893, pp. 370-371.

Manufacturers in the inland towns had their own reasons for following the examples of London and Bristol, and needed little urging. The merchants, however, were ready to force the manufacturers to coöperate, if need be, and refused to give a single order for goods to those who failed to support the movement for repeal.[59] In Birmingham a committee of twenty drew up a petition to parliament, and carried on necessary correspondence. They wrote pleading letters to influential members of parliament who might help their cause, especially to members of the nobility. In a letter to Lord Dartmouth, for example, they described conditions in Birmingham resulting from loss of colonial orders, and begged him to use the facts "to prevent the frightful consequences which might ensue from so many necessitous workmen being suddenly unemployed."[60] The idea of petitioning parliament spread like a disease from one town to another, wherever financial loss, unemployment, and hunger made the people susceptible. On January 17 the House of Commons received ten petitions for the repeal of the Stamp Act; on the twentieth, seven more; and by February 27, eight more—thirty-five in all.[61]

Members of parliament could scarcely ignore these complaints from all parts of the kingdom; but lest the written word be insufficient, the outports and inland towns had sent special deputies to plead their cause. Horace Walpole declared that "A nod from the ministers would have let loose all the manufacturers of Bristol, Liverpool, Manchester, and such populous and discontented towns who threatened to send hosts to Westminster to back their demand of repeal."[62] Fortunately

---

[59] "Commerce of Rhode Island," I, 145 [*Massachusetts Historical Society Collections*, Seventh Series, vol. IX].

[60] *Historical Manuscripts Commission Report*, XIV, 10, pp. 28 and 32.

[61] *Commons Journals*, XXX, 462, 463, 465, 484, 489, 501, 503, 611.

[62] Walpole, *Memoirs of George III*, London, 1894, II, 212.

the representatives of commerce who appeared in London were sober and discreet; but they were nevertheless determined. Henry Cruger, one of their number, expressed a popular sentiment when he declared: "I am no politician, but in this matter of America, and its trade, I embarked body and soul."[63] The merchants did not fail to make themselves known in those days when the House of Commons was debating the question of repeal. Day after day they dined together, one hundred strong. From the King's Arms Tavern in Palace Yard they went *en masse* to hear the debates in the house.[64] With what breathless eagerness they must have craned forward from the gallery benches, anxious lest they lose a word in the battle fought on the floor below! When on March 4 the house listened for the third time to the reading of the bill, and then divided 250 to 122, not only the gallery, but the lobbies were crammed with British traders who through the long hours of the winter night had waited to learn their fate. Years afterward Burke recalled to the memory of that same house the moment when their doors were at last thrown open and "from the whole of that grave multitude there arose an involuntary burst of gratitude and transport."[65]

Indeed the merchants felt that parliament had saved them from impending ruin. On the seventeenth of March the bill to repeal the Stamp Act passed the House of Lords, and next day received the royal assent.[66] The mer-

---

63 *Commerce of Rhode Island*, I, 146.

64 *Lloyd's*, Feb. 17-19 and 21-24, 1766.

65 *Speech on American Taxation*, April 19, 1774, 4th edition, London, 1783, p. 65. The resolution to repeal was brought in Feb. 24, 1766. The bill was presented on the 26, had its second reading on the 27, and was sent to committee. The latter reported on Mar. 3, the bill was passed on March 4 and sent up to the Lords. There it passed the readings on Mar. 5, 11, and 17 and received the royal assent on March 18.

66 *Commons Journals*, XXX, 664; *Lords Journals*, XXXI, 311.

chants, however, did not need this final assurance that
parliament had abandoned the American stamp tax. On
February 24 the resolution to introduce the bill passed the
House of Commons.[67] Twenty men, booted and spurred,
were waiting in the lobby and immediately galloped away
over the roads to Sheffield, Birmingham, Leeds—all the
manufacturing towns—spreading the joyful news as they
rode, while several light ships set sail at once to carry the
news to America. At the prospect of repeal the merchants
could face their creditors with more assurance; and the
destitute mechanics were encouraged with promises of
immediate employment. Contemporaries said "there was
an universal joy to be seen in the countenance of every
lover of trade in the city."[68]

Bristol was no less exultant. When the news reached
that port, bells were rung; for the first time in months
captains flew the colors on the ships lying idle in the har-
bors and fired their guns saluting the prospect of an early
voyage. Crowds in holiday mood thronged the streets of
the old seaport town, and scrambled in good-humored
rivalry for the coins which merchants tossed from the
windows of the American Coffee-house. In the evening a
galaxy of candles made the houses bright within, while
outside bonfires defied the night and furnished torches
for the gay processions.[69] And every port and inland town
where the London riders brought the news repeated the
Bristol celebration. When royal assent gave the final
sanction to repeal, messengers again rode posthaste into
the country and to Falmouth where captains were only
waiting for the final word before setting sail for America.
In London, sailors and mechanics thronged St. James's
Park to cheer the king for his share in bringing them

[67] *Commons Journal*, XXX, 602.
[68] *Jopson's*, Mar. 3, 1766.
[69] *Lloyd's*, Feb. 28—Mar. 3, 1766.

MERCANTILE CLASSES

Arms Tavern—this time to prepare an address of gratitude to his Majesty. They then rode in a triumphant pro-
cession of fifty coaches to the House of Lords. That evening they dined at the Half Moon Tavern in Cheapside
with the aldermen and members of parliament who were
most responsible for the success of the merchants' appeal.
They congratulated each other on the end of their troubles, and drank to "The Gentlemen of the North American Committee," "Trade and Navigation," and "Unanimity between Great Britain and the Colonies."[71] In the
last days of April they were still celebrating. West Indian
and North American merchants entertained at Drapers'
Hall the chief state officials and other members of the
administration which had carried through repeal. A brilliant and distinguished company, nobility and commoners, enjoyed the "magnificent" feast and the music of the
band which Sheriff Trecothick had planned for their
amusement. The many toasts which they drank at the
close of the banquet were, needless to say, "loyal and
constitutional."[72]

In the weeks that followed repeal, the mercantile and
manufacturing towns also showed their gratitude to
parliamentary leaders. The Society of Merchants in Bristol presented the freedom of their company to the Duke
of Grafton, William Dowdeswell, William Pitt, Sir William Meredith, and Sir George Savile.[73] Coventry was
enthusiastic in its approval of Archer and Hewitt, members of parliament for that city. Meeting in St. Mary's
Hall, the corporation voted an address to the two men,
thanking them for their work in pushing through parlia-

[70] *Jopson's*, March 24, 1766.
[71] *Lloyd's*, Mar. 17-19 and 19-21, 1766.
[72] *Ibid.*, Apr. 25-28, 1766.
[73] *Ibid.*, Apr. 7-9, 1766.

ment the bill for repeal, beneficial to the whole country, but to Coventry in particular.[74] Letters and addresses from all parts of the kingdom overwhelmed the Marquis of Rockingham and Lord Dartmouth, inadvertently two of the principals in the drama. To Lord Dartmouth Liverpool offered the freedom of the borough.[75] Superseded by another minister in August, the Marquis of Rockingham retired to his estates in Yorkshire; but merchants and manufacturers did not forget the great act of his ministry. On the Sunday evening of his return two hundred citizens of York rode out upon the highway to welcome him home. Bells rang a greeting as he entered the city. Next day the citizens presented an address which in formal but sincere language thanked the marquis for ''signal services done to the commercial interest of this nation . . . the repeal of an act equally oppressive to Great Britain and her colonies.'' Manchester, Leeds, Halifax, Kingston-upon-Hull, Wakefield, Sheffield, Lancaster, and Liverpool sent similar addresses to Rockingham, congratulating him upon the harmony which he had been able to restore to Great Britain and America.[76] William Pitt, however, was still the national hero; and the repeal of the Stamp Act raised him even higher in popular estimation. Medals, which bore his head in relief, honored him as ''The man who, having saved the parent, pleaded with success for her children.''[77]

Business revival following repeal justified popular re-

[74] *Lloyd's*, Apr. 9-11, 1766.

[75] *Hist. MSS. Com. Rep.*, XIV, 10, pp. 44, 46, and 47.

[76] *Lloyd's*, Aug. 20-22; 27-29; 29-Sept. 1; Sept. 3-5; 8-10, 1766. *Jopson's*, Aug. 25, 1766.

[77] *Ibid.*, Apr. 18-21, 1766. Opinion was not unanimous in favor of Pitt or repeal. Verses in the *Gentleman's Magazine* for February, 1766, p. 140, represent Pitt as forcing Goody Bull to her knees to ask her daughter's pardon.

''No thanks to you, mother, the daughter reply'd:
    But thanks to my friend here, I've humbled your pride.''

joicing. Merchants had not even waited for the final passage of the bill. The mere introduction of the measure set
the wheels of industry in motion. On March third weavers
in Colchester were working on orders for baize to the
value of £11,000. In Birmingham hundreds of iron workers took up the hammers which they had dropped five
months before.[78] Shoemakers and hat manufacturers soon
had more orders than they could fill.[79] At Newcastle-upon-
Tyne one factor alone gave orders for window glass and
bottles to the value of £4,000.[80] The ports were noisy
again with the shouting of orders as captains loaded their
ships for the American voyage. During the last few days
of February merchants signed contracts for thirty vessels
lying in the Thames; and in a single week they did four
times as much business as in any one month since October.[81] Many captains who had cleared their ships in November, and were only waiting for repeal, set sail on the
eighteenth of March, racing to reach the colonies before
their rivals. The repeal of the Stamp Act called from the
taverns three hundred shipwrights, carpenters, and rig-
gers.[82] On the first of April Glasgow reported eighteen
ships sailing to the West Indies or North America.[83] In
Bristol and Liverpool seamen no longer complained of
unemployment. In fact there were not enough ships to
handle commerce; and London merchants commissioned
colonial shipbuilders to supply them with vessels.[84] Within
a few weeks British merchants received orders directly
from America. But most welcome was the sterling—payment on American debts. In November, 1767, a contribu-

---

[78] *Jopson's,* March 3, 1766.
[79] *Lloyd's,* March 26-28, 1766.
[80] *Ibid.*
[81] *Ibid.,* Feb. 26-28; Feb. 28—March 3, 1766.
[82] *Ibid.,* March 26-28, 1766.
[83] *Ibid.,* April 2-4, 1766.
[84] *Ibid.,* April 18-21, 1766.

48   BRITISH OPINION

tor to *Jopson's* declared that since the repeal of the
Stamp Act British merchants had received £10,000 in
payment of colonial debts.[85] British industry quickly re-
covered from the depression of 1766.

Parliament repealed the Stamp Act because British
merchants, manufacturers, merchants, and everyone interested in commerce united to demand repeal.[86] In the
period of non-importation both Englishmen and colonists
realized the commercial interdependence of their countries as they never had before. At the same time fundamental differences in their thought appeared. British
merchants had no sympathy with the independent claims
of colonial legislators. British traders could not forget
that parliament had protected them from the paper
money of the colonies, and had helped them to collect
their debts. They saw no objection to an expedient and
discreet use of parliamentary control over the colonies;
and they did not oppose the Declaratory Act. This "Bill
for the better securing the Dependency of His Majesty's
Dominion in America upon the Crown and Parliament of
Great Britain," receiving the royal assent on the same
day as the repeal of the Stamp Act, stated that parliament had the right "to bind the colonies . . . in all cases
whatsoever."[87] Americans, on the other hand, deeply resented this suggestion that they were utterly dependent
upon the British government.

London merchants carefully explained their idea of
the correct American attitude when they wrote to John
Hancock announcing the repeal of the Stamp Act. The
merchants reproached the Bostonians for the lawless and
riotous methods by which they had resisted the tax. "We

[85] *Jopson's*, Nov. 23, 1767.

[86] Chapter V, *post*, explains how their arguments affected the country
gentlemen.

[87] 6 George III, c. 12.

CHART OF TRADE BETWEEN ENGLAND AND THE THIRTEEN ORIGINAL COLONIES IN AMERICA

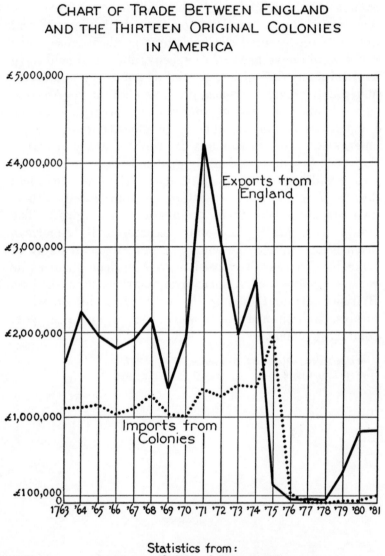

Exports from England

Imports from Colonies

Statistics from:
Anderson, Origin of Commerce
Sheffield, Observations on Commerce

cannot but acquaint you," they wrote, "that had the Americans endeavoured to acquiesce with the law, and dutifully represented the hardships as they arose, your relief would have been more speedy, and we should have avoided many difficulties, as well as not a few unanswerable mortifying reproaches on your account."[88] An attitude of just submission and respect, according to the London merchants, would be more effective in any future emergency. The Bostonians in reply frankly declared that they saw no occasion for gratitude or submission. A wrong had been righted, and that was all. Americans had decided to ignore the Declaratory Act, but placed on their own statute books their declarations of rights.[89] The "natural rights" philosophy expressed in American declarations united the colonists, but alienated many of their British friends. Hostility to American theories as well as jealousy of American enterprises flourished on British soil; and during the next crisis in American affairs, British merchants were less eager to support colonial demands.

[88] *Gentleman's Magazine*, September, 1766, p. 397.
[89] *Ibid.*, p. 612, ff.

CHAPTER III

INTERESTS, ACTIVITIES, AND OPINIONS OF THE MERCANTILE CLASSES.

II. PERIOD OF DECLINE AND FAILURE, 1767-1775.

In the taverns and coffee-houses, at the King's Arms and the Half Moon, British merchants hailed the repeal of the Stamp Act and toasted American commerce; but their joy was short-lived. In 1767 parliament once more sacrificed American goodwill, and wrecked colonial trade. Grenville's scheme had failed, but British officials still believed that some means of colonial taxation might succeed.

In 1767 Charles Townshend, chancellor of the exchequer under Chatham, proposed a new plan to tax America. Members of parliament were so ready to welcome the suggestion that they responded quickly to Townshend's brilliant and persuasive arguments. The treasury was still in urgent need of funds to pay the costs of new colonial projects; and the country gentlemen refused to raise the land tax. To pay the interest on the national debt and to provide revenue for the ordinary expenses of government strained England's own resources. Naturally Townshend was tempted to seek again in America contributions for defense. He did not anticipate serious opposition. In 1766 the colonies had objected only to internal taxation; they had admitted, in theory at least, that parliament could rightfully impose customs duties on America. Townshend respected this distinction; and the acts of 1767 provided for duties upon colonial imports

of tea, glass, paper, painters' colors, red and white lead.[1]
But Townshend was not aware that by 1767 many American patriots had begun to deny the constitutionality of all taxes except those laid by their own legislatures. His death in September left to Lord North the duty of enforcing the act, which became effective in October.

The colonists had every reason to believe that Great Britain was in earnest this time. British laws legalizing writs of assistance, increasing the jurisdiction of the admiralty courts, and reorganizing the customs system, had only one aim—to prevent smuggling and to ensure the collection of the customs. Business depression in America, attributed to restrictive trade acts and lack of currency, made the colonists particularly sensitive to the new customs duties; and every measure taken by Great Britain made the colonists more resolute in their resistance. In 1767 a movement for economy began in the New England town meetings. The colonists decided to boycott British manufactures and encourage home industries, while colonial merchants resorted again to non-importation measures similar to those which had secured the repeal of the Stamp Act in 1766. Boston started the movement, and New York and Philadelphia followed somewhat more slowly. In the southern colonies, the planters, in debt to British merchants, were most active in organizing associations for non-importation. By 1769 there was an association for non-importation in every colony except New Hampshire.[2] Agreements varied; but all required as the minimum concession from Great Britain the repeal of the Townshend Acts. American importers expected their

---

[1] 7 George III, c. 46.

[2] Schlesinger, *The Colonial Merchants and the American Revolution, 1763-1776,* chapter II; C. M. Andrews, "The Boston Merchants and the Non-importation Movement," *Publications of the Colonial Society of Massachusetts,* vol. XIX.

merchant friends in England to influence parliament in their behalf; but the colonists knew that British merchants would act more promptly and work more persistently under the pressure of non-importation. There is no doubt that British merchants were alarmed at the possibility of facing another season like that preceding the repeal of the Stamp Act.

Even in the spring of 1768, before colonial agreements became effective, British merchants began to worry. The balance of trade between England and America was greatly in favor of the mother country. British merchants declared it the height of folly to risk loss of trade in a quarrel over taxation.[3] During the year 1768, the colonists stopped payment on their debts to British merchants. Business men in England, working with small reserves of capital, became hard pressed by their creditors, and were glad to sell their claims against colonial debtors at the rate of four shillings on the pound.[4] Large orders from America only tantalized and aggravated British merchants, for the orders were conditional upon the repeal of the Townshend Acts. To be sure, some of the merchants refused to believe that the colonists would persist in non-importation. They expected that colonial housewives would be unable to forego their cups of fragrant Ceylon and that the opportunity for profit would tempt colonial merchants to violate their trade agreements. A correspondent for *Jopson's* wrote: "Although the merchants of New York and Boston have agreed to decline giving orders for British goods, yet we are now assured by the most recent advice from North America . . . that now is the time for any of the natives of this island to make his fortune, by exporting our manufac-

---

[3] *Gentleman's Magazine*, Nov., 1768, "State of our Trade with the Northern Colonies" by F. B., p. 513 ff.   [4] *Jopson's*, Sept. 19, 1768.

tures to the western continent, as there is no doubt but
they would find in these colonies a readier sale and better
prices than usual.''[5] In succeeding years speculators
adopted the suggestion eagerly. The old conservative
practice of shipping goods to America only upon definite
orders from colonial importers or British factors stationed in the colonies gave place to newer methods. ''Adventurers'' borrowed capital to purchase articles from
the manufacturers, then shipped these goods to the colonies on the chance of a possible sale.[6] Though the risk of
loss was great, unusually high prices tempted even the
conservative merchant, and the speculator was in his
element. British traders found many loopholes in the
non-importation system. Colonial ports were not completely closed to British goods; but irregular sales could
never equal the business done in normal times.

Conscientious observers of the non-importation agreements were numerous enough to make the speculator's
trade precarious. Many a British captain was refused
permission even to unload his cargo. With his lading still
intact he set sail for the return voyage. Within a few
weeks his vessel was riding heavily on the Thames or
the Mersey. There ships lay for months, their holds still
packed with British merchandise, waiting for the repeal
of the Townshend Acts.[7] It is not surprising that the
price of merchant ships posted for sale at the coffee-
houses near the Exchange fell twenty-five per cent in six
months.[8] Sailors haunted the docks in vain hopes of a
berth; or, despairing of better fortune, drowned their
woes at the ale-house.

Manufacturers, on the other hand, found that Ameri-

---

[5] *Jopson's,* Feb. 6, 1769.

[6] *Lloyd's,* Mar. 5-7, 1770; *Middlesex Journal,* Mar. 8, 1770.

[7] *Lloyd's,* Feb. 5-7, 1770.

[8] *Middlesex Journal,* Nov. 30—Dec. 2, 1769.

can non-importation affected them much less seriously than had the colonial agreements of 1766. According to the *Middlesex Journal*, "After the American stamp-act had passed, in the year 1766, great complaints were made that the trade of England was at a stand, on account of the orders from New York and Boston being counter-manded; upon which that act was repealed, as it was supposed it might be detrimental to the various manufac-turers. The shoe-makers and weavers, it was said, would be totally ruined; but now in three years afterwards, when there are counter orders from almost every part of America, the complaints are totally different. The leather cutters alledge that there are not hides enough in the kingdom for home-consumption, and pray leave to bring in foreign ones; and the weavers, instead of being distressed for work, at this time insist upon the full wages which they have been deprived of for some years back; and their masters to induce them to go to work, have agreed to give it."[9]

Increase in foreign and domestic markets partly ex-plains the comparative prosperity of British manufac-turers in 1769 and 1770. In the summer of 1770 the Russian War created an unusual demand for British manufactures in that country.[10] Merchants were more in-clined to place orders, regardless of the non-importation agreements. Speculators demanded wares for immediate exportation; and conservative traders, expecting parlia-ment to grant their petitions for repeal, wished to have goods on hand to fill the conditional orders. Certainly the weight of business depression fell less heavily upon the manufacturer than upon the merchant. Common artisans, especially, suffered less from lack of work in 1769 than in 1766. Some of the enterprisers, however, risked their

[9] *Ibid.*   [10] *Lloyd's*, July 23-25, 1770.

own funds in producing goods for an uncertain market. An observer in Manchester wrote: "This town and neighborhood already feel the severe stroke, having conditional orders by them to the amount of at least one hundred and thirty thousand pounds, the greatest part of which sum, in manufactures, now lies dormant in their warehouses, ready to be packed up; and some have larger quantities ready cased for shipping."[11] Evidently serious financial difficulties would result if colonial ports were not soon opened to British trade. If parliament would repeal the Townshend Acts, colonial importers would once more buy from British merchants. Again English trading towns petitioned parliament to rescind the American duties.

The movement in 1770, however, lacked the unanimity which had characterized the merchants' demand for the repeal of the Stamp Act. Dissension broke up many meetings called to instruct members of parliament to vote for repeal. Most traders urged the abolition of the American taxes as a measure of expediency, a practical measure, which would increase British prosperity. A few individuals adopted the latest colonial theory, complaining that the acts which injured their business were not only impolitic, but unconstitutional.[12] Another element in many cities and towns had purely political aims. This group supported the party in power, and opposed all petitions to the king or to parliament, and all instructions to members of the House of Commons, that might embarrass their party. A study of conditions in Bristol in the spring of 1769 shows that the citizens there were already divided into these three groups, according to their attitude toward colonial taxation.

Bristol probably had a greater interest in American

11 *Lloyd's*, Mar. 21-23, 1770.   12 *Middlesex Journal*, Nov. 22, 1769.

trade than any city in England except London; but citizens of Bristol disagreed on the question of repealing the Townshend Acts. In spite of the injury to trade resulting from non-importation, a majority of the corporation voted against instructing Lord Clare and Matthew Brickdale, members of parliament from Bristol, to vote for repeal. On the other hand, three-fourths of the city, as distinguished from the corporation, approved the instructions. Contemporaries ascribed the opposition in the corporation to the large number of elderly and conservative members, and to the influence of a certain person who was an "implicit follower of Lord C . . . . ."[13] Lord Clare was a well-known government supporter who was not inclined to help the merchants. In his reply to the letter of instructions he said: ". . . I could not help remarking that the names of a very great majority of the most respectable of our fellow citizens are not to be found among the subscribers. . . . Several points contained in the instructions from some of my constituents seem to hint at evils which in my opinion do not exist."[14] In later months Bristol traders concentrated their efforts on Matthew Brickdale, the other representative of Bristol. Lord Clare's letter and the development in the political situation in Bristol indicate that opposition to the instructions of 1769 was partly the result of the wording of the instructions. Clauses accusing the government of depriving the people of their rights and liberties confused the issue which in England was primarily commercial—the expediency of the Townshend Acts. Yet in the autumn of 1769 petitioners to the king insisted upon describing the colonial measures which had ruined their business as "impolitic and unconstitutional."[15] By so doing Bristol

13 *Jopson's,* March 20, 1769.   14 *Ibid.,* April 3, 1769.
15 *Middlesex Journal,* Nov. 22, 1769.

petitioners lost many of their former supporters. In
April, 1770, the merchants of that city met a ''powerful
opposition'' when they proposed a remonstrance to the
throne.[16]

Newcastle-upon-Tyne and Southwark experienced less
difficulty in gaining approval of letters instructing their
representatives to vote for repeal of the Townshend Acts;
but in Canterbury the mayor was strongly opposed to
repeal, and denied that instructions ascribed to his town
had really been delivered to members of parliament.[17]
Only a dozen citizens of Southwark, it was said, opposed
instructions to their representatives, Sir Joseph Mawbey
and Henry Thrale. These instructions, however, were
truly mercantilist in character, for they emphasized the
necessity of maintaining a monoply of colonial trade.[18]

In London, merchants trading with the colonies again
met at the King's Arms Tavern. They collected statistics
of countermanded orders from America and of goods
actually returned from the colonies, in order to convince
Hillsborough, secretary of the state for the colonies, that
the effects of recent American measures were disastrous.[19] They petitioned parliament; and other trading
towns followed London's example. There was little dissension among London merchants; but they did not wait
for parliamentary relief as anxiously as they had waited
in 1766. Indeed it was not until two years after the passage of the Townshend Acts that British merchants began an active campaign for repeal. In the meantime
American colonists petitioned and remonstrated in vain.
Only colonial non-importation succeeded in arousing
Great Britain against acts so unpopular in America; and

---

[16] *Lloyd's*, April 11-13, 1770.

[17] *London Magazine*, March, 1769, p. 136.

[18] *Ibid.*, pp. 132-133.   [19] *Middlesex Journal*, Feb. 3, 1770.

in 1770 even non-importation failed to succeed as non-importation had succeeded in 1766. On April 12, 1770, the influence of British merchants finally won from parliament a partial repeal. The tax on tea remained. In 1766 parliament had temporarily renounced the practice of taxing America, while reserving to itself the right to make laws binding the colonies in all cases whatsoever. In 1770 parliament took pains to maintain not only the principle of taxation, but also the practice. British merchants were perplexed. Conditional orders from America depended upon a total repeal of the objectionable acts. Yet fifteen London merchants declared that they were satisfied with the decision of parliament.[20] Naturally the merchants who continued to work for the repeal of the tax on tea could accomplish nothing. The prorogation of parliament was the final blow to mercantile hopes.

For several months the difficulties of both American and British traders multiplied. "The Boston Massacre," occurring in February, strengthened colonial resistance to British measures, and increased American loyalty to the non-importation movement. Shipping showed the effects earlier than other branches of trade. While parliament debated the subject of repeal, ships were lying in the harbor, freighted, ready to set sail. When the final vote was announced, captains of trading vessels or the merchant owners were obliged either to store their goods in warehouses to wait for a change in parliamentary sentiment or to risk rebuff on reaching America with their unwelcome news. Experience in earlier years made them cautious. Demand for ships declined; and the best river-built vessels sold for less than the original cost of the materials.[21] In June ships which had ventured to defy the American non-importation agreement began to re-

[20] *Jopson's*, Jan. 27, 1766.   [21] *Middlesex Journal*, April 3, 1770.

turn to their docks in the Thames or in Bristol harbor, their ladings untouched.[22] Apparently the colonists had no intention of relaxing their vigilance against the importation and consumption of British goods, as long as parliament persisted in taxing America. Factors and merchants who had been so indiscreet as to risk trade with America under such conditions lost forty per cent on their investments.[23] During the summer of 1770 prudent captains limited their cargoes to colonial necessities.[24] According to British regulations, unfortunate masters who returned with ladings of tea risked the loss of ship and cargo. For that reason a captain arriving in America with a shipload of the forbidden article would sometimes prevail upon the colonists to allow him to store his tea in an American warehouse.[25] Merchants felt the effects of American resistance immediately, and it was inevitable that manufacturers should eventually share the losses of the merchants.

At first the inland towns suffered less than the ports. Orders given on the assumption that repeal would be complete carried the manufacturers over the first period of disappointment. But the value of exports to America in 1769 was at least £400,000 less than in 1768;[26] and Barlow Trecothick declared that the prospect for 1770 was still more discouraging.[27] Merchants ordered the manu-

---

[22] *Lloyd's*, June 27-29, 1770. [23] *Ibid.*, June 20-22, 1770.

[24] It is interesting to note that the colonists considered books necessities. One reads in *Jopson's*, June 11, 1770: ''The Captains of ships in the American trade have got such positive orders from their several owners at the other side of the Atlantic, in regard to carrying out any goods from Great Britain, except books, cutlery, and a few articles that they cannot possibly do without, that they will not even carry the usual presents from their friends here, till they first make an affidavit that they are not for sale.''

[25] *Middlesex Journal*, June 15, 1770.

[26] According to customhouse accounts. See graph *ante*, p. 49.

[27] Trecothick, according to *Jopson's*, April 23, 1770, estimated the difference at over £700,000.

facturers to postpone filling their commissions. Finished
goods were stored in warehouses, and laborers were dismissed. The common people suffered somewhat less than
in 1766, for unemployment was not so general; and imported wheat kept down the price of bread. Nevertheless,
the situation was alarming. In July *Lloyd's* stated au-
thoritatively that the balance of North American trade
was beginning to be in favor of that country and that the
value of colonial exports exceeded the value of their imports.[28] On the other hand, the difference between British exports to America and imports from the colonies,
only about £300,000 in 1769, had probably never been so
small.[29] British mercantilists feared that England was
losing her favorable balance of trade with the colonies;
and to mercantilists an unfavorable trade balance was a
sign of national decline. America, by contrast, seemed to
show every sign of prosperity. British traders believed
the Americans were making fortunes at the expense of
the mother country. American trade with European countries was growing. Recent floods in France had increased
the demand for American flour and Indian corn; and
these articles, together with fish, found a ready market
in Cadiz and Lisbon. Instead of changing their foreign
gold for British manufactures on the return voyage, as
formerly, American traders were now taking specie directly to the colonies; and British merchants complained
of a scarcity of gold in their own country.[30]

Unsatisfactory trade conditions in India added to British commercial misfortunes. According to letters from
Madras, the markets there were so overstocked that factors were returning goods to England or storing them till
the market should recover.[31] British merchants com-

---

28 *Lloyd's*, July 23-25, 1770.   29 See graph *ante*, p. 49.
30 *Lloyd's*, July 23-25; Aug. 10-13, 1770.   31 *Ibid.*, April 25-27, 1770.

62   BRITISH OPINION

plained also of loss of trade in Portugal, and accused
Spain of cheating them of their privileges under "the
most favored nation clause."[32] A heavy gloom enveloped
British traders, and deepened on the threat of war with
Spain and on the report that an American returning to
the colonies had taken firearms, bayonets, and swords—
the only articles of British manufacture for which he had
orders.[33] When conditions seemed most desperate, however, help came from an unexpected quarter—from the
colonies themselves.

In 1770 American plans for concerted action against
Great Britain broke down under the strain of intercolonial jealousy and the temptation for one colony to profit
at the expense of its neighbors. London merchants had
an inkling of the situation, for they knew that American
ports were still partly open to British trade. A popular
pamphlet, eagerly discussed in the coffee-houses, stated
that British vessels had entered Boston harbor even before parliament made its concession to American demands; and that the Bostonians had accepted consignments of tea, glass, lead, and other dutiable commodities.[34]
In August came the first real encouragement for British
hopes with the news that New York suspected Boston of
violating the non-importation rules, and that the New
York merchants had consequently dissolved their agreement.[35] The same ship that brought this report to Bristol carried orders for British manufactures—a sufficient
confirmation of the news. New York traders strengthened
their credit and hastened the filling of their orders by
sending bills of exchange to pay some of their outstand-

[32] *Lloyd's,* June 13-15, 1770.   [33] *Middlesex Journal,* Aug. 24, 1770.
[34] *Ibid.,* Sept. 22, 1770. *Lloyd's,* Oct. 1-3, 1770.
[35] *Middlesex Journal,* Aug. 30, 1770. C. M. Andrews, *The Boston Merchants and the Non-importation Movement;* and A. M. Schlesinger, *The Colonial Merchants and the American Revolution, 1763-1776,* especially pp. 156-
236.

ing debts.[36] By the middle of August the iron manufacturers in Birmingham had engaged several hundred
workmen to complete goods for the New York demand;[37]
and by the end of the month vessels laden with these
goods were setting sail from London.[38] North Carolina
soon followed the example of New York in breaking her
compact, furnishing more business for British workers.
In September the new orders were ready, and captains
were signing contracts for shipment.[39] London merchants
tried to hasten the end of American non-importation by
agreeing to give unlimited credit to merchants in any
colony that followed the precedent set by New York and
North Carolina.[40] Merchants became so confident of better
business, and competition among them became so keen,
that they paid Yorkshire manufacturers for their cloth
while it was still on the loom.[41] Throughout England industry responded to renewed colonial demand.

In America, in the meantime, one town after another
yielded to economic pressure, and abandoned the non-
importation movement. Early in September *Lloyd's* reported that Philadelphia had voted to import British
goods again.[42] Londoners then realized that Boston could
not long persist in non-importation, even with irregulari-
ties of enforcement. The odds at the coffee-houses were
three to eight that Boston would be importing goods by
the end of October;[43] and early in that month the town
succumbed, insisting only that the importation of tea
should still be forbidden.[44] One by one the other colonies,
agricultural and commercial alike, resumed trade with
Great Britain. On November 17 the British press reported

[36] *Lloyd's*, Aug. 29-31, 1770.   [37] *Middlesex Journal*, Sept. 1, 1770.
[38] *Lloyd's*, Aug. 29-31, 1770.   [39] *Middlesex Journal*, Sept. 1, 1770.
[40] *Ibid.*, Sept. 4, 1770.   [41] *Lloyd's*, Sept. 10-12, 1770.
[42] *Ibid.*   [43] *Ibid.*, Sept. 19-21, 1770.
[44] Reported in *Lloyd's*, Nov. 16-19, 1770.

that the colonies had universally agreed to import all
articles except Asia tea.[45] Although the decision of the
Philadelphia merchants did not go into effect until January 16, 1771, and there was a rumor that the "patriotic
party" in New York was regaining influence, British
fears were dispelled. By the end of November London
merchants held commissions worth £300,000.[46] British
policy had prevailed in spite of colonial resistance. In
1770 the Declaratory Act was still on the statute books,
and there was also the provision for a tax on tea, evidence
that parliament retained the practice of binding the colonies, regardless of American objections.

The period of commercial uncertainty following the
passage of the Townshend Acts differed from the years
of the Stamp Act dispute. In the later years British mercantile classes were better prepared for trouble than they
had been in 1766. Shipping was the branch of trade most
severely affected. The merchants' chief loss resulted from
the difficulty of collecting debts; and the manufacturers
suffered comparatively little. Consequently the trading
classes were less interested in securing the reforms which
America demanded. At the same time they were handi-
capped in their campaign for repeal by the confusion of
issues. American complaints were based upon constitutional as well as economic arguments. British merchants
were not convinced that the colonists were justified in
resisting parliament on constitutional grounds. British
traders and manufacturers based their arguments for
opposing parliament on grounds of expediency, and derived their evidence from statistics of Great Britain's
trade. Such arguments were much more effective than
were the suggestions that parliament, in taxing America,
had overstepped its legitimate powers. In fact the con-

45 *Middlesex Journal*, Nov. 17, 1770.
46 *Ibid.*, Nov. 20, 1770.

stitutional issue, first raised in America, where it divided merchant opinion, antagonized many erstwhile friends of America in England; and when that issue was repeated in Bristol and other trading centers, it split the party of American sympathizers into two irreconcilable groups. Thus weakened, advocates of repeal were only partly successful. British merchants, as a class, were deaf to American constitutional claims; whereas to trade grievances, complaints of disastrous restrictions, heavy taxes, and lack of currency, they turned a willing ear. In 1769 London merchants writing to their fellow merchants in Philadelphia said: "Had a petition come over from your merchants on the principle of inexpediency instead of from your assembly denying the right, the law would ere now have been repealed."[47] British merchants grew less sympathetic toward America as they grew more suspicious of colonial constitutional claims; and their interest in American complaints naturally waned as business revived.

The increase of trade in 1770 and 1771 was phenomenal. Too many manufacturers and traders, however, financed their business ventures in a dishonest way, or at least by unsound methods; and in 1772 there came a business crash which shook the whole trading structure of Great Britain to its foundation. Statistics of trade tell their own story. According to the reports of the customhouse, the value of exports to America rose from about £1,325,000 in 1769 to about £4,200,000 in 1771. In the next year the value of exports to the colonies dropped £1,200,000, and in 1773, another £1,000,000. The following year exports increased slightly, but in 1775, on the outbreak of war with America, they became a negligible factor in British

[47] *Pennsylvania Chronicle*, Apr. 3, 1769, cited by C. M. Andrews, *The Boston Merchants and Non-importation*, p. 210, note 3.

trade.[48] An explanation of these violent fluctuations in commerce is essential to an understanding of the attitude of British merchants toward the colonies.

The uncertainties of the period, 1767-1770, fostered a spirit of speculation among the less conservative traders, that flourished in succeeding years. British merchants overestimated the demand which would follow the cancelling of the colonial non-importation agreements, and accumulated great stocks of goods, both domestic and foreign.[49] Conditions in America led to exaggerated optimism. Currency was more plentiful than usual, for the colonists had increased their supply of bullion by their European trade. Then, too, British merchants passed on to colonial importers the credit which they secured so easily at home. Under these circumstances the Americans probably indulged a feeling of greater prosperity than was justified by facts. In the winter of 1770-1771 heavy colonial orders stimulated unprecedented production in England. To the uncritical observer all business conditions were good. Even as late as the spring of 1772 a correspondent from Maryland wrote: "This last year the Americans have imported above double the usual quantities of British goods, yet the prices, instead of falling, have risen from 25 to 30 percent above what they formerly brought in the stores, which plainly proves an increasing opulence, as well as an increasing population, and the face of things daily changes here for the better."[50] In the meantime all sections of the British population that de-

[48] John, Lord Sheffield, *Observations on the Commerce of the American States,* Appendix, especially Table XIII.

[49] *The Parliamentary History of England,* XVII, 1119. Statement by Richard Glover, son of a Hamburg merchant doing business in London. The son was a member of the House of Commons before 1768. He had a share in his father's business. *Dict. Nat. Biog.,* vol. VII.

[50] *Lloyd's,* June 19-22, 1772, quoting letter of April 15.

pended upon American trade enjoyed the results of the boom.

In the spring of 1771 ordinary seamen were earning £3 10s. a month, an exorbitant wage.[51] Even the recall of press warrants late in February caused only a slight and temporary drop in wages.[52] Sailors were so much in demand that Liverpool merchants could scarcely fit their ships for sea.[53] Manufacturers, both masters and laborers, enjoyed good times. Large orders kept them busy, and made it possible to raise the price of finished goods. For example, frame-work knitters and hosiers, meeting at Nottingham in July, agreed to raise the price of men's hose a penny a pair, and the price of women's, a halfpenny.[54] The prosperity which smiled upon colonial trade seemed to shed its benign influence over all sorts of business undertakings—great building projects, the cultivation of distant islands, vast manufacturing schemes.[55] Credit, based upon false capital, supported most of these enterprises.

In the eighteenth century business men were experimenting with various forms of credit. The science of banking was undeveloped. Even the Bank of England was not founded until the end of the seventeenth century. Big business enterprises, however, were increasing rapidly; and the normal credit facilities of the country could not keep pace with the need. Business men held the instruments of credit in their hands; but these instruments became dangerous when used by ignorant men or rascals. One favorite scheme for raising capital involved the circulation of domestic bills of exchange. To give a simple illustration: A through an arrangement with B might

[51] Earlier in the year merchants who yielded to the demand for £3 feared a loss. *Ibid.*, Jan. 30—Feb. 1, 1771.

[52] *Ibid.*, Feb. 25-27, 1771.   [53] *Ibid.*, May 17-20, 1771.

[54] *Ibid.*, July 1-3, 1771.   [55] *Parl. Hist.*, XVII, 1113.

draw a bill upon B, though B owed A nothing. B would accept the bill on condition that he could within a certain time re-draw upon A for the original sum plus interest and commission. Before the second bill fell due, A would draw a new and larger bill upon B or upon some other man in the same game. The larger the number concerned, the less likely was detection by the banks. The latter used their own paper to discount these bills, and the bank paper was frequently poorly secured. Consequently business rested on a very weak foundation. The banks uncovered the system of circulating bills too late to prevent the mischief. They tried to withdraw their capital from such precarious business gradually, by raising the discount rate. Then a Scottish firm, that of Douglas, Heron and Company, established the Ayr Bank, for the purpose of offering more liberal discount rates, and relieving the situation. The new bank took part of the burden from the older institutions but enabled speculators to involve themselves even more deeply in debt.[56]

The circulation of domestic bills of exchange, "made bills" as they were called, was at its height just at the time when the breaking of American non-importation agreements encouraged British adventurers to undertake an export business.[57] Unsound finance intensified the evils of overproduction and speculation. When colonial trade ceased to bring in the expected profits, and when the banks raised their discount rates, business men were hard pressed for cash to meet their immediate requirements. Banks also felt the pressure. In the winter of 1771-1772 credit contracted rapidly. A few of the weaker business houses failed; but the great crash came in June of the latter year.[58] The Ayr Bank barely escaped complete

[56] Adam Smith, *The Wealth of Nations*, London, 1887, I, 313-317.
[57] *Parl. Hist.*, XVII, 1119.
[58] Many failures resulted from the bankruptcy of Alexander Fordyce of

disaster, and even the Bank of England stopped its discount business for a few weeks. Private credit had to support these two banking organizations. In June, 1772, London merchants met at the King's Arms Tavern, and chose Beeston Long, an eminent trader to the West Indies, as chairman. At this meeting about fifty merchants signed a resolution to raise a subscription for indemnifying the Bank of England against any loss it might sustain from discounting the bills of Douglas, Heron and Company.[59]

Although the banks were saved, nothing could protect the smaller business houses from collapse. In a period of seventeen days, forty-six commissions for bankruptcy passed the great seal, and the number of failures grew in succeeding weeks.[60] The panic and consequent liquidation affected all forms of business enterprise, including trade with America. The difficulty of getting money from America, a difficulty enhanced by the distance that separated the two countries, placed British merchants in a peculiarly perilous position when credit at home failed. In July "a very considerable House in the American trade stopt for between sixty and seventy thousand pounds, owing to the slow circulation of money from that continent."[61] Accounts of bankruptcies filled the papers, and suicides and insanity accompanied the failures.[62] According to contemporary computation, between June, 1772, and August, 1773, one hundred and twenty important merchants, bankers, and traders were completely ruined, owing to "speculation, made bills, and other species of

Clement's Lane, who left for France when he found his case was hopeless. Speculation seems to have been the cause of failure. His partners paid 4s. in the pound, and he finally returned to face charges. *Lloyd's,* June to December, 1772.

59 *Ibid.,* June 22-24; 24-26, 1772.　　60 *Ibid.,* July 15-17, 1772.
61 *Ibid.,* July 22-24, 1772.　　62 *Ibid.,* July 1-3, 1772.

deceitful credit."[63] Distrust was so prevalent even in
January, 1773, that respectable houses found difficulty in
getting good bills of exchange discounted. In one case
private individuals raised £100,000 to discount the bills
of certain houses whose books showed that they were not
only solvent but prosperous.[64] Bankers and traders tended
to profit by the sad experience of those months.

At the beginning of the new year the Bank of England
decided upon stricter regulations for the discounting of
bills, "the growing insecurity of public credit rendering
an additional share of caution absolutely necessary."[65]
Early in the history of the panic business men made two
important decisions. Conservative traders resolved in
the first place to take their money out of private hands
and to deposit it with the Bank of England; and in the
second place, "to keep their cash at no bankers, who
jointly or separately, by themselves or their agents, are
known to sport in the Alley, in what are called bulls and
bears, since by an unlucky stroke in this illegal traffic,
usually called speculation, hundreds of their creditors
may be ruined. . . ."[66] The financial perils of 1772 and
1773 aroused an unwonted caution and circumspection in
the merchants who traded with America, and caused them
to study and criticise the conditions under which they did
business with the colonies. In the period when colonial
trade was at a low ebb, England's latent jealousy of the
colonies rose to the surface.

In the eighteenth century Englishmen constantly complained of the emigration of artisans to the new world.
The exodus naturally increased when business in Great
Britain was dull. In 1772, for example, the newspapers
reported that plush weavers from Coventry had been

63 *Lloyd's*, Aug. 23-25, 1773.   64 *Ibid.*, Jan. 22-25, 1773.
65 *Ibid.*, Jan. 1-4, 1773.   66 *Ibid.*, June 19-22, 1772.

hired to go to New England.[67] Since at that very time
Boston was importing looms, the conclusion was obvious
that the colonists were planning to weave their own cloth.
Although the colonists could scarcely manufacture all
their own goods, Englishmen were convinced that the
Americans would smuggle from France or Holland the
articles which they could not produce. Bankrupt merchants were quick to find fault with the colonists, and
placed the blame for their own losses upon America
rather than upon their own shoulders. Embittered by
failures, a small number of Englishmen arrived at the
conclusion that colonies were from all points of view a
disadvantage to the mother country; but this opinion was
still rare enough to cause comment.[68] During the depression of 1772 and 1773 artisans had little encouragement
for remaining in England. They were in a miserable state.
Laboring men had to bear the brunt of all the evils connected with a period of agricultural as well as commercial
and industrial readjustment. Critics could not agree upon
the cause of the workers' misery. Some blamed the en-
grossing of farms; others, the manipulation of the provision market; still others, the corn law.[69] But merchants
generally agreed that parliament's failure to settle the
quarrel with America prevented stability of trade, and

[67] *Ibid.*, Aug. 17-19, 1772.
[68] *Ibid.*, Aug. 19-21, 1772. Lord Hillsborough opposed grants of land
in the Ohio Valley because they would increase the difficulty of defense, but
a supporter made the following general assertion: ''It may be questioned
whether it be sound policy in any state to establish any colonies at all; we
have the best political writers on our side, who all concur in censuring the
measure as injudicious, and tending to weaken and finally destroy the mother
country.''
[69] Parliament sought to remedy conditions by a corn law which allowed
the importation of wheat at a duty of 6d. per quarter when the price reached
48s. and the exportation when the price fell to 44s. *Lloyd's*, May 10-12; Jan.
8-11, 1773. L. Levi, *History of British Commerce, 1763-1870*, London, 1872,
part I, p. 24. 13 George III, c. 43.

was consequently at the root of most commercial difficulties. Convinced of the need for parliamentary action, merchants and manufacturers again appealed to the government.

London merchants took the initiative, as usual, and interviewed Lord Dartmouth, secretary of state for the colonies and president of the Board of Trade.[70] Lace and linen manufacturers, petitioning parliament for duties on competing imports, suggested that the decrease in the American demand was one cause of their poverty.[71] Merchants and freemen of Worcester appealed to parliament for relief in a period of declining trade and credit.[72] The most poignant plea came from the journeymen weavers of London, a class usually silent in regard to their own needs. Their petition was significant because the authors without hesitation proclaimed the trouble with America responsible for their distress.[73] Undoubtedly the people of Great Britain and America needed a wise and comprehensive settlement of their disagreements, a sort of panacea for the mercantile distresses of the empire; but

---

[70] *Lloyd's*, Jan. 25-27, 1773.   [71] *Commons Journals*, XXXIV, 127.
[72] *Lloyd's*, Nov. 8-10; 10-13, 1773.

[73] ''That Divine Providence which hath been pleased to place us in the humble rank we hold amongst the rest of your Majesty's subjects, hath been mercifully pleased at the same time not to deny us the gift of common understanding by which to discern the causes that have produced the afflictions we experience; the most obvious of these, were it not a presumption, we would humbly beg leave to represent, are founded in that insatiable venality which those entrusted with the executive administration of your Majesty's government make the sole rule of their conduct. The same spirit of rapacity originally laid the foundation of and continues to cultivate, that destructive contention which has so long prevailed between the Parent State and the British Colonies in America; a contention which tends totally to alienate the affections of our distant fellow-subjects, is pregnant with every future commercial evil, and is the principal immediate cause of the prevailing distress amongst the British Merchants, and which, through them, extends to us, your Majesty's miserable subjects, who, for want of the usual circulation of their operations, are reduced to the utmost degree of destitution and wretchedness.'' *Ibid.*, Apr. 30—May 3, 1773.

the superman with the superbrain fitted for the task was
lacking. The ministers of George III had little breadth
of vision. Their medicine was intended only as a sedative,
and it affected merely one branch of traders, the East
India Company.

As was the case with other organizations trading with
America, the East India Company overestimated the colonial demand for their goods on the breakdown of the
non-importation agreements. Consequently, their warehouses were full of tea which they could not sell. The
company was on the verge of bankruptcy when parliament came to its relief with the East India Tea Act of
1773. Before the passage of the Townshend Acts in 1767
the company sold £600,000 worth of tea in the colonies
annually; but when America boycotted English tea, Holland and Denmark took over the trade. In January, 1773,
a correspondent for *Lloyd's* wrote that the failure of the
colonial market made a difference of three millions in the
cash account of the company, accounted for a loss in the
national revenue, and was an important factor in producing the scarcity of money and business stagnation in
the country.[74] Speculators naturally blamed the ministry
for its blunder in taxing colonial imports of tea.[75] The
colonists had been more punctilious in refusing to purchase British tea than they had been in refusing to receive any other British commodity. On giving up the
non-importation agreements colonial merchants almost
invariably stipulated that they would still refuse to buy
English tea. Members of the general court of the East
India Company knew that it would be necessary to offer
the colonists a real inducement for trading with them
rather than with the Dutch. The company proposed that

[74] *Ibid.*, Jan. 20-22, 1773.

[75] J. Burgh, *Political Disquisitions or An Enquiry into Public Errors,
Defects, and Abuses*, Philadelphia, 1775, II, 322.

parliament remove the threepenny duty on tea in America, and allow the same drawback on export from Great Britain to America as on export to any foreign country. In that case American merchants could have bought tea from England more cheaply than from Holland.[76] The government ignored this proposal of the company, and introduced its own measure for relief. By the terms of the East India Act of May, 1773, parliament retained the duty on tea in America, thus perpetuating a principle involved in the Declaratory Act of 1766; but provided for a drawback on tea exported from England to America. As a result British tea actually sold for less in America than in England, and also for less than the Dutch smuggler demanded when delivering tea to his American customers.[77] The American colonists, however, were not quarreling over a price, but over a principle.

The members of Lord North's ministry failed to gauge the temper of the colonists, if they believed for one minute that America could be bribed into paying a duty. Even the conservative merchants in America, those who particularly dreaded a break with England, were enraged by the act because parliament had practically given to the East India Company a monopoly of the transportation and distribution of tea, thus destroying the business of the American tea merchant. The East India Act successfully united radicals and conservatives in the colonies, aroused the slumbering antagonism of American patriots, and provoked a revolution. From 1773 events moved swiftly both in England and America. The colonists refused to receive English tea. In Boston a few hot-headed radicals enjoyed their tea party, and gave the home government an excuse to inaugurate its new policy

[76] *Lloyd's*, Feb. 22-24; Feb. 26—Mar. 1, 1773.
[77] 13 George III, c. 44. Schlesinger, *The Colonial Merchants and the American Revolution, 1763-1776*, pp. 263-264.

of coercion. In spite of warnings that British merchants owned colonial property worth four million pounds, and that foreign trade was dull, the government proceeded to carry through parliament the "Intolerable Acts." The ministry remained deaf to such advice as the following: "Let authority give way to prudence. Dignity is supported best by justice; . . . one hundred thousand manufacturers [are] . . . of more importance than a shadowy authority."[78] Parliament first closed the port of Boston, then made changes in the government and in the administration of justice in Massachusetts Bay, and provided for the quartering of soldiers in the colonies. The use of coercion in America endangered the business of British merchants and was contrary to their policy. The adoption of coercive measures by the British government was conclusive proof that British merchants had lost most of their influence with the administration. But several months passed before merchants and manufacturers realized the seriousness of the American revolt.

Large commissions from America continued to reach England. Although there were exaggerated reports of colonial agreements for resuming non-importation, the British public was loath to believe that the new agreements would amount to any more than the old.[79] News that Norfolk, Virginia, had refused to accept non-importation, because Boston had failed to live up to her earlier agreement, increased the optimism of the British merchants.[80] An encouraging number of ships cleared regularly from the customhouse in London; and for several months business continued to flourish. At the autumn

[78] *Lloyd's*, Oct. 21-24, 1774.

[79] *Ibid.*, June 15-17, 1774. British fears at first exaggerated the facts in the new non-importation movement. Compare Schlesinger, *The Colonial Merchants and the American Revolution, 1763-1776*, pp. 325-327.

[80] *Lloyd's*, June 29—July 1, 1774. The temper of Norfolk was less radical than that of rural Virginia. Schlesinger, pp. 364-365.

fair in Bristol there was a brisk trade in coarse cloths and low-priced woolen goods for the American market.[81] Long intervals passed without the passage through the great seal of a single commission for bankruptcy. Nevertheless, the period of temporary business prosperity came to a sudden close on the first of December.

Fifty-six colonial patriots, meeting at Philadelphia in September as the first Continental Congress, had adopted the Continental Association, a more systematic and more nearly universal scheme of non-importation than any that had been previously tried. Their plan was to go into effect in December. British trade increased during the intervening months, for American merchants were determined to have available a large store of British commodities before trade ceased. British merchants were more cautious than usual about extending credit,[82] but in spite of their unwillingness to trust the colonists, the value of exports to America rose about £600,000 between 1773 and 1774. The volume of American business in these few months perhaps exaggerated in the minds of British merchants the real importance of colonial trade. Recent imports of grain from America suggested another advantage to be derived from the colonies.[83] Imported grain meant cheaper bread for the laborer, more contentment, and better work. All the mercantile classes tended to profit from cheap provisions. The country gentlemen, on the other hand, naturally wanted high prices for their own products, and resented competition from America. When the year 1774 came to a close merchants and manufacturers were deeply impressed with the necessity of maintaining peace with America, while the country gentlemen were inclined to approve the ministerial policy of coercion.

[81] *Lloyd's*, Sept. 9-12; 12-14, 1774.
[82] *Ibid.*, June 27-29, 1774.   [83] *Ibid.*, Oct. 12-14, 1774.

Reports of dull times in England followed almost immediately upon the closing of colonial trade. In Birmingham manufacturers began to discharge their workmen.[84] In London a shoemaker's orders dropped to one-tenth of his previous business.[85] In Wolverhampton manufacturers of iron and steel repeated the complaint.[86] But from Leeds, Derby, Manchester, and Nottingham came contradictory reports.[87] While one house mentioned a loss of £12,000 from American non-importation, other firms insisted they were as busy as ever.[88] As a matter of fact, the lack of the usual American demand did not have such disastrous material effects as one might have supposed; and consequently merchants and manufacturers remained cheerful in the face of a colonial policy that was rapidly alienating America.

Merchants still hoped that the colonists would not be able to enforce their non-importation agreement. Orders received by a "very respectable House in the Boston and Salem trade" encouraged them in this happy belief.[89] British merchants found in Georgia, Florida, and Quebec an increased demand for goods which were destined eventually to find their way into the rebellious colonies.[90] Soldiers, who had to be clothed and armed to go out on the spring transports, furnished more business for British workers. On the transports British merchants shipped other goods intended for sale in America. Sound political policy lay behind this venture, for not only did the increase of business keep the manufacturers at home satisfied, but the sale of British goods in America would help to destroy the Continental Association and produce dis-

84 *Ibid.*, Dec. 19-21, 1774.   85 *Ibid.*, Dec. 26-28, 1774.
86 *Commons Journals*, XXXV, 81.
87 *Lloyd's*, Jan. 11-13; 16-18; 23-25; 25-27, 1775.
88 *London Chronicle*, Jan. 3-5, 1775.
89 *Lloyd's*, Dec. 12-14, 1775.   90 *Ibid.*, Mar. 24-27, 1775.

union in the colonies.[91] Fortunately for the British merchants they did not rely solely upon the American market.
On December 5, 1774, the king announced to parliament
the conclusion of the war between Russia and the Porte.[92]
Although the war itself had created a Russian demand
for certain British goods, peace opened up greater opportunities for trade with Persia and other countries
reached through Russian trade routes. England had long
enjoyed a commercial treaty with Russia which proved
of great value now that the colonial trade was declining.
American orders, given in spite of the non-importation
agreements; larger sales to the American colonies which
were not included in the Continental Association; contracts for supplying the army; increased trade with Europe—all furnished business for British merchants and
tempered their criticism of the government policy. Indeed
strict mercantilists were inclined to approve the course
which government officials were following.

According to the mercantilists the mother country must
monopolize the trade of the colonies in order to realize
any advantages from their possession. According to one
contemporary, "The colonies may be considered as the
great farms of the public, and the colonists as our tenants
whom we wish to treat kindly whilst they act as such;
but when they usurp the inheritance, and tell us they are,
and will be independent of us, it is time to look about us
and keep them to the terms of their leases."[93] After 1765
the suspicion on the part of the British merchants that
the colonies were becoming too self-sufficient increased
steadily. When the colonists were resisting the enforcement of the Stamp Act Englishmen questioned which
would establish independence sooner, enforcing or repeal-

[91] *Lloyd's* Feb. 1-3; Apr. 12-14; May 24-26, 1775.
[92] *Commons Journals*, XXXV, 8.   [93] *Lloyd's*, Jan. 9-11, 1775.

ing the act.[94] By 1774 when the report of the first Continental Congress reached Great Britain Englishmen were convinced that the Americans wanted freedom of trade, if not independence; and because of that conviction they were inclined to support the policy of coercion.

Even as early as 1768, when New England was refusing to import British goods, a contributor to the *Gentleman's Magazine* suggested that parliament retaliate by economic restrictions on America. He declared that if no New England vessel could enter the port of any British dominion, if no New Englander were allowed to fish off the Banks of Newfoundland, carry lumber to any British possession, sell rum to any British subject, trade beyond the borders of New England with American Indians in alliance with Great Britain—if all these things were forbidden to New Englanders, they would soon come to terms.[95] By 1775 the spirit of retaliation had grown stronger. Two important facts underlie both the suggestion in the *Gentleman's Magazine* and the coercive acts of later years. First, the British considered New England the source of most of their trouble in America, the leader in revolt. Secondly, they no longer believed implicitly that the loss of the colonial market would spell complete disaster for British trade. Indeed, the losses directly due to speculation in American trade, and to the extensive credit demanded by the colonists had forced British merchants to consider the superior advantages in other enterprises. Englishmen resented the fact that the colonists had "used" British merchants to further their own end in past disputes with the mother country. Conservative merchants realized that the speculative character of colonial trade in recent years detracted from its value. In 1775 the "malcontents," those dissatisfied with the gov-

[94] Add. MSS., 33030, f. 105.   [95] Oct., 1768, p. 467.

ernmental policy, were said to be adventurers who "are well known to be of desperate circumstances and principles, whose aim is to profit by the public confusion, and not by a legal honest way of trade."[96] If George III's ministers really believed that the petitioners for leniency were all speculative traders, it is no wonder that they ignored the petitions. There were, however, serious merchants who honestly believed that it would be better to abandon parliamentary control and keep the friendship and unregulated trade of America. Consciously or not, they had accepted the doctrine of free trade. Disciples of free trade had no influence on governmental policy in the years of the American Revolution, but they did affect the merchants' campaign for peace.

British merchants, regardless of the varying opinions of individuals, were as a group doing what they could to keep peace with America. War, as they knew, would mean destruction of much American property, including their own. No one could foretell what conditions would follow a war to subjugate the colonies; but the American confiscation of British property early in the Revolution justified the fears of British merchants. They were far from confident that the temporarily increased demand from Europe for British manufactures would prove permanent.[97] When all other arguments for conciliating America failed, there was always the dread of seeing French merchants gain what the British were losing. In the fall of 1774 letters from France had told of increasing commerce between that country and the British colonies

[96] Lloyd's, Jan. 25-27, 1775.

[97] Merchants from Norwich, petitioning parliament against coercion, said: ". . . if the demand of Norwich stuffs to any several parts of Europe (of late plentifully supplied) should by any means be lessened, the petitioners are fearful of the consequences which must inevitably happen to the said city from the stoppage of the American trade." Commons Journals, XXXV, 77.

in America. Vergennes, called the Sully of that age, was said to be taking advantage of the mistakes of the British government.[98] Even though British merchants might question whether or not they had valued colonial trade too highly, they were not prepared to toss any possible advantage lightly away into the laps of their ancient enemies. For these reasons the merchants were anxious for parliament to act slowly in the crisis following the Boston tea party.

The merchants urged parliament to give the people of Boston time to hold an assembly and vote on the question of repaying the East India Company. Perhaps the merchants imagined that the people of New England were more tractable than they proved to be. At any rate, they were so sure that the Bostonians would pay for the tea destroyed that they themselves offered to compensate the company, and asked only six months to settle with the town. According to the invoice of the company, the value of the tea in Boston harbor was £8,000. The Lord Mayor of London offered to furnish £20,000 as security for the payment of the £8,000. Lord North, however, required in addition that the merchants should be responsible for the "future peaceable conduct and entire acquiescence of the town" in receiving tea. The merchants refused Lord North's demand, as he must have intended they should, on the ground that it was absurd and impossible.[99] In spite of their confidence in the ultimate reasonableness of the Bostonians, London merchants wished no one to misunderstand their own attitude. They did not in the least condone the rash action of the Boston radicals, but they did want the people of Boston to have an opportunity to reconsider and to pay for the injuries committed

[98] *Lloyd's*, Sept. 5-7, 1774. *London Magazine*, Oct., 1774, p. 509.
[99] Public Record Office, Chatham Papers, 97, Amer., No. 5. *Lloyd's*, Mar. 16-18, 1774.

in a reckless moment. In October when all Britain was waiting for news of the American congress, the merchants hoped that the first decision of congress would be to settle with the East India Company. They knew that if the colonists refused to take this step, any petitions or remonstrances on their part would be worthless;[100] but they were doomed to disappointment. In November a correspondent for *Lloyd's* wrote: "The real friends of America are greatly disappointed that the Congress have not resolved on paying for the tea destroyed. They were in hopes that however just or unjust the complaints of the colonies against the illegality or oppression of parliament, that they should at least have had that piece of common honesty to have urged in their favor, that they had agreed to pay for the goods they had destroyed. As it now stands, they are at a loss what they can say in favour of the Colonies, and such a deliberate piece of mischief as this is known to be, will be immediately urged against them, whenever they plead in their favour."[101] Nevertheless, in spite of the feeling that the tide was moving relentlessly against them, merchants and manufacturers made another effort to reconcile the mother country and her colonies.

London merchants again took the lead, but they were not alone in dreading a "civil war" and a total loss of the American trade.[102] When they met at the King's Arms Tavern on January 4, they heard resolutions and letters from a meeting of West India merchants, as well as from the merchants of Bristol, asking for their coöperation. Letters from the council of commerce at Liverpool, from Manchester, Leeds, and other manufacturing towns, encouraged the London merchants to petition parliament

---

100 *Lloyd's*, Oct. 28-31, 1774.
101 *Ibid.*, Nov. 11-14, 1774.   102 *Ibid.*, Dec. 16-19, 1774.

again.[103] In 1766 they had forced parliament to repeal the Stamp Act; in 1770 they had been less successful; in 1775 they could at least test their influence again. The merchants were almost as insistent as the ministers that Great Britain must rule her colonies; and there was perhaps some misgiving in the minds of the merchants as they studied the problem. They encouraged themselves as best they could with the belief that the colonies did not question the supreme legislative power of parliament or the acts of trade and navigation.[104] They insisted, too, that their petition should exclude all reference to any matter that verged on a political or constitutional question. When a committee had drafted the petition and presented it to the assembly for approval, merchants trading to Quebec complained that the petition made no reference to the objectionable Quebec Act, and that Quebec merchants had not been represented on the drafting committee.[105] One merchant, by the name of Sharp, declared that "Canada was universally looked upon as a cudgel in the hands of Government against the rest of the Americans." The majority of the merchants, however, refused to consider any amendment to the petition or the resolutions, though they did name three Quebec merchants on the committee that was to present the petition to the House of Commons.[106] They knew they would have to be most discreet if they were to receive any consideration from the government; and their petition was as tactful as possible under the circumstances.

West India merchants and planters had their own rea-

[103] *London Chronicle*, Jan. 5-7, 1775. *London Magazine*, Jan., 1775, pp. 42-43. *Lloyd's*, Jan. 6-9, 1775.

[104] *Lloyd's*, Dec. 16-19, 1774.

[105] In the summer of 1774 merchants had petitioned the king against the Quebec Act, protesting that property would be endangered by a return to French law and trial. *Ibid.*, June 20-22, 1774.

[106] *Ibid.*, Jan. 11-13, 1775.

sons for petitioning parliament against the acts which had caused the American "Articles of Association." Good business in the West Indies depended upon a supply of lumber and provisions from North America; but the first Continental Congress had voted to stop exportation to Great Britian and the British West Indies in September, 1775, unless parliament yielded to their demands before that time. Property in the West Indies, owned largely by planters resident in England, would certainly drop in value; and British merchants would find it hard to collect their debts. A few merchants declared they were already having trouble with their West India business, and all agreed that they should not wait for harder times before petitioning parliament. Anxious to offend neither the colonists nor the home government, West India merchants could not decide what term to use in speaking of the Philadelphia assembly. The American word, "Congress," would certainly antagonize the ministry, and the expression, "called a Congress," would of course displease the colonists. This seeming quibbling over a word suggests that their loyalties tended to draw British merchants into one course of action, while business interests impelled them to take another. They were in that uncomfortable position which demands a compromise. In the final draft of the petition presented by the West India merchants the first Continental Congress became merely "a meeting held at Philadelphia."[107]

By whatever name it was known the meeting at Philadelphia brought consternation to the hearts of British merchants and manufacturers. Other petitions quickly followed those from London. There were two from Bristol, one from the Merchant Venturers, and one from other merchants, traders, and manufacturers; there were others from merchants at Liverpool, Leeds, and White-

[107] *Lloyd's,* Jan. 6-9; 18-20, 1775.

haven; from merchants and manufacturers in Norwich,
Manchester, Dudley, and Birmingham; from manufacturers in Bridport and Nottingham; from the pottery
makers in Staffordshire; and another from the manufacturers of hats and shoes in the same county.[108] The
people of Bridport were especially disconsolate. They
manufactured nets, lines, twine, and canvas, for use in
the American fisheries; and they declared that in their
community no other industry was possible. Several thousand workmen were entirely dependent upon trade with
America; but for a whole season, they wrote, there had
not been an order of the value of a shilling. They had
been confident that the colonists were dependent upon
supplies for fishing and would except these articles from
their non-importation agreement. They were too optimistic, however, and continued to manufacture until they
had on hand a large stock of goods which could be used
only in America. They were unable to sell the goods already in stock, and they were sure the colonies must be
manufacturing supplies for themselves, in which case
Bridport had lost its market forever.[109] At least fifteen
different petitions from English towns, and others from
Scotland and Ireland, described almost as feelingly as
the petition of Bridport the suffering resulting from
parliament's failure to conciliate the colonies. But parliament treated the fifteen petitions with less consideration
than it showed to one of the thirty-five petitions presented
in 1766.

For more than two months London merchants tried
their influence with every branch of government, but in
every case they failed. The House of Commons referred
the petitions to one committee and the papers from Lord
North on American affairs to another. Since this action

108 *Commons Journals*, XXXV, 72-186.
109 *Ibid.*, p. 123.

prevented the petitions from having any influence upon
American measures, London merchants withdrew their
original petition and substituted another, asking the
House of Commons to grant them a hearing before considering the American question.[110] When the House of
Commons persisted in its decision to examine the American papers and to hear the merchants in separate committees, Thomas Wooldridge announced that the merchants waived their right to a hearing.[111] Disappointed in
their attempt to influence the lower house of parliament,
the merchants next petitioned the House of Lords to
grant them a hearing before the Lords' conference with
the House of Commons.[112] Failing in this move, the merchants decided to wait until they could learn what bills
the ministers would propose as a result of the address to
the king.[113] Another petition to the House of Commons
followed the news that the ministers were planning to
restrict the trade of New England to the British Isles
and the British possessions in the West Indies, and to
prevent New Englanders from fishing off the Banks of
Newfoundland. This second petition explained how seriously the proposed act would affect British merchants,
whose debts were in large part paid from the proceeds
of the fishery.[114] The failure of this petition and of one
to the king convinced the London merchants that their
cause was hopeless.

When in February the West India merchants presented
their carefully worded petition they fared no better, although their advocate at the bar of the House of Commons was Richard Glover, merchant and son of a merchant and experienced in the ways of parliament.[115]
Neither eloquence nor statistics could change the settled

[110] Lloyd's, Jan. 25-27, 1775.   [111] Parl. Hist., XVIII, 194.
[112] Lloyd's, Feb. 6-8, 1775.   [113] Ibid., Feb. 8-10; 15-17, 1775.
[114] Commons Journals, XXXV, 145.   [115] Ibid., p. 91.

determination of the ministers.[116] Merchants and traders who really valued the friendship of America resorted to more direct means of expressing their good-will; and in February a subscription fund for the people of New England was started.[117] When the ministers and members of parliament failed to answer the petitions of the merchants, they were probably influenced by the fact that the mercantile classes were no longer unanimous on the question of American policy. Indeed the loyal petitions from members of the mercantile classes completely destroyed the effect of the remonstrances.

In 1775 many British merchants realized that the time had come when Great Britain could no longer make concessions to America without sacrificing that very parliamentary supremacy which had protected British traders in their relations with the colonies. This idea formed the main theme of the petitions to parliament from Birmingham, Leeds, Nottingham, Huddersfield, and Trowbridge.[118] Petitioners from these towns declared that they preferred to suffer temporary inconvenience rather than to submit to conditions which would lead sooner or later to colonial independence. The clothiers of Trowbridge even stated that it was only just for America to contribute to the revenue, because heavy taxes in Great Britain were driving woolen manufacturers out of England into the colonies.[119] It is difficult to say how sincere these petitioners in support of government were, or how truly they represented the mercantile classes.

Members of the opposition in the House of Commons declared that the petitioners for strict enforcement of colonial laws were trying to win favors from the government; and they called witnesses before the bar of the

---

[116] *Parl. Hist.*, XVIII, 461.   [117] *Lloyd's*, Feb. 17-20, 1775.
[118] *Commons Journals*, XXXV, 77, 89, 141, 186, 198.
[119] *Ibid.*, p. 198.

house to give evidence of the way in which signatures
had been obtained for the Nottingham petitions. According to newspaper reports, the merchants who protested
against American measures had formerly depended upon
the colonial demand for British manufactures; but the
signers of the counter petitions had no direct interest in
American trade.[120] Government supporters defeated a
motion to inquire into the methods used in securing
signatures for the loyal petition from Birmingham;[121]
but Edmund Burke told the opposition's side of the story.
He declared that a certain Dr. Roebuck, after vainly trying to persuade the merchants not to petition parliament
in favor of America, had started another petition in
support of the administration. According to Burke, the
doctor had personally taken the petition from house to
house soliciting signatures. Burke described this method
as "clandestine" in contrast to the usual practice of
leaving a document at some public place for all who were
interested to sign.[122] Merchants who opposed governmental measures suspected that the loyal petitioners were
trying to secure government orders for firearms.[123] Whatever the reason for the second petition, it received little
support for Birmingham was strongly "anti-ministeri-
alist."[124] Merchants and manufacturers of that city united
in thanking Burke for his services in supporting their
petition, and for his effort to secure an investigation of
the counter petition.[125]

The increase in European trade was probably more
effective than any other factor in making the merchants
lose interest in the American cause. Norwich citizens who

120 *Lloyd's*, Mar. 22-24, 1775.   121 *Commons Journals*, XXXV, p. 87.
122 *Parl. Hist.*, XVIII, 195-196.
123 *Lloyd's*, Jan. 25-27, 1775. Horace Walpole, *Letters*, London, 1857, VI,
184.
124 Curwen, *Journal and Letters*, p. 80.
125 *Lloyd's*, Feb. 13-15, 1775. *London Magazine*, July, 1775, p. 338.

opposed a suggestion for a petition to parliament on
American matters objected to "intermeddling in an affair
of such high importance to the honour and interest of the
whole nation, and particularly so, as our trade with North
America is not very considerable and our manufacturers
fully employed."[126] Governor Hutchinson wrote to his
brother that the decrease in American trade seemed to
have lost all its terror. He even claimed that London merchants had been playing a part in their recent petitioning,
and that their petitions to parliament were mere matters
of form, intended to please their American correspondents. He quoted the tale that one of the London merchants
who presented the petition to the king had remarked in
tones loud enough for the queen to hear, "I am glad I am
clear of it."[127] To whatever lengths of duplicity the uncertainty of their position may have led the merchants,
they were much less aggressive than formerly in opposing the government.

One section of the mercantile interests gave positive
and undivided support to the governmental policy of coercion. The fishermen of Poole had long been jealous of
New England because of her successes off the Banks of
Newfoundland; and they welcomed wholeheartedly the
governmental plan of restricting colonial trade and forbidding the colonists to fish in Newfoundland waters.[128]

126 *Lloyd's*, Jan. 27-30, 1775.
127 Thomas Hutchinson, *Diary and Letters*, Boston, 1884, I, 431-432.
128 *Commons Journals*, XXXV, 164. Force's *American Archives*, Fourth
Series, I, 1637. In 1771 Englishmen engaged in the fisheries in the bays of
Chaleur and Gaspé and other places on the coast of Nova Scotia and Quebec
complained of the practices of the New Englanders. They said that the colonists came in decked vessels to the grounds allotted for boat fishing, used
seines contrary to an act of parliament, and threw overboard parts of the
fish, which would soon ruin the fishery. They doubted whether by the charter
of Massachusetts Bay the colonists had the right to fish there, but would
tolerate them if they observed the regulations and restrictions. C.O. 5: 115, f.
128.

The strongest argument in the petition from Poole was the plea that the colonists prevented the fisheries from fulfilling their function as a "nursery for seamen," a school for the British navy. In the first place, a law of William III's reign which compelled every British captain of a fishing vessel to employ one inexperienced man in five did not apply to the colonies.[129] In the second place, according to the law of 1708, seamen in America were not liable to impressment; and for this reason British fishermen were tempted to go with the colonists to America when the fishing season was over, rather than return to England where they were likely to be seized for service in the British navy.[130]

The right of impressing seamen in colonial waters or on the mainland was a much debated question in the eighteenth century. After 1709 the general instructions to provincial governors omitted the clause directing them to impress seamen for the navy,[131] and until 1722 the British Admiralty ordered captains of men-of-war to refrain from the practice.[132] The law officers of the crown, however, declared that the act did not prevent colonial governors from exercising powers of impressment,[133] and that the act expired with the conclusion of the war in 1713.[134] In 1722 the Admiralty accepted the opinion of the law officers, and after that date the warning against impressment was omitted from the Admiralty instructions, and press warrants were issued to commanders in American waters.[135] When necessary the navy resorted to impress-

[129] 10 William III, c. 25, ¶ 9.   [130] 6 Anne, c. 37, ¶ 9.

[131] C.O. 391: 21, pp. 220 and 228 for decision to omit the clause. *N. Y. Col. Doc.*, V, 98-99, 124 ff.

[132] Public Record Office, Admiralty 2: 37, p. 42; 48, p. 178, for examples of instructions to commanders attending on American stations.

[133] Add. MSS., 21497, ff. 110 and 159.

[134] Admiralty 2: 50, p. 247, marginal note. *Pa. Arch.*, I, 638. *Correspondence of William Shirley*, I, 418.   [135] Admiralty 2: 51, pp. 3-6, 76, 204, etc.

ment in the colonies to secure the quota of seamen, and in time of war colonial governors received special instructions to aid commanders in securing mariners.[136] The colonists resisted the press and demanded exemption under the act of 1708.[137] The British public also believed that the act was still in force, and deplored the fact that the Americans were legally favored by freedom from the press.[138] In 1766 the lords in minority on the question of the repeal of the Stamp Act referred to the privilege which the Americans enjoyed in the matter of impressment, and expressed the fear that in the future the colonists would also be free from all financial obligations.[139] Englishmen in general felt that the Americans were failing to bear their share of burdens, and they shouldered their own the more unwillingly. The men of Poole, for example, were always annoyed by the press when they returned from their fishing expeditions, especially in time of war. Their aggravation was increased by the thought that the colonists, although contributing nothing to the naval defense of the empire, had a large share in the profits of the fishing industry. It is small wonder that Poole supported the government in its policy of coercion.

Even the merchants who had been most devoted to the colonial cause in earlier years were faced by a dilemma in the crisis of 1775. As a contemporary writer explained the situation, if the merchants refused to petition parliament for the Americans, the latter would have a pretext for refusing to pay their debts; if the Americans were

[136] Jameson, *Privateering and Piracy*, p. 449. *Correspondence of William Shirley*, I, 155-156.

[137] *Correspondence of William Shirley*, I, 417. Admiralty 1: 3676. *Mass. Hist. Soc. Pro.*, LV, 250 ff.

[138] The impressment clause of 6 Anne was not repealed until 1775— 15 George III, c. 31, § 19.

[139] *Correct Copies of the Two Protests against the Bill to Repeal the American Stamp Act of Last Session*, Paris, 1767, pp. 21-22.

successful, British merchants would then be subject to their caprice.[140] The conviction that radicals at home were taking advantage of trouble in America to demand something for themselves helped to convert the more conservative merchants to the governmental program. The increasing demand for British manufactures in Europe partly reconciled the mercantile classes to the loss of the colonial market. Since the disasters of 1772 and 1773 British merchants had been overwhelmed by the difficulty of collecting colonial debts. The combination of these various factors weakened the efforts of the mercantile classes to obtain parliamentary relief for the colonies in 1775. Furthermore, regardless of opposition, the government was now determined to follow its own policy of coercion.

On March 30, 1775, Lord North's first retaliatory measure became law. Parliament restricted the trade of New England to the British Isles and the British West Indies, and forbade the people of New England to fish off the Banks of Newfoundland. A later act extended these provisions to the rest of the colonies. Then in December came the main prohibitory act which attempted to deprive the colonies of all their commerce; but in the meantime Americans and Englishmen had met in the battles of Concord, Lexington, and Bunker Hill, and war had begun. Merchants who favored conciliation had fought a losing fight, both with the government and with public opinion, for in 1775 coercion was a popular policy. During the war, merchants occasionally renewed their demands for conciliation, but in a half-hearted fashion. For the most part, they concentrated on making the best of a bad situation.

140 *Lloyd's*, Jan. 27-30, 1775.

CHAPTER IV

INTERESTS, ACTIVITIES, AND OPINIONS OF THE MERCANTILE CLASSES.

III. DURING THE WAR.

DURING the period of armed conflict the rebellious American colonies became for Great Britain not only a hostile but in effect an alien country. Many existing evils increased as the breach between the two countries grew wider. On the other hand one benefit resulted from the war. Merchants and manufacturers were forced to diversify their business, to adjust themselves to new situations, and to seek compensations for their American losses in a variety of ways.

The merchants, however, were first concerned with the unfortunate results of the war with America. After 1775 British traders found it impossible to collect their debts in America. Those who pressed the colonists for payment in the summer of 1775 were fairly successful. A London merchant wrote from New York that he had no difficulty in collecting what was due him; and Glasgow merchants reported that they had collected from America a debt of half a million, and that outstanding debts were trifling.[1] Merchants who depended upon correspondence for all their business transactions were less fortunate, and after 1775 there was little possibility of collecting by any method. Bankruptcies increased among the American traders in Great Britain. A man might as well cross from

---

[1] *Lloyd's,* Aug. 16-18, 1775. *London Magazine,* Aug., 1775, p. 435.

his list of assets all colonial book debts; and land and buildings in America were worth very little to British merchants when the new state governments were seizing British property.

Few bankrupts were as fortunate as the merchant whose creditors admitted that his failure was due to the war rather than to mismanagement. Finding that American importers owed him £70,000, while he owed only £27,-000 in England, his creditors gave him a letter of credit for three years, hoping that in the meantime he might be able to improve his situation.[2] Richard Neave and his son furnish another illustration of the effects of the war. They were among the exporters whose business began to suffer in 1766. In that year payments from America ceased, and as a result the Neaves were heavily in debt. For several years they managed to pay the interest on their indebtedness and a part of the principal. In 1772, the year of the panic, they temporarily stopped payment, although their assets were £50,000 more than their liabilities. After an interval they again paid something until the British statute restraining commerce with America increased the difficulty of collecting from the colonies. The Neaves held real property in America as security for their debts; and when in 1777 their English creditors began to make life miserable for them, they decided to sail for the colonies where they could either dispose of their land or manage it themselves.[3] The end of the story is not told, but they were probably more comfortable among their enemies in America than among their creditors at home.

In parliament his Majesty's opposition tried to harry the government by talking about the business failures

2 *London Magazine*, Sept., 1776, pp. 501-502.
3 State Papers Domestic, George III, 12, no. 106.

caused by the war. In 1778 Thomas Wooldridge, a London merchant, declared before the House of Lords that the average debt of the colonies to British merchants was worth only five shillings in the pound. Where comparatively little property had been destroyed, as in North and South Carolina, debts were still valuable; but in New York and Pennsylvania they were practically worthless.[4]

Although British manufacturers suffered far less than the merchants, the loss of the colonial market brought misfortune to many an enterpriser and hardship to the laborers. Woolen workers in Norwich and linen weavers in Chester were idle when the colonies stopped purchasing their goods.[5] For a time the makers of earthenware expected to sell enough products in Spain to compensate for the loss of the colonial market, but in 1777 this seemed a forlorn hope.[6] Richard Champion, a china manufacturer of Bristol, finally acknowledged that under the circumstances the struggle for success was too severe. He had depended upon selling his cheaper products in America, but during the war that market failed. He found it difficult to borrow sufficient capital for his business, and the competition with Wedgwood was too keen for comfort. In 1781, financially embarrassed, he sold his share of the business, and three years later he moved to America to start life anew.[7] A man might well hesitate before risking a new venture in an unknown country, but in America he was at least safe from his creditors and from a debtors' prison.

Mechanics in the pottery and hardware industries, both affected by colonial disputes, filled the jails of Stafford County, while parliament wrestled with the problem of

[4] *Parl. Hist.*, XIX, 710.
[5] *Lloyd's*, June 9-12, 1775; July 18-21, 1777.
[6] *Ibid.*, Feb. 28—March 3, 1777.
[7] Latimer, *Annals of Bristol in the Eighteenth Century*, p. 383.

insolvent debtors.[8] Idle laborers who managed to elude
the debtors' prison were perhaps in even greater physical
distress. Lancashire cotton spinners complained bitterly
of injuries caused by the American war, the closing of
the Spanish market, the cessation of the African trade,
the disturbance in West Indian traffic, and finally the
exclusion of British ships from the Mediterranean. Combined with these misfortunes, however, was another, "a
domestic evil of very great magnitude," "the introduction of patent machines and engines of various descriptions."[9] Historians call this "evil" the beginning of the
industrial era. Unemployment was bound to result from
the industrial changes of the period, but the American
war aggravated conditions, serious at best.

When merchants and manufacturers were losing their
colonial trade, and when laborers were idle, shipowners
necessarily suffered, too. If vessels set sail for America
loaded with army supplies or the goods of speculative
traders, their owners were taking the gravest chances.
American privateers were daring. Farmers on the western coast trembled at their bold raids, and even feared an
organized invasion. Naturally commerce was in danger.
In October, 1776, *Lloyd's* stated that the Americans had
captured sixty-one British ships; but that thirteen of
these had been retaken.[10] A few days later the number of
captures rose to ninety, and the total value of the large
ships alone was said to be £576,000.[11] Insurance rates rose
rapidly. Before the war the rate of insurance on goods

---

[8] C.O. 5: 116, f. 229.

[9] *Commons Journals*, XXXVI, 834-835. The ignorant workmen of Wigan
tried to wreak their revenge upon the machines; and the result was an orgy
of destruction. Magistrates and manufacturers, to pacify the workers, agreed
to submit the grievances of the laborers to parliament; and promised not
to use machines or engines, worked by water or horses, for carding, roving,
or spinning cotton until they could learn the attitude of parliament.

[10] *Lloyd's*, Oct. 23-25, 1776.   [11] *Ibid.*, Nov. 6-8; Dec. 6-9, 1776.

bound for the West Indies or North Carolina was two or two and one half per cent; in 1778 it was double that amount with convoy, or fifteen per cent without.[12] Seamen feared impressment for the royal navy, and for that reason hesitated to ship on a merchant vessel where they would be in particular danger.[13] Commerce with the West Indies and Africa, as well as with North America, suffered from the high insurance rates and the scarcity of seamen.[14]

Even the fisheries felt the effects of war in the colonies. The people of Great Britain, jealous of the New Englanders, found that they could not do without them on the Banks of Newfoundland as easily as they had hoped. British fishermen missed the supplies which they used to obtain from the New Englanders; and they were hampered by exclusion from American ports. Although the British people had valued the fishery at £1,500,000 and cherished it as a "nursery for their seamen," pessimists nevertheless suggested that they must abandon this source of wealth. When in 1777 news circulated in England that the Americans had scattered the ships on the Grand Banks, sinking some, and practically ruining the fleet, the port towns grew very restless. Even Englishmen who were most loyal to the government questioned the wisdom of forcing the colonial issue to a point where their own business might be ruined.[15]

Not only did the British mercantile classes lose business because of the war in America, but to their chagrin they saw France and Holland gaining what they had lost. Letters from European ports described the profits that foreigners were making from British misfortunes.[16]

12 *Parl. Hist.*, XIX, 709.
13 *Lloyd's*, Oct. 28-30; Oct. 30—Nov. 1, 1776.
14 *Ibid.*, May 28-30, 1777.   15 Curwen, *Journal and Letters*, p. 159.
16 *Lloyd's*, June 28—July 1, 1776.

France, for example, was buying tobacco from Virginia and Maryland, one of the enumerated commodities long monopolized by England.[17] Holland was trading lumber, barrel-staves, hoops, and other supplies for the products of the West Indies.[18] Under ordinary conditions the islands would have purchased these goods from New England, furnishing American traders with specie which they could use in exchange for British manufactures.

[As the enmity of the colonies increased, Great Britain lost a plentiful source of provisions.] The mercantile classes, who were most seriously affected by dearness and scarcity of food, appreciated the fact that imports from America had helped to keep down the price of grain. Bristol merchants declared that supplies from America had not only helped to lower the price of bread, but had also been "the means of preserving multitudes from the calamitous consequences of famine." The American "Articles of Association" provided for the export of goods to Great Britain until September, 1775, several months after imports from England had ceased. The people of Bristol attributed this provision to the friendliness of the colonists, who did not wish to see their friends in England starve.[19] When direct exportation from the colonies to Great Britain was discontinued, Governor Hutchinson wrote that the French were buying American flour to sell to London contractors. One French firm imported 20,000 barrels.[20] As England was becoming increasingly dependent upon imported food supplies, all old-school economists could see the advantage of trading directly with the colonies instead of building up the commerce of England's ancient enemy, the French.

[In 1775 merchants and manufacturers were so anxious

---

[17] *Lloyd's*, Aug. 16-18, 1780.   [18] *Ibid.*, Apr. 16-18, 1777.
[19] *Ibid.*, Sept. 29—Oct. 2; Oct. 11-13, 1775.
[20] Hutchinson, *Diary*, I, 339.

for reconciliation with the colonies, that they addressed numerous petitions to king and parliament. Bristol merchants again enumerated the advantages of peace with America, and the disasters resulting from war. Eager to assure his Majesty that they had no sympathy for the constitutional claims of the colonists, they declared: "No part of your Majesty's subjects can wish more earnestly to preserve the constitutional superiority of the British legislature over all parts of your dominions than the citizens of Bristol." They were sure, however, that force would never have the desired effect, and so pleaded for a return to the "ancient indulgent customs."[21]

London merchants met as usual at the King's Arms Tavern. Eleven hundred and seventy-one protested against the American contest and asked for peace.[22] Their influence extended beyond the city limits, for wealthy merchants were accustomed to improve their social position by buying country estates and becoming freeholders. Thomas Wooldridge, one of the most important of the London merchants, owned estates in Staffordshire where he opposed a loyal address, but supported a freeholders' petition for conciliating the colonies.[23] The presence of merchants among the freeholders of the counties may partly explain the freeholders' addresses which expressed sympathy for America. A union of mercantile and landed interests was an exception to the rule, however. More characteristic of the period was the conflict of economic interests, the clashes between country gentlemen and merchants or manufacturers—on colonial questions as well as on matters of domestic interest. Consequently, in 1775, one may feel sure, the country gentlemen who signed the petitions for clemency had interests which seemed to

[21] *Lloyd's*, Sept. 29—Oct. 2; Oct. 11-13, 1775.
[22] *Ibid.*, Oct. 2-4; 13-16, 1775.　　[23] *Ibid.*, Oct. 23-25, 1775.

them more important than their landed estates. Land-holders were usually loyal to the government and sanctioned coercion, while merchants and manufacturers from the ports and from the inland towns pestered their representatives in the House of Commons with warnings of the disasters which would inevitably overwhelm them if America remained hostile.[24]

[Heedless of the pleas of the mercantile classes, parliament passed the act of December 22, 1775, which prohibited America from carrying on trade, and even forbade intercourse among the colonies and between Great Britain and America. That act convinced the merchants that government officials had forgotten the interests of commerce, and had some ulterior purpose of their own. From that time the merchants put all their effort into finding new outlets for their trade, and making the most of whatever compensation they could find for their American losses.

The possibility of a domestic market looked bright to the West Indian merchants who could no longer send their molasses to New England. They hoped to substitute molasses for grain in home distilleries, and in a memorial to Lord North and Lord George Germain asked for a removal of the duty on imported rum and the tax on spirits distilled from molasses in Great Britain and Ireland.[25] Unfortunately, the country gentlemen were interested in the sale of grain, and they ruined the merchants' scheme. Merchants who looked to foreign countries for a substitute for the American market were more successful than those who depended upon an increase in

[24] *Lloyd's*, Nov. 1-3, 3-6, 6-8, 1775. *Commons Journals*, XXXV, 447. Petitions were from Nottingham, Halifax, Leeds, Westbury, Warminster and Trowbridge. In addition there were the petitions from the Lancashire cotton spinners and the debtors in Staffordshire, already mentioned.

[25] *Lloyd's*, Feb. 15-16, 1776.

the home demand. Both Russia and Spain offered to British merchants and manufacturers compensation for American losses.

Russia and eastern lands reached through that friendly country were an inviting field for British enterprise. Anthony Brough, writing in 1789, declared that the increase in trade with Russia and the Levant was more than equal to that lost in America. Ports on the northeastern coast of England, most conveniently located to carry on this branch of commerce, depended upon it for their livelihood, as the people of Bristol and Liverpool had been accustomed to depend upon trade with America.[26] Due to the treaty of commerce between Russia and England, dating from 1734, Russia purchased most of her manufactured goods from Great Britain. British merchants continued to enjoy this trade for many years, although in 1776 they feared that Russia herself would soon start manufacturing and would learn to do without British products. The peace treaty between Russia and the Porte granted to Russian ships free navigation of the Black Sea; and as a result Holland, France, and Italy lost much of their trade with Turkey and Persia, while Russian traders were carrying British manufactures into those countries.[27] In January, 1778, *Lloyd's* reported: "The people of Yorkshire in the narrow cloth way, never had more to do than at present; . . . the orders from Russia and Germany are greater than ever were known."[28] Letters from Elsinor confirmed the story of the increase of British shipping through the Sound into the Baltic.[29] Many of the ships for this trade were built in Russia. At the beginning of the American war, British merchants

26 Brough, *A View of the Importance of the Trade between Great Britain and Russia*, London, 1789, p. 33.
27 *Lloyd's*, Sept. 20-23, 1776; June 2-4, 1777.
28 *Ibid.*, Jan. 28-30, 1778.   29 *Ibid.*, June 2-4, 1777.

missed the vessels which the colonies had built; but the
friendly Russian empress, Catherine the Great, allowed
ships for Great Britain to be built within her realm. England received from there annually about ten sail of large
vessels, each of the average burden of 1200 tons.[30]

In 1776 an unusual demand from Spain helped to tide
British merchants over the first difficult year of the
American war. Spanish traders needed an unusually
large supply of goods for the Spanish West Indies, because the previous year no flota had sailed from Cadiz to
those islands. Manufacturers in Exeter declared that the
trade for serges, duroys, and long ells, had never been
more brisk; and they attributed their unusual business to
the Spanish demand.[31] Possibly some of these goods found
their way by devious routes to the British colonies in
America. Even the London packers felt the rush of business and were obliged to hire extra hands to get their
goods on shipboard by the time of contract.[32] Although in
succeeding years the demand from Spain somewhat
diminished, the Spanish trade continued until the outbreak of the war with that country. In July, 1779, London
merchants were busy filling Spanish orders, but those
were probably the last until the war was ended.[33] The
merchants regretted the loss of another market; and
while it lasted the Spanish trade had served well to reconcile the British to a decline in the colonial demand.

England's trade with foreign countries during the
American war was apparently profitable. Contemporaries
quoted the rate of exchange as a sign of England's prosperity. One student of the subject studied the rates of exchange for the period 1775 to 1778 between London and
Paris, Bordeaux, Madrid, Bilboa, Leghorn, Genoa, Ven-

30 Brough, p. 33.   31 *Lloyd's*, Apr. 10-12, 1776.
32 *Ibid.*, June 24-26, 1776.   33 *Ibid.*, July 2-5, 1779.

ice, and Lisbon; then concluded that the advantage to
England was equal to one hundred thousand pounds
annually. Unlike the states of Europe, "America," he
wrote, "exclusive of the other expenses of our fostering
care was a dead weight upon our trade, and not only
clogged the wheels of our national prosperity, by invei-
gling away our industrious subjects, but likewise left us
a balance to pay foreign nations upon her account."[34]
William Eden made a similar investigation, but discreetly
decided that so many factors were involved in fixing rates
of exchange between countries that he could draw no
trustworthy conclusions from them. He did believe, however, regardless of opinion to the contrary, that the national wealth of Great Britain was undiminished.[35] British merchants contributed a large share to the wealth of
the country, and it was fortunate for Great Britain that
her trade was not entirely dependent upon America.

The few merchants who made spectacular fortunes during the war took advantage of the misfortunes of others.
They profited from the peculiar conditions incident to the
war. To this class of business men belonged government
contractors, merchants trading under government licenses, and speculators. Next to the new European markets, the needs of the army for clothes and equipment
were most effective in reconciling the mercantile classes
to the partial loss of American trade. But contractors
were a favored class. A contract with the government
gave to a merchant a sort of monopoly. Independent merchants and the public generally were inclined to hold
government contractors in ill repute, both because of the
fortunes they occasionally made (at public expense, it was

[34] *Ibid.*, Aug. 5-7, 1778.
[35] William Eden, *Four Letters to the Earl of Carlisle*, London, 1779, p. 84.

said) and because the government expected unqualified support in return for special privileges.[36]

The licensing system was another device of the war period subject to contemporary criticism. The army continued to require supplies after it reached the colonies; and this demand opened the door to renewed trade with America and to another form of monopoly. According to the terms of the Prohibitory Act, merchants, although forbidden to trade with America as formerly, could obtain licenses from the government "for conveying stores and provisions to the forces upon the American service." There was a grave suspicion at the time that merchants favored by government permits abused their privileges and under cover of their licenses carried on an illicit commerce with the rebellious colonists.[37] Although the business derived from extra-legal commerce and from army contracts helped to keep manufacturers contented, the merchants who had no special privileges grew more dissatisfied and more bitterly opposed to governmental measures. Some of the London merchants took the risk of trying to trade in America without a license, but they could expect no protection from the home government.[38] Finally in February, 1780, London merchants petitioned the House of Commons, complaining of the licensing system, and asking for open ports in America wherever the British forces were in possession.[39] An investigation of trade under the government licenses and an attempt at greater strictness followed the merchants' complaints; but graft was as difficult to eradicate in the eighteenth as it is in the twentieth century.[40]

[36] John Horne, *Facts Addressed to the Landholders, Stockholders, Merchants* . . ., London, 1780, 3d edition, published anonymously, pp. 48 ff. Horne criticises the method of granting government contracts.

[37] *Lords Journals*, XXXV, 12-13. Anderson, *Origin of Commerce*, V, 255.

[38] C.O. 5: 116, f. 331.

[39] *Lloyd's*, Feb. 21-23, 1780.   [40] *Lords Journals*, XXXV, 12-13.

To a large extent, the ordinary merchant carried on trade with America through the loyal colonies. In 1776, when exports to the thirteen rebellious colonies were few, there was a remarkable increase in the value of goods sent to Canada, Florida, and the other parts of British America. New York continued to sustain a more or less constant traffic in British goods, in spite of British prohibitory acts; and after 1780 when the British took Charleston, South Carolina, British merchants received more orders from the southern colonies. Certainly sales to the colonies did not entirely cease during the war. Possibly through various agencies enough manufactures reached the colonies to give some basis to Lord Sheffield's statement that the army in America was supported by British manufactures instead of money. By that explanation Lord Sheffield intended to account for the fact that very little specie was circulating in America, although the British army had incurred great expense there.[41] Yet during the early years of the war, at least, government officials frequently found it necessary to send specie to the colonies. In 1775 the deputy paymaster of the forces at Boston wrote to John Robinson, secretary to the Treasury, that the suspension of trade had made it impossible for him to raise the necessary supply by draft on the contractors. As a result, £20,000 in specie was sent out to America.[42] In 1777 Robinson wrote to the king that £350,000 was on its way to Lord Howe for the service of the army.[43] Although the American demand increased slightly between 1778 and 1781, it could hardly have been equal to the normal orders from the colonies in years of peace. At the

[41] Sheffield, *Observations on the Commerce of the American States*, p. 209, note.
[42] *The Correspondence of King George the Third*, III, 219.
[43] *Ibid.*, p. 475.

same time, imports from America were also few and their arrival most uncertain.

The difficulty of bringing goods from the colonies offered an unusual opportunity for speculation. Merchants who purchased goods from America at the beginning of the war, and then held them for a rise in prices, made spectacular profits. Probably the largest fortunes were realized in the tobacco market. Glasgow, the chief port of importation, was a good field;[44] but Glasgow merchants were not the only profiteers. In 1777 a sudden increase in prices enabled a tobacco merchant of Southwark to clear "upwards of 14,000l.," according to popular report.[45] The next year a London merchant was said to have made £20,000 in the same way.[46] But in 1779 fortune took a swing in the opposite direction. The capture of several prize ships laden with tobacco brought down the price from £100 to £50 a hogshead.[47]

The average merchant could find little consolation for the loss of American trade in the fortunes of a few speculators; but there was salve for wounded feelings in some of the reports from foreign countries trading with America. Foreigners were finding disadvantages in American commerce similar to those which British merchants had experienced before the war. Several French houses doing business with the American colonies had been obliged to close because they had given too large credit. They had been generous with credit because they wished to secure the colonial trade; but they then complained, in terms long familiar to British ears, that they could get no remittances. One house alone, it was said, had "stopped for £300,000."[48] These reports of French experiences must have helped to convince the merchants

[44] *Lloyd's*, July 22-24, 1776; Jan. 14-16, 1778.
[45] *Ibid.*, Sept. 10-13, 1777.   [46] *Ibid.*, Oct. 21-23, 1778.
[47] *Ibid.*, Mar. 8-10, 1779.   [48] *Ibid.*, Apr. 9-12, 1779.

that the loss of American commerce was not an unalloyed evil.

Every means found by the merchants to expand their trade gave more work to the manufacturers, for one business was dependent upon the other. Unlike the merchants, manufacturers never complained that a few of their number were monopolizing all the business. For that reason, perhaps, manufacturers remained much better contented during the war than did the merchants. European markets absorbed nearly as wide a variety of goods as did the colonies. Contracts for the army also were varied. They included deal boxes for shot, blankets, linen, shirts, flannel waistcoats, hose, and shoes.[49] In order to assure every advantage to British manufacturers, the government ordered contractors to purchase their woolen cloths, hose, and hats from firms in Great Britain.[50] Journeymen shoemakers from all parts of England hastened to London to make shoes for the army.[51] In Nottingham stocking manufacturers were busy with army orders.[52] The navy had its own needs, increased by the war. Sailmakers in Chatham worked "double days" on sails for ships fitting at that port for America, while ropemakers worked "one day and a half."[53] If manufacturers regretted for a moment the fact that the troops were spending their pay on the other side of the Atlantic, they soon remembered that the army purchased goods made in Great Britain.[54]

Evidently the manufacturers in general were prosperous, in spite of occasional misfortunes due to the war. In 1775 Charles Irving made a tour of the manufacturing

[49] *Ibid.*, Mar. 13-15, 1776.

[50] *Ibid.*, Mar. 25-27, 1776. But in the case of the Hessian troops, the government made an agreement with the Landgrave of Hesse that all clothing and equipment should be made in Germany. Trevelyan, *The American Revolution*, New York, 1909, II, 54.

[51] *Lloyd's*, May 31—June 3, 1776.   [52] *Ibid.*, Feb. 21-23, 1776.
[53] *Ibid.*, Mar. 13-15, 1776.   [54] *Ibid.*, Nov. 3-6, 1780.

towns and reported to John Pownall, undersecretary of
state, on the conditions which he found. The iron and
steel industry seemed to be especially thriving. Exports
from Birmingham, he wrote, were greater than ever before. In Staffordshire the nail trade seemed less brisk,
but any hands that could be spared readily found employment in other hardware manufactories. In Derbyshire silk
throwsters and manufacturers of woolen stockings were
making money, and Derby had a larger demand than
usual for its pottery. In Manchester cotton manufacturing
flourished; and improvements in English velvets had
opened new European markets, as for example, Naples
and Messina. British manufacturers had always considered the colonies the chief market for coarse cloths,
but manufacturers of these goods in Yorkshire, especially
in Halifax, Bradford, and Leeds, were never more prosperous than in 1775. Irving explained that this healthful
state of industry was due to improvements in machinery,
cheapness of fuel, and the cultivation of the potato, which
was proving to be a cheap and satisfactory food. These
reasons for prosperity had nothing to do with the American situation, but Irving decided that the unusual consumption of English manufactures by the Continent
accounted for the fact that manufacturers felt the inter-
ruption in American commerce so little.[55]

These favorable conditions in most of Britain's manufacturing industries continued for several years. In 1777
prices were high because of the large demand, and merchants were obliged to order from the manufacturers a
long time in advance in order to have finished goods when
they needed them.[56] In August, 1780, manufacturers in

[55] C.O. 5: 154, f. 88. *Calendar of Home Office Papers of the Reign of
George III*, 1773-1775, § 1164.
[56] *Lloyd's*, June 9-11, 1777.

Manchester wrote that they had received so many orders from London that they could not hope to complete them by Christmas.[57] The increasing number of England's enemies and her growing misfortunes finally injured her trade and consequently her industry; but on the whole the American war affected both merchants and manufacturers less disastrously than they had feared. A conservative writer of the time said: "It would be absurd to suppose that our commerce does not materially suffer by the present unfortunate contest; yet it certainly is not injured in such a degree as might be apprehended." The same author suggested that improvements in mechanism, in internal navigation, and in increase of "elegance" might explain the flourishing condition of manufactures.[58] One might just as reasonably infer that the manufacturers were prosperous from the fact that they had capital to spend on new machinery for their industries and on the building of canals for transportation—improvements which characterize that period of English history.

As in the case of commerce and manufacturing, shipping suffered from the American war, but at the same time found certain compensations. Although insurance rates were high and losses were numerous, there was plenty of business for shipowners who wished to run the risks of transportation, incident to war. Captains of merchant ships, temporarily thrown out of work by the war, could enter the transport service. In some cases captains, who for years had sailed vessels between England and America, refused to carry troops to fight against their former friends, although they were in danger of losing

[57] *Ibid.*, Aug. 2-4, 1780.
[58] *A Letter to the Noblemen, Gentlemen, etc., who have addressed His Majesty on the Subject of the American Rebellion*, London, 1776, pp. 32-33.

their ships by their refusal.[59] In 1776 the price of tonnage
rose to more than one-fourth of its usual rate, paying the
shipowners for the hazards they endured.[60] So great was
the demand for government service that merchants had
difficulty in securing ships to carry supplies to America.[61]
Sailors' wages doubled.[62] The sinking and capturing of
vessels by the Americans had a pleasant reaction upon
the shipbuilding industry at a time when merchants were
cut off from their usual supply of colonial-built vessels.
Charles Irving noticed the growth of the shipbuilding
trade in Whitby, and the increased tonnage at Hull—both
probably due to a more extensive trade with northern
Europe.[63] In other shipbuilding centers the docks were so
busy fitting out ships that contractors purchased the sails,
ropes, and other materials ready-made. The manufacture
of sails for example, became an industry in itself—a business in which the town of Poole specialized.[64] Losses from
the attacks of American privateers were so serious that
the British Admiralty granted letters of marque and reprisal to owners of private merchant ships.[65] Privateering
by the British gave an impetus to business in some of the
coast towns, which, in the case of Liverpool at least, was
more than temporary. In 1778 the Earl of Derby declared
that had it not been for privateering and the success at-
tained in that enterprise, Liverpool would have been
ruined during the war.[66]

Compensated in various ways for their American
losses, and more than a little vexed at colonial tactics,

[59] *Lloyd's*, Sept. 13-15, 1775; Apr. 24-26, 1776.

[60] Anderson, *Origin of Commerce*, V, 261.

[61] *Lloyd's*, Aug. 2-5, 1776.   [62] *Ibid.*, Feb. 16-19, 1776.

[63] C.O. 5: 154, f. 88. *Calendar of Home Office Papers of the Reign of George III*, 1773-1775, § 1164.

[64] *Lloyd's*, Apr. 8-10, 1778.

[65] Anderson, *Origin of Commerce*, V, 266.

[66] *Parl. Hist.*, XIX, 1292.

merchants from some of the towns expressed their approval of governmental measures by loyal addresses. Even Bristol, in spite of its interest in American trade, had many citizens who were supporters of Lord North's administration. In 1775 the mayor, burgesses, clergy, and others addressed the king in words approving the colonial policy of coercion.[67] By 1777 even the Merchant Venturers were ready to support the government.[68] During the war officials found Bristol merchants willing to contribute to election funds and to other loyal subscriptions.[69] Yet controversy over American affairs was so bitter that loyal citizens blamed friends of America for mysterious fires that broke out about the time a loyal address was being planned.[70] Popular opinion was divided also in Liverpool. When in 1775 some of the citizens sent a loyal address to the king, the *Liverpool Advertiser* printed an "Address to Liverpool Addressers," which expressed the opinion of government opponents. "Our once extensive trade to Africa is at a stand; all commerce with America at an end. Peace, harmony, and mutual confidence must constitute the balm that can restore to health the body politick. Survey our dock; count there the gallant ships laid up, and useless. When will they be again refitted? What will become of the sailor, the tradesman, the poor labourer, during the approaching winter? Answer me this, and then again address."[71] The obvious answer was a reference to the development of privateering, but the gains in this hazardous employment could scarcely compensate for the loss of regular trade.[72]

[67] *Gentleman's Magazine*, Oct., 1775, p. 478.

[68] Latimer, *The History of the Society of Merchant Venturers of the City of Bristol*, p. 190.

[69] *The Correspondence of King George the Third*, V, 479.

[70] *London Magazine*, Jan., 1777, pp. 50-51.

[71] *Ibid.*, Oct., 1775, p. 543. *Lloyd's*, Oct. 4-6, 1775.

[72] Gomer Williams, *History of the Liverpool Privateers*, p. 179; and

London merchants caused government officials, and even King George himself, most annoyance. The king was anxious to secure a loyal address from the city, for the effect it would have upon popular opinion throughout the country.[73] In 1775 eleven hundred and seventy-one merchants signed the London remonstrance against governmental measures, but friends of government could muster only nine hundred and forty-one signatures for the pro-government address.[74] Of course it was worth something to show that the merchants of the city were not unanimously pro-American; but the ratio between the number of signatures to the two addresses was scarcely satisfactory. Time and again during the war London merchants disappointed the government by their hostile attitude. Manchester, on the other hand, expressed such unquestioning allegiance to the government that cynics suspected government officials of using bribery there.[75] As a matter of fact, however, Manchester's petition was unsolicited; but in other instances government officials asked for an expression of loyalty.[76] During the war, British merchants, with a few exceptions, were not enthusiastic supporters of government. In spite of the fact that British industry and commerce survived the war with surprisingly little net loss, British merchants were the first to hail prospects of peace.

In the spring of 1778 London merchants received private letters from America, which caused them to purchase several thousand pounds worth of goods to store in ware-

Ramsay Muir, *A History of Liverpool*, p. 218, agree as to commercial ruin, decrease of population, and increase of poverty in Liverpool during the American war.

[73] *Correspondence of King George III with Lord North*, London, 1867, I, 272.

[74] *Ibid.*, p. 270. *Gentleman's Magazine*, Oct. 1775, pp. 476-477.

[75] *Correspondence of King George III with Lord North*, I, 272.

[76] The subject of solicited petitions is treated in chapter VIII, *post*.

houses ready for shipment at the first news of peace.[77]
Merchants who expected the war to end in 1778 were over-
optimistic.; but their very optimism was a sign that they
were tired of war. They hoped for peace because commerce is one of the pursuits of peace. They looked forward to re-opened ports in America all the more appreciatively because in recent years the European war had
closed many of their best continental markets. In 1782,
when the country learned of a change in ministry, the
first preliminary to treating with the revolted colonies,
the celebrations were reminiscent of the rejoicing on the
repeal of the Stamp Act. In Norwich, for example, houses
were illumined, bonfires flared, and bells rang gaily.[78] The
iron and steel manufacturers soon learned that the Americans were sadly in need of sharp tools and all other kinds
of hardware. Immediately business boomed in Birmingham, Sheffield, and Manchester.[79] Orders from the West
Indies and from North America confirmed the rumors of
American needs.[80] As the prospects of peace grew
brighter, London merchants agreed to send to America
several ships laden with woolen cloth and other clothing,
much needed in that country. In every manufacturing and
trading center there was " a hurry and bustle unknown at
any former time."[81] But the uncertainties of the period
before peace was formally concluded hindered trade.

The merchants did not know through what ports they
could enter merchandise; and both they and the underwriters were hesitant about insurance rates.[82] There was
chance for speculation, but merchants had grown wise
through their own misfortunes and through tales of the
recent experiences of French traders in America.[83] Specu-

[77] Lloyd's, April 17-20, 1778.   [78] Ibid., Mar. 25-27, 1782.
[79] Ibid., June 12-14, 1782.   [80] Ibid., Oct. 4-7, 1782.
[81] Ibid., Aug. 16-19, 1782; Jan. 24-27, 1783.
[82] Ibid., Dec. 9-11, 1782.   [83] Ibid., Aug. 16-19, 1782.

lators took their chances, while conservative merchants agreed among themselves to send to the United States only implements of husbandry, wearing apparel, materials needed in the handicraft trades—in other words, goods which were necessary for comfort or would serve as capital for industry.[84] They decided, too, upon a safer mode of business. In the future they would fill no more orders or commissions, but would freight their own ships and employ supercargoes to sell the goods in America, to collect the cash, and to make immediate payment to their employers in Great Britain.[85] Merchants who before the war had traded to South Carolina, for example, were counting their losses in bad debts at £700,000 sterling.[86] They were determined to avoid similar experiences in the future. A healthfully conservative but hopeful attitude characterized the British mercantile class when commerce with America re-opened. The merchants confidently expected that friendly intercourse would accompany peace, that trade with the United States would expand, and that commerce with an independent people would be more regular and systematic than was possible with colonies constantly rebelling against parliamentary control.[87]

To be sure, many British merchants hoped for special commercial privileges in the United States. They thought that Great Britain ought to grant independence only as a concession for a monopoly of trade, not realizing that such an arrangement would mean independence in nothing but name. Mercantilists, who expressed the greatest alarm at the slightest relaxation of the acts of trade and navigation in favor of Ireland, considered that since America was lost the days of England's commercial glory were gone. "In these advantages . . .," they said,

[84] *Lloyd's*, Feb. 3-5, 1783.   [85] *Ibid.*, Jan. 27-29, 1783.
[86] *Ibid.*, Jan. 24-27, 1783.   [87] *Ibid.*, Jan. 27-29, 1783.

MERCANTILE CLASSES   115

"which heretofore we exclusively enjoyed, other Powers
will in future partake; so that though peace will partially
relieve us from the difficulties under which we have labored for many years, it will not restore our commerce to
that respectable state which once excited the envy of all
the great trading Powers of Europe."[88]

On the other hand, the theories of free trade, which
Adam Smith developed in his *Wealth of Nations,* were
finding many practical exponents among the merchants,
loath though they might be to acknowledge it. That is,
merchants were adapting themselves to new conditions
in a way that older mercantilists would have believed
impossible. Even the newspapers were publishing articles
which exposed the fallacies of mercantilism. When politicians and business men were discussing the status of
Ireland and her relation to Great Britain, one might read
in *Lloyd's Evening Post:* "It is one of the rawest, and
most indigested systems of policy imaginable, to suppose,
that by granting indulgences in trade to the People of
Ireland, they would impoverish England. When trade is
mutual, there can be no rivalship but for the good of the
whole. Ireland and England should be as one county is to
another county, in either kingdom, each pursuing their
own industry and interest, according to the situation of
places, and disposition of inhabitants."[89] In 1780 a contributor to the same paper declared that "it would be for
the benefit, the peace, and for the happiness of mankind,
that all commercial restraints, all monopolies, should be
removed and abolished."[90] The more modern economists
knew that as long as British manufactures exceeded those
of foreign countries in the quality of materials and work-
manship, Great Britain would never be at a loss for a

[88] *Ibid.,* Dec. 13-16, 1782.
[89] *Ibid.,* July 15-17, 1778.   [90] *Ibid.,* Sept. 22-25, 1780.

market, and that even a politically independent America
would continue to be economically dependent upon England for cloth, tools, all sorts of hardware, and other
things which they could neither make so well themselves
nor find so cheap elsewhere.[91] Mercantilism was not dead,
but it had received its death wound. Great Britain com-
promised with the theory to meet the exigencies of the
case in Ireland. America forced upon Great Britain the
proof that a monopoly of her trade was not indispensable.
Then in 1786, by a treaty of commerce with France, England came to terms with her ancient rival, who, under the
strictest theory of mercantilism, was an enemy with whom
no terms could be made.

During the war British merchants also learned that they
had depended too much upon American trade. The population of the colonies had been neither large enough nor
rich enough to furnish sufficient business for all England's merchants and manufacturers. Another difficulty
arose from the fact that many of the British colonies had
little to exchange for manufactured goods from England.
They were constantly in debt. British merchants were
partly responsible for this condition, because they had
given more than generous credit to the Americans, placing a heavy burden upon American trade. The merchants
were slow to learn that it did not pay to get rid of all
kinds of goods in America, regardless of the ability of the
colonists to pay for them. The war was probably useful
to the extent that it taught caution to British merchants
and encouraged them to seek wider markets in other parts
of the world. Fortunately for both Great Britain and
America, and necessarily for America, at least, commerce
revived after the war. Then the merchants of Great Britain continued, but in a somewhat wiser way, to show their
friendship for the people of the United States.

[91] *Lloyd's*, July 29-31, 1782.

In one sense the merchants had always been the best friends of America. The colonies had grown with the aid of British capital; and many a British trader had been harassed by his creditors, until he had finally succumbed to bankruptcy because he could not collect the debts owed him from America. In 1766 the merchants were unanimous in favor of the repeal of the Stamp Act, and London thronged with their representatives from all parts of the kingdom. If the mercantile classes had been in control of government in the pre-Revolutionary period there would probably have been no thought of taxing the colonies. Merchants, manufacturers, and men in the shipping business were interested in the colonies because of trade and trade alone. If the question of parliamentary control in America had arisen on a purely commercial matter, the group would have backed parliament to a man. To this extent there was unity in the group. There were few Englishmen who did not regard the subordination of the colonies to parliamentary legislation as the only logical relationship. A very small minority among the merchants questioned the power of parliament to tax or to pass other laws for the Americans. The vast majority allowed their own ideas of expediency to weigh against their natural political and mercantile beliefs.

Three years after the repeal of the Stamp Act, however, the merchants were discouraged by the difficulties of trading with rebellious colonies; and they were beginning to be suspicious of colonial aims. The merchants were less ready than formerly to abandon principles for the sake of keeping American ports open to their trade. Manufacturers, especially, became lukewarm in their attitude toward the colonies when they were busy filling orders for the European demand. Even before war broke out in America, the ranks of British merchants were broken. When the Americans boldly declared that they were seeking independence, honest mercantilists could no longer find any excuse for refusing to support Great Britain's attempts to hold the colonies in subjection. But the merchants had weakened England's control in the colonies by their repeated demands for concessions to America, for the purpose of stimulating trade. Merchants who realized how ultimately useless such concessions were became government supporters. Others abandoned their former creeds of trade and politics. Then the unity of the group was completely broken; and the power of the merchants to influence government was gone.

As the war progressed, and as it became more and more evident that Great Britain could never completely sub- ject the colonies to her control, the mercantilists saw no use in continuing the struggle. They resented a useless expenditure of money as heartily as did the landed gentry. Merchants who had abandoned mercantilist theories, who expected to profit quite as much from trade with independent states as from commerce with subject colo- nies, had consistently opposed coercion. At the end of the war the merchants were once more a solid group in favor of peace. They could again influence government. To the merchants America owed the favorable terms on which commerce was resumed between the two countries.

Peace came, finally, as a result of the combined efforts of several groups, including not only the mercantile classes, but also the country gentlemen. These groups represented widely different desires except on the one matter of peace; for great as had been the differences of opinion within the ranks of the merchants, those differ- ences were as nothing in comparison to the conflicting interests of merchants and country gentlemen.

CHAPTER V

OPINIONS AND PREJUDICES OF THE COUNTRY GENTLEMEN.

SEVERAL years of strife between British merchants and the country gentlemen preceded the union of these two groups in a movement to end the American war. They disagreed over revenue acts and economic legislation of all kinds, because measures that helped one class seemed to injure the other. In particular, they were at odds over methods of handling colonial problems. Antagonism between these two classes was not new. The age-old feud between land and personal property had always lain very near the surface of British politics; but both landholders and merchants had tried to suppress their differences for the sake of their common aims and interests.

For example: landowners, manufacturers, and merchants shared the profits from the wool industry, and were interested in the success of all phases of the business, although their individual wishes sometimes clashed. England's ancient staple, wool, was the product of the sheep farm and the raw material for manufacture, while woolen goods were among the country's most important exports. Landowners and sheep raisers naturally wanted high prices for their product; but manufacturers and merchants wished to pay as little as possible. Parliament had favored the manufacturer by forbidding the export of raw wool. As a result of this encouragement, industry had thrived, the sheep growers had been able to sell all their wool for a good price at home, and the value of sheep land had risen. If for any reason, however, British merchants failed to sell their cloth, there was no market for wool, the value of land fell, and landlords were obliged to reduce their rents. At such times sheep raisers and landowners learned to their sorrow that they were dependent upon commerce.

Unlike the producers of wool, the grain growers were almost independent of the home market and the demands of the mercantile classes. Since the early seventeenth century when seasons of abundance and low prices made the country gentlemen complain that England was growing poor, parliament had tried to raise the value of land and its products.[1] Bounties on exports made it possible at times to buy English wheat more cheaply in France than in the British market. Duties on imports, on the other hand, gave the English farmers a practical monopoly at home. During the American war, although thousands of unemployed were cutting their rations to a minimum, provisions were scarce and prices were high. Merchants and manufacturers protested against the corn laws, which made such conditions possible, and demanded cheaper food. Cheap provisions would reduce the cost of living for manufacturers and merchants; but lower prices, according to the landholders, meant that their land would be less valuable. Parliament found it difficult to harmonize these conflicting interests. The country gentlemen were determined to protect their profits; but the manufacturers insisted they could not pay wages high enough to buy provisions at current prices. Through the eighteenth and early nineteenth centuries, the clashes between the manufacturers and the landowners grew more bitter, and their problems became more serious. When manufactur-

1 James E. Thorold Rogers, *Six Centuries of Work and Wages*, New York, 1884, p. 483.

ing centered in large towns, the laborers were more dependent upon the provision market, for they no longer
had plots of ground where they could raise a few vege-
tables to supply their own wants. The corn laws were not
repealed until the middle of the nineteenth century, but
during the American Revolution parliament was obliged
to modify the acts in order to bring down the price of
food.

In 1765 and 1766 poor harvests caused such a scarcity
of grain that prices soared even beyond the high limits
previously reached; and the poor people of England were
suffering from hunger. For a limited time parliament removed the bounty on the export, and the duty on the import, of wheat. A later act permitted the king in council
to prohibit entirely the export of wheat, if the price
reached a certain figure. In 1766 parliament allowed the
importation of grain from America duty free. The next
year another act provided for the importation of grain
from Europe as well as America. Variations of these
measures were repeated from time to time as necessity
demanded.[2] In 1772 a committee of the House of Commons
reported in favor of a permanent law regulating foreign
traffic in grain;[3] but parliament continued to legislate only
for the need of the moment. From 1773 on, however, England was a regular importer of foreign grain. Although
the country gentlemen were loath to yield to the demands
of the merchants and manufacturers, they all had a common interest in the welfare of the country. Some change
in the corn laws was necessary; but the landowners had

[2] 5 George III, c. 31, c. 32; 6 George III, c. 3, c. 5; 7 George III, c. 3,
etc. Charles Smith, *Three Tracts on the Corn Trade and Corn Laws*, London,
1804 (a new edition with additions from the manuscripts of Catherwood),
pp. 44-45.

[3] *Commons Journals*, XXXIII, 698.

special reasons for opposing every new regulation for the sale or purchase of grain.

Country gentlemen protested against the acts which temporarily forbade the exportation of grain from England, because they were afraid of losing a very valuable market in the West Indies. The North American colonies were taking advantage of the British restrictions to sell more of their own grain in the islands. Governor Pownall thought the government had made a grave mistake in cutting off the West Indies from supplies of English grain, because that market had given the British people annually an income of half a million pounds. Now American merchants were making £600,000 from the business which Englishmen had lost.[4] British merchants were probably the gainers in the end, for the Americans could use the specie, which they received from the West Indies, in purchasing British manufactures or in paying their outstanding debts. British landowners, however, were jealous of colonial successes; and they found in the amendments to the corn laws an additional reason for their resentment against the merchants of their own country.[5]

Another emergency measure, which delighted the merchants and manufacturers but distressed the country gentlemen, was the act permitting the merchants to buy grain from America. British wheat growers who had mourned the loss of the West Indian market were in despair when they saw the Americans invading the English market. British merchants, on the other hand, were fortunate, for they could now take American grain in exchange

[4] *Lloyd's*, Jan. 26-28, 1774.

[5] The protests of the country gentlemen finally persuaded parliament to allow them to export to the West Indies a limited quantity of wheat flour, biscuits, and starch, and an unlimited amount of barley, rye, oats, beans, and similar products. 13 George III, c. 5. *Lloyd's*, Jan. 26-28, 1774.

for manufactured goods or in payment of their debts. American wheat was a boon to the whole manufacturing population, for the price of English grain had risen thirty-five per cent in the course of twenty years.[6] In 1774, within a period of two months, a single American house shipped to England 140,000 bushels of wheat; 15,-000 bushels of Indian corn; and 16,000 barrels of flour.[7] Between September, 1774, and the following year, when the Americans stopped their exports to Great Britain, British merchants imported more than one million bushels of wheat.[8] Grain from the colonies was so important for British industry that Bristol merchants mentioned the protection of the grain supply as one of the strong arguments for conciliating America.[9] The merchants' reason for wishing peace with the colonies made no impression upon the country gentry nor upon the government, which represented land. Grain producers failed to appreciate colonies that competed with them in the markets of the West Indies, Europe, and at home. But in 1775 poor rates were rising. This fact convinced the country gentlemen it would be wiser for them to sacrifice the protection of grain. Poverty increased when provisions were costly; and landowners bore the burden of the poor rates.

In the middle of the eighteenth century and during the period of colonial revolt, the complaint of heavy taxes was constantly on the lips of the country gentlemen. Although in the middle of the eighteenth century approximately one-fourth of the taxes collected by the central government came from the customs, nearly one-half from the excise, and less than one-sixth from the tax on land, which at that time was only two shillings in the pound,

6 Rowland E. Prothero (Lord Ernle), *English Farming Past and Present*, London, 1917, Appendix II, p. 435.

7 *Lloyd's*, Oct. 12-14, 1774.

8 *Ibid.*, Oct. 11-13, 1775.   9 *Ibid.*, Sept. 29—Oct. 2, 1775.

country gentry felt that they were bearing the burden of
the revenue.[10] By 1780 the rate had risen; and in that year
the supply included £2,000,000 from the land tax and
£6,694,321 from other sources.[11] In other words, in 1780
nearly a quarter of the revenue came from the land tax.
The normal rate for times of peace was three shillings
in the pound, and in time of war, four.[12] Whether or not
the country gentlemen paid more than their just share
of the revenue was a matter of dispute at the time, and
is still uncertain, for statistics of population and of the
distribution of wealth are too unreliable to use as proof.
According to some accounts, the landed classes formed
about forty-two per cent of the population;[13] and they
certainly had a large proportion of the wealth of the
country. Arthur Young said the wealth and income of the
landed interests was ten times as great as that of other
business interests. Perhaps the land tax alone would not
have seemed a burden if it had been justly assessed. Unfortunately the assessment was based upon an unfair
evaluation made in the seventeenth century. Since that
time inequalities had increased, for land values had
changed, rising in some sections, declining in others.[14]
Another objection occasionally made to the tax was that
the proportion of the tax paid by each county bore no

[10] Stephen Dowell, *History of Taxation and Taxes in England*, London,
1884, II, 130.

[11] State Papers Domestic, George III, 14, Budget for 1780.

[12] The expenses following the Seven Years' War kept the tax at four shillings until Townshend lowered it to three in 1767.

[13] Statistics are from Arthur Young's *Northern Tour*, London, 1770, IV,
543-547. These, according to Gibbins' *Industry in England*, New York, 1914,
p. 334, though high in totals are probably correct in proportions. But Young
also said: ". . . the landed interest of this country is of ten times the
importance of all other interests, and this in every respect . . ., wealth, income, population, stability." *The Expediency of a Free Exportation of
Corn*, London, 1770, p. 41.

[14] *Commons Journals*, XXXIII, 468. Dowell, *History of Taxation*, II, 100.

relation to the number of representatives in parliament from that county.[15] The country gentlemen also felt that they were paying heavily because the land tax was a direct tax, always a more noticeable burden than the customs or the excise which may be passed on from one person to another, until the tax itself is disguised as part of the selling price paid by the consumer. Only in the case of a tax on agricultural or sheep land could the country gentlemen get back their tax in the price of their product. The land tax was essentially a class obligation. For all these reasons the land tax was unpopular.

In some respects the local poor rates and the church tithes, paid almost exclusively by landholders, were more oppressive than the land tax. Local rates varied at the discretion of local officials. Merchants and manufacturers were usually exempt, for stocks and personal estates were seldom rated. Arthur Young, champion of the farmer, declared that the shopkeeper paid only one shilling in taxes for every forty shillings paid by the farmer of similar station.[16] The tithes averaged three shillings, threepence in the pound; but the amount is not as important as the way in which it was assessed. Officials were accustomed to increase the tax as the value of the property rose. This practice served effectually to hinder improvements both on the soil and on other property.[17] This much could be said for the land tax, by contrast—that it, at least, was fixed. With local rates doubling in a period of twenty, or even ten years, it is not strange that the country gentlemen should have become uneasy, and that they should have wondered if the mercantile classes were paying their share of taxes.[18] The landed classes had no

15 Burgh, *Political Disquisitions*, Philadelphia, 1775, p. 38.
16 A. Young, *The Farmer's Letters to the People of England*, London, 1767, I, 270-271.
17 *Ibid.*, p. 323.   18 A. Young, *Eastern Tour*, London, 1771, II, 394.

sympathy for any of the complaints of the manufacturers, for the Dutch manufacturer paid a third of his earnings in taxes, while the British paid at most one-tenth.[19] The country gentlemen became more and more annoyed with their own position as they considered the favors which the mercantile classes seemed to enjoy in the matter of taxation, the manufacture of woolen goods, and more recently, in the importation of grain. Vexation grew as the expense of maintaining the colonies increased. In the eighteenth century the most serious clash between merchants and country gentlemen was over the problems of colonial administration. Regardless of the justification for the country gentlemen's resentment and feeling of injustice, their prejudices are significant in explaining their attitude toward colonial problems.

The colonies had always been of special importance to the merchants; but country gentlemen had grudgingly accepted the mercantilist proposition that the landed interests were dependent upon commerce. Mercantilists taught that the colonies gave business not only to merchants and manufacturers, to shipbuilders and seamen, but also indirectly to the British "husbandman who raises provisions to feed all these useful people."[20] In 1764, however, the country gentry were more impressed by the costs of the colonies than by the profits to be derived from them. British taxpayers were groaning under burdens left by the Seven Years' War, waged, supposedly, in the interests of the colonies; and they resented additions to the normal charges of maintaining the American plantations. The British government had long been accustomed to encourage certain colonial industries by granting bounties on products imported into England.

[19] A. Young, *The Farmer's Letters*, p. 33.
[20] George Heathcote, *A Letter to the Right Honourable the Lord Mayor, the Worshipful Aldermen and Common Council*, London, 1762, p. 10.

The British exchequer shared the expense of civil government and of provincial military forces in the younger colonies, while forces of the establishment had been stationed in America even before the French and Indian War. The colonial customs system, strangely enough, cost more than it brought in, until after its reorganization in 1768. Englishmen who had no special interest in America quite naturally begrudged to the Americans naval stations and fleets, supplies for the army, parliamentary grants to the colonies that had given special service in the war, presents for the red men exchanged for promises of peace, and all the other charges upon the British exchequer. In particular, the country gentlemen rebelled against the new expenses in America after 1763, for they objected to the terms of the peace, and wondered why Great Britain had taken Canada instead of rich islands in the West Indies. The merchants looked forward to expanding markets for British manufactures, but the country gentlemen were intent upon their present distresses.

To organize the new territory was a vast and expensive undertaking. The colonies needed protection from jealous foreign states and from Indian hordes on their borders. So costly were the plans for managing Indian affairs that the government finally abandoned them in almost every detail, and left this important phase of colonial administration to the vagaries of individual colonies. But increased military forces and fortifications were indispensable.[21] Experience had shown that all schemes for colonial self-defense were apt to end in failure. Time after time, because of intercolonial jealousy, the Americans had refused to supply quotas of men and money. Each

21 Clarence Alvord, *The Mississippi Valley in British Politics*, treats most comprehensively the problems of the new territory.

colony was ready to protect its own lands and firesides; but attempts at coöperation were never really successful. Everywhere the Quakers refused to fight, and in Pennsylvania their pacifism dangerously reduced the number of fighting men. In 1763 Great Britain decided to depend no longer upon colonial supplies or promises, but to deal with problems of colonial protection in her own way. Many Englishmen, however, assumed that the colonists should help to pay for their own defense as well as for the war from which they had benefited.

Merchants and country gentlemen agreed that the colonies ought to be useful to the mother country; but they disagreed as to how they could make them so. The mercantile classes expected the colonies to pay for themselves by commerce. They knew that what the Americans paid in taxes could not be spent for British manufactures. But because the proceeds of commerce went directly into the pockets of the merchants, country gentlemen were rather skeptical about receiving much of it themselves. What they especially wanted was some relief from taxation. They were determined to avoid an increase in their own burdens; and Grenville's plan to tax America appealed to the country gentlemen as being entirely reasonable.

Landowners were ready with a list of arguments to justify the experiment. More important than England's need, or the obligations of the colonists, was the ability of the Americans to pay for what they enjoyed. In the eighteenth century Englishmen thought of America as a land of prosperity. While British merchants were going bankrupt, the colonists were ordering luxuries that the ordinary Englishman could not afford. Nowhere in America was there the bitter poverty that was becoming an ever increasing problem in England and the states of Europe. In the colonies laborers' wages were so high that

artisans were attracted from England. Although the
frontier had its hardships, land was cheap, and success
was the reward of toil. Impressed by these facts, English
country gentlemen thought it only just for America to
share expenses.

Taxing America, however, provided another element
of discord between the merchants and the country gentlemen. In this case the country gentry were to profit; but
the merchants suffered such unfortunate consequences
from the Stamp Act that parliament was obliged to repeal
it. To be sure the stamp tax had no direct effect upon
commerce, but the colonists emphasized their indignation
at being taxed by stopping all commercial intercourse
with Great Britain. In this way they easily persuaded the
British merchants to oppose the Stamp Act, too. The merchants had few representatives in parliament, but in 1766
they had influence. Country gentry made up the majority
of the House of Commons as well as the House of Lords.
To secure the repeal of the Stamp Act, British merchants
were obliged to show the country gentry that the tax was
injuring the nation—landed and mercantile interests
alike. Henry Cruger, Jr., of Bristol, who like many other
merchants trading to America, spent the anxious weeks
of February, 1766, in London, wrote to his father how the
country gentry were won over.

The fear of rising poor rates was the immediate consideration which caused the landowners in parliament to
vote for repeal. A manufacturer of Leeds reported to the
House of Commons that of six hundred families whom he
ordinarily employed, he had been obliged to dismiss three
hundred since the decline of the American trade. "This
fact," wrote Cruger, "will have great weight when added
to more evidences of the like kind. The country members
are somewhat alarmed at so many people losing employ,

if anything repeals the act, it must be this. The present
ministry see and have declared the expediency of repealing on this ground; if the late ministers come in again,
and enforce the act, they will have 20,000 unemployed
poor in a suppliant manner petitioning a repeal of the S:
Act, otherwise they must starve, or [*sic*] : so I think there
is no doubt but it must be repealed on some grounds, or
some cause or other.''[22] Added to the facts of unemployment and rising poor rates was the failure of the act as
a means of securing revenue. During the few months the
act was in force, the amount collected was insufficient to
pay the costs of enforcement.[23] The act furnished places
for British patronage, but there were too many sinecures
already. From every point of view the act seemed impractical.

The repeal of the Stamp Act restored to British merchants their American market; but left Great Britain
with a deficit in her revenue. In 1767 matters were worse.
Under the leadership of William Dowdeswell, formerly
chancellor of the exchequer under Rockingham, country
gentlemen carried through parliament a reduction in the
land tax.[24] This step cut £500,000 off the revenue, and
drove Townshend to try another experiment in American
taxation.[25] The arguments for taxing the colonies were the
same as in 1765; but the government respected American
prejudices in fixing the form of the impost. The Townshend Acts were in the nature of commercial regulations,
for which there were plenty of precedents. When the colo-

[22] *Commerce of Rhode Island*, I, 140.
[23] Dowell, *A History of Taxation and Taxes in England*, II, 154, says
that £4,000 were collected and that the costs of execution were £6,837. The
estimate for collections had been £60,000 to £100,000. *Parl. Hist.*, XVI, 89
and 183.
[24] Dowdeswell refused the presidency of the Board of Trade under Rockingham's successors. *Dict. Nat. Biog.*, vol. V.
[25] *Jopson's*, Mar. 9, 1767.

nists objected to these additional customs duties, provided by the act of 1767, and again tried to force repeal by the methods which had proved successful in 1766, the government and its supporters, the country gentry, were firm.

For three years, in spite of the fact that business was uncertain, that merchants and manufacturers were complaining, and that the value of stocks fell, the government persisted in pressing American taxation. In the spring of 1769, Lord North, who had succeeded Townshend, admitted that the tax instead of producing the expected £150,-000 or even £70,000 would yield only £30,000. In 1768 the actual revenue from the tax had been only £20,000; but North assured his supporters that the establishment of troops in the colonies would quiet the turmoil there, and would make it easier to collect the duties. Although Governor Pownall declared that the net proceeds of the Townshend Acts were only £295 and a few shillings, Lord North's assurance temporarily satisfied the country gentry.[26] Landowners, however, were growing nervous about the loss of their provision markets. Report of American sales of flour and Indian corn to Portugal, Spain, and France were disturbing. Traders complained that bullion was scarce in England, because European gold, formerly exchanged for British corn, was now going to America. "The landed gentlemen," it was said, "will . . . soon be made sensible of the loss of the corn trade, if that trade is suffered long to remain in another channel."[27] Such arguments were convincing because they were self-evident. In 1770 the government, influenced by the merchants, and supported by the country gentlemen, repealed all the Townshend taxes except the one on tea. By making that one exception, the British government supported parliament's claim to the right of taxing America, and pre-

[26] *Parl. Hist.*, XVI, 608.　　　　[27] *Lloyd's*, July 23-25, 1770.

served for the country gentlemen their illusion that
America might lighten the British financial burden.

Although the colonies became daily more independent,
English country gentry still cherished the idea that Great
Britain could force America to pay taxes into the British
treasury. Even landowners who held no places and received no favors from the government supported the colonial policy of coercion as long as they believed that they
would eventually receive a revenue from America. When
parliament was debating the question of repealing the tax
on tea, Edmund Burke said: "Country Gentlemen, the
great patrons of economy, and the great resisters of a
standing armed force, would not have entered with much
alacrity into the vote for so large and so expensive an
army, if they had been very sure that they were to continue
to pay for it. But hopes of another kind were held out to
them; and in particular, I well remember, that Mr. Townshend, in a brilliant harangue on the subject, did dazzle
them by playing before their eyes the image of a revenue
to be raised in America."[28] The costs of the struggle in
America naturally increased the need for money. The
problem of the national debt caused serious worry. The
Seven Years' War had added about one hundred million
pounds to the debt, which in 1775 was only ten million
pounds less than at the close of the war.[29] In 1773 the
government had been unable to pay off any part of the
debt; and the grants were insufficient to cover the necessary expenses of government.[30] In spite of these financial
embarrassments, with the exception of one year when
Spain threatened war, the country gentry refused to
raise the land tax until Lord North included an increase

[28] *Parl. Hist.*, XVII, 1238.
[29] Price, *Additional Observations on the Nature and Value of Civil Liberty
and the War with America*, London, 1777 (3d edition), part II, p. 147.
[30] *York Chronicle*, June 25, 1773; Dec. 17, 1773.

to four shillings in his budget for the first year of the war.[31]

When the ministers first suggested a four shilling land tax, some of the landholders in parliament threatened to desert the government. Having heard the rumor that the ministry had abandoned the idea of taxing America, the country gentry were opposed to spending more money on the contest.[32] Lord North reassured them, however, saying the government had only temporarily dropped the idea of taxing America and was planning some means by which the colonies could contribute to the British treasury.[33] Lord Lyttelton also denied that government had renounced the claim to the right of taxing America, for he knew the country gentlemen had supported American measures in the hope of getting revenue from there.[34]

The same hope kept the landowners outside of parliament quiet, even in the face of rising taxes. The landed classes "out of doors" seldom expressed their opinion until the later years of the war, but their ideas were well known. They agreed with the Wiltshire farmer who told Shelburne that he wished peace with the colonies, but thought they should be taxed as well as Great Britain.[35] In 1775 the landholders' chief criticism of the government was that it had delayed the use of force in America, and had for that reason prolonged the contest and increased the expense.[36] The government had the support of the country at large in its policy of coercion. Loyal addresses encouraged the ministers in their course, but the addresses prove little as to public opinion, because many of them were solicited by government agents. Landholders' signatures were most prominent on the loyal

[31] Parl. Hist., XVII, 165.
[32] Ibid., XVIII, 939.
[33] Ibid., p. 949.
[34] Ibid., p. 1072.
[35] Fitzmaurice, Life of Shelburne, II, 5.
[36] Lloyd's, Nov. 6-8, 1775.

addresses, however, while merchants and manufacturers
signed the protests against governmental policy. The
signs of approval usually came from the towns where opposition was strong, and where the government wished to
prove its own strength. Generally speaking, the landholders or country gentlemen were slow to make any
demonstration.

As a class the country gentry troubled themselves very
little about colonial problems. Their share of responsibility for the American conflict rests upon these two
facts: they insisted upon sparing themselves additional
taxation and they silently acquiesced in governmental
policies. Ordinarily the country gentry took little interest
in parliamentary business. They left London for their estates as early as possible. They were characteristically un-
interested in every phase of American affairs except the
ones which lay closest to their pockets, questions of taxation and expense. They were quite ready to forget
America except when it was forced upon their attention.
So slight had been their share in colonial business that
Governor Pownall suggested they might act as mediator
between the British government and America.[37] Soame
Jenyns wrote in vexation: "The landed interest of this
nation, like the silly and defenseless sheep, in silence
offers its throat to the butchery of every administration,
and is eat up by every ravenous profession; while the
trading interest, like the hungry and unmannerly hog
devours everything, and if a finger is but laid upon it the
whole country is distracted with the outcry."[38] But the
interests and sympathies of the landed classes were usually with the government. The country gentry could afford
to be silent, because government most truly represented

[37] *Parl. Hist.*, XVIII, 325.
[38] Soame Jenyns, "Reflections on Several Subjects," *Works*, Dublin,
1791, I, 349-350.

land. Since the Revolution of 1689 the landed aristocracy had controlled the administration of government. They had at their disposal not only offices of state, but high positions in church and army; and they also had under their control lower education and the universities. They naturally trusted the members of parliament to look out for the interests of their own class; and for several years governmental policy, even in America, seemed to suit the interests of the landowners as well as the plans of the administration.

There were, however, two groups within the landed class: first, those who had some business or profession aside from land; and second, those who drew their total income from the soil.[39] Many of the first group held positions under the ministry, and supported the administration in return for the salaries which they received. They continued to vote for the government's measures long after the second group had begun to denounce the ministers for their failures in America. The independent country gentlemen at first approved American taxation, and thought coercion was justified. Had the war proved successful, they would have continued to support Lord North and his administration. They joined the opposition one by one as they realized that for them the war with America was useless. Instead of relieving them of their burden of taxation, the war laid heavier ones upon their shoulders. "About Christmas, 1777, . . .," said John Wilmot, M. P. from Tiverton in Devonshire, "after an expenditure of about twenty millions of money, the eyes of many independent Gentlemen, and of the nation in general, began to open, and to see clearly the fatal tendency of the past measures, into which they had been deceived, and the too certain prospect of future calami-

[39] *A Prospect of the Consequences of the Present Conduct of Great Britain toward America*, London, 1776, p. 65.

ties.''[40] The failure of the campaigns of 1778 and the declaration of war by France convinced the country gentry that the war was to become still more unprofitable. Although the entrance of France into the conflict caused a burst of patriotism in England, which strengthened the hand of the government, expenses increased. The war with France was one of a long line of calamities which followed the employment of coercive measures in America; and the contest with America became increasingly unpopular.

The opposition left no stone unturned to show the country gentry that they were waging an expensive war with little chance of recovering their fortunes. The minority in parliament repeatedly introduced resolutions regarding the extravagance of government, and they demanded drastic reforms. The newspapers published items concerning British financial reverses. According to one estimate, Great Britain was losing one hundred thousand pounds in revenue because Americans were buying Holland instead of English tea.[41] As the need for money increased, the income from America declined. The capture of homeward bound ships meant a loss not only to the merchants who owned the goods, but also to the government in the matter of import duties.[42] The first year of the war added nearly three and one-half millions to the debt, and there were other expenses not provided for. In that year the government took one million nine hundred thousand pounds from the sinking fund to use for current expenses. Unable to wait for the quarterly collections of the land tax, the ministry borrowed from the Bank of

---

[40] John Eardley Wilmot, *A Short Defence of the Opposition*, London, 1778 (printed anonymously), p. 16.

[41] *Lloyd's*, Sept. 8-10, 1773.   [42] *Ibid.*, Oct. 23-25, 1776.

England, mortgaging the land tax from 1775 down to Lady Day, 1777, inclusive.[43] In 1776, the country gentlemen, groaning under new luxury taxes and the increase in the land tax, observed the state of the treasury with apprehension.

Writers on public finance, such as Dr. Price, John Dalrymple, and Matthew Robinson-Morris, to mention only three, helped to awaken the public to the extravagance of the government and to the costs of the American war. Dr. Price wrote long and exhaustive treatises on the state of public affairs. He advised the adoption of political as well as economic reforms, but an anonymous sympathizer wisely said: "It is your State of the National Debt that has gained you readers; more, I fear, than your arguments, however clear and conclusive. The horrors of civil war and impending slavery have been lost in the more interesting dread of Public Bankruptcy."[44] Writers with very different opinions as to the value of colonies were coming to the same conclusion in regard to the foolishness of continuing the war. Matthew Robinson-Morris, second baron Rokeby in the peerage of Ireland, was a mercantilist of the old school. He tried to arouse the country gentlemen from their apathy by saying: "It may be depended upon that there will be found no possible safety or welfare for this now happy and fortunate as well as most respectable order of men, except by the preservation of all the essential parts of our great empire in peace, in union, and in harmony with each other. . . . Should two such very considerable portions of this empire, as the mother country and our colonies of North America separate from each other only to meet again in a contention of

---

[43] Matthew Robinson-Morris, *A Further Examination of our Present American Measures*, Bath, 1776 (printed anonymously), p. 31.

[44] *A Letter to the Rev. Dr. Price*, London, 1776, p. 10.

arms; all English estates cannot but be broken by the shock and the conflict."[45]

Dean Tucker, on the contrary, declared in 1776, as he had been insisting for many years, that colonies were a handicap to the mother country. Like Robinson-Morris, however, Tucker urged the government to make peace with America—but for very different reasons. "Every man now plainly sees," he said, "that we shall never be able to retain the Americans in due and constitutional subjection (even supposing that we conquered them in the present war) but at such an expense both of men and money as would in the event prove our ruin."[46] Another writer expressed a similar opinion in this way: "If successful, we *must* be ruined; if unsuccessful, we *may* be ruined."[47] Even if Great Britain should conquer America, the colonies would be so weakened by the war that they would be in greater need of protection and support than before, and would be unable to contribute to the British exchequer.

The effect of the war upon the rental value of their estates was another important factor turning the independent country gentlemen against the government and its war policy. In 1769 English papers reported that the disputes between the colonies and the mother country were causing a twenty per cent decline in the value of American land.[48] Toward the close of the war, there was a similar situation in England. Land investments failed

[45] *A Further Examination of Our Present American Measures*, p. 171. Although this prophecy did not prove true in 1812, it reminds one of the breaking up of English estates at the close of the World War, when a greater shock broke the hold of the landed classes.

[46] *A Series of Answers to Certain Popular Objections against separating from the Rebellious Colonies*, Gloucester, 1776, pp. 85-86.

[47] *A Prospect of the Consequences of the Present Conduct of Great Britain toward America*, p. 38.

[48] *Middlesex Journal*, Aug. 8; Oct. 13, 1769.

because capital became scarce in comparison with the demand, interest rates increased, taxes were heavy, and prices of land fell.[49] The small landholder who had mortgaged his lands found it almost impossible to pay the interest on his mortgage, to say nothing of the principal. A forced sale meant a heavy sacrifice, probably ruin. Before the war the average value of land had been thirty to thirty-three and a half years' purchase; during the war, it fell to twenty, eighteen, and even fifteen.[50] The unfortunate experience of a merchant who invested his whole fortune in land illustrates the way in which the war affected English landlords. In 1770 the merchant retired to North Essex where he purchased a small estate. When he had an opportunity to buy another at a bargain, he put the remainder of his savings into land. As his income from these investments was six and one-half per cent, he found it profitable to borrow money for further purchases. Then came the American war and, after a few years, an end to his prosperity. Interest rates rose, and land values fell from thirty-two years' purchase to twenty-eight. He waited hopefully, but when the prices fell to twenty-five, he could not think of selling. Prices continued to decline to twenty-three years, and at last to twenty.

---

[49] Arthur Young, *Northern Tour*, IV, 393. Land values were ordinarily quoted in terms of the rate of interest. The number of years' purchase was found by dividing one hundred pounds by the rate, and adding three years to allow for the advantages that land had over money or stock in being a more secure investment. The money value of the land would be the number of years' purchase multiplied by the annual income from the land. When the rate of interest was four per cent, the average value of land was twenty-eight years' purchase. As money rose in value, the price of other things, of course, including land, decreased, other influences remaining unchanged. Nicholas Barbon, *A Discourse of Trade*, London, 1690 (reprint by J. H. Hollander, Johns Hopkins Press, 1905), p. 21, explains how land values were calculated. See also Jeremy Bentham, *Defence of Usury*, Philadelphia, 1796.

[50] *Lloyd's*, Aug. 26-28, 1782. Bentham, *Defence of Usury*.

Some of his tenants failed, and he was obliged to lower rents. Forced to pay increased interest on his mortgages, while he received less rent from his farmers, this unfortunate investor faced ruin. In 1782, in contrast to the income of £1100 which he enjoyed when he first settled in the country, the "neat income" from his whole fortune was only £150 a year.[51]

The less influential landlords felt the effects of the war before the men of capital. The increasing cost of living, high money rates, and heavy taxes bore most heavily upon the small landholders, for whom the eighteenth and nineteenth centuries were difficult at best. The financial hardships of the period of the American war speeded up the process of eliminating the small landholder, which had begun before the war and continued somewhat more slowly for many years after.[52] New methods of farming, bringing about the agricultural revolution, made enclosures profitable; but the small landowner lacked the scientific knowledge and the capital to compete with the capitalist or moneyed landholder, or to face such obstacles as fluctuation in the price of corn and increasing taxes. The poor man finally sold his lands to the rich, and wealthy landholders were able to consolidate their estates when making enclosures.[53] In the eighteenth century the ownership, and consequently the loss of land, had a political significance which it lacks in this day of universal suffrage. The forty shilling freeholder had a vote for the shire representative, when the wealthy but landless merchant in the town had none. The independent country

[51] *Lloyd's*, Aug. 26-28, 1782.

[52] Arthur Johnson, *Disappearance of the Small Landowner*, Oxford, 1909, p. 114. Hasbach, *A History of the English Agricultural Labourer*, translation by Ruth Kenyon, London, 1908, p. 104.

[53] See a rare pamphlet by Nathaniel Kent, *Hints to Gentlemen of Landed Property*, London, 1775, p. 211, for the effect of the destruction of small farms.

voters cherished their franchise, although it meant comparatively little when the aristocracy of the country held
the administration of government in their hands. When
the small landholders saw their estates, and with them
the last vestige of their political power, melting away,
they began to rebel against the government which they
held responsible for their misfortunes.

By 1778 the large landholders—country gentlemen and
capitalists—were also beginning to tire of war and the
results of war. When tenants were on the verge of bankruptcy, landlords were obliged to lower rents and econo-
mize. Before the end of the war, the scarcity of capital
and high interest rates began to affect the progress of
agricultural improvements. In the years from 1780 to
1789 the number of enclosures by act of parliament was
much smaller than the number made in any other decade
between 1760 and 1810.[54] The landed classes, rich and
poor alike, gradually learned that the war was injuring
their interests. The independent country gentlemen then
deserted the ranks of government. The landowners joined
the opposition much later than the mercantile classes,
because the landed interests were slower to show the effect
of the war. At the beginning of colonial troubles, the merchants lost their trade, but land values did not decline
until the last years of the war. Furthermore, until 1778
the country gentlemen expected America to repay them
for what they were losing in extraordinary taxes. As late
as the autumn of 1777 Colonel Barré wondered that not
a single country gentleman had risen either to speak of
peace or to complain of war.[55] Lord Ongley replied that
there was just one motive which kept the country gentlemen in their seats. "We are heavily taxed ourselves," he

[54] Edward P. Cheyney, *Introduction to the Industrial and Social History
of England*, New York, 1921, p. 218.
[55] *Parl. Hist.*, XIX, 468.

said, ''and it is but reasonable that when we shall compel the colonies to return to their duty they should contribute in common with the rest of their fellow subjects in support of the government whose protection they will equally partake of.''[56]

The propositions for American conciliation introduced by Lord North in 1778 took the country gentlemen by surprise, and showed them that they had been cherishing a vain hope. If, as the conciliatory proposals suggested, the government was willing to abandon forever the plan of taxing America, the only motive for the support of the independent country gentlemen was gone.[57] Their anger at having been so long deceived by the government roused them from their inertia. But for four more years the officeholders, the placemen, the protégés of the government, furnished the ministry with a majority in parliament.

Lord North's conciliatory proposition disillusioned the country gentlemen outside of parliament as well as those within, and for the rest of the war the ministry faced not only a growing opposition in the House of Commons, but hostile popular opinion outside. As soon as landowners throughout the country realized that they were paying heavily for the war with no chance of securing anything in return, they joined the merchants in demanding peace.[58]

---

[56] *Parl. Hist.*, XIX, 469.   [57] *Ibid.*, p. 772.

[58] A petition to parliament of gentlemen, merchants, traders, and others, shows the attitude of those outside parliament at this time. ''. . . the Petitioners are impressed with the deepest concern, on perceiving that the war in which we have for three years been involved with our brethren in North America, has been attended with successes from which we derived no advantage, and disasters which admit of no remedy; that, in the present miserable and uncertain state of our affairs, the only circumstances of which we have no doubt, are burthens intolerable and impending ruin, that it is no longer from any speculative opinions we had formed of the rights of either party in this unhappy dispute, or of the nature and extent of their

When the ministry persisted in its colonial policy, the public became suspicious of a government which so obviously failed to reflect popular opinion. The country gentlemen could not understand why landowners in parliament allowed the war to continue. Apparently parliament was subservient to the ministers, instead of protecting the rights and interests of the country gentlemen. For centuries the power of parliament had rested upon its right of making or withholding grants of men and money; but during the later years of the American Revolution, private supporters of the government raised regiments at their own expense, and contributed funds for the conduct of the war. In 1778 five thousand four hundred gentlemen and freeholders of Norfolk protested against the practice, and begged parliament to prevent such an "invasion of its prerogative."[59]

The growing dissatisfaction with the government led the various groups that were suffering from the war to come together and discuss their grievances. All agreed that there ought to be some change in the government of the nation. The country gentlemen were especially concerned about the extravagance of the ministry; and they demanded economy which would make lower taxes possible. The first step in economy would naturally be to make peace with America, as war created vast and unusual expenses. The merchants also wanted peace, both for the sake of economy and to reopen trade with America. In addition to these two classes, who were interested in economic reform, there was a group of liberals who de-

respective resources, that we are led to condemn the cause or conduct of this war, since it now stands confessed that the very authors of it themselves, convinced of the error or impracticability of their measures, have abandoned the objects which first gave rise to the contest, and appear anxious to conciliate the enemy they affected to despise. . . ." *Commons Journals*, XXXVI, 824-825.

[59] *Parl. Hist.*, XIX, 759-762.

manded constitutional changes—in particular, a more
equal representation of the people in parliament. The
liberals believed that true representatives of the people
would of their own accord declare peace with America,
and introduce a series of economies in government. All
three groups were represented in an extensive reform
movement, which began in the county of York, but finally
spread over the whole country.

In 1779 independent country gentlemen of the North
Riding suggested a county association to work for reform. Two hundred and ten prominent men of the county
signed an advertisement in the *York Courant* which notified nobility and freeholders of a meeting to be held on
December 30 at the Assembly Room in York.[60] Even
George III heard of the proposed assembly, and urged
Lord North to have friends of the government present
to use their influence against radical measures.[61] On the
appointed day the Rev. Christopher Wyvill gave the
opening address before a serious audience. Wyvill, a
clergyman and a liberal in politics, was destined to be one
of the leading spirits in the county association movement. A political career was closed to him, because he had
taken orders; but he welcomed an opportunity to use his
influence in political matters. At the meeting on December
30, however, he tried to allay a suspicion that the opposition was responsible for that assembly; and he absolutely
denied the report that Lord Rockingham had made the
original suggestion for the meeting. After the formalities
of opening, the country gentry proceeded to describe their
own economic ills, the "large addition to the national
debt," and the "rapid decline of . . . land rents," and
also the plight of the merchants and manufacturers, suf-

---

[60] "Wyvill Papers," printed in *Excerpta Antiqua*, York, 1797, pp. 1 ff.
[61] *Correspondence of George III with Lord North*, II, 296.

fering from loss of trade.[62] A resolution for a petition to
the House of Commons criticising the administration
and asking for reform, was the signal for the King's
Friends to rise to the defense of the crown. Leonard
Smelt, at one time sub-governor to the Prince of Wales
and long a pensioner, was the spokesman for the group.
He tried to absolve the government from the charge of
gross expenditures, and decried the suggestion that the
king had acquired an unconstitutional influence in government. Interrupted by shouts and hisses, he was at last
compelled to stop; but the public was soon able to read his
speech in a pamphlet, which, according to rumor, issued
from a press in Buckingham House.[63] Because the King's
Friends were too few in number to influence the assembly,
they refused to show their weakness by casting any vote
upon the resolution for the petition, which was carried
without difficulty.[64] The assembly then turned its attention
to the business of permanent organization. Wyvill became
chairman of a committee of sixty-one members, which was
to carry on the work begun in the county meeting, and to
urge landholders in other counties to join the movement
for reform. Smelt declared that the assembly passed the
resolutions giving authority to the committee at the close
of the session and in great haste, implying that the members of the association did not give the same approval
to the committee that they had given to the petition.[65] In

[62] *Wyvill Papers*, p. 7.

[63] *An Account of some Particulars, which passed at the Meeting held at
York, on Thursday, the 30th December,* 1779, the original edition, anonymous
and undated. The New York Library copy of the second edition with slight
changes in the title, *An Account of Some Particulars Relative to the Meeting
held at York* . . ., London, 1780, with the author's name on the title page,
contains a clipping with the reference to Buckingham House.

[64] *The Yorkshire Question, or Petition, or Address* . . ., London, 1780.

[65] *An Account of Some Particulars, which passed at the Meeting* . . ., p.
29.

following months the severe criticism of the work of the committee, heard among the country gentry, gave some color to Smelt's assertion. A sub-committee of twenty-one, having authority to act for the larger group, included the most enthusiastic leaders, who gave character to the association movement. The York assembly, after completing the business of organization, adjourned to meet again in the next Easter week.

In the meantime, leaders in the York association were busy securing signatures for their petition. This was not a difficult matter, for the subject of economy was popular. Yorkshire freeholders heartily approved the statement that the misfortunes from which the British people were suffering were the result of an expensive and unsuccessful war with their colonies, and of the alliance which those colonies had formed with France and Spain, the "inveterate enemies of Great Britain."[66] They were also inclined to sympathize with the criticisms of the government heard at the December meeting, culminating in the phrase, "the unconstitutional influence of the crown" in British politics. Even freeholders who had not attended the York meeting were glad to address parliament on these matters. Yorkshire landholders who were spending the winter in London learned through the newspapers that they could sign duplicates of the original petition at Gray's Inn, the King's Arms Tavern, or at some convenient spot in the west end of the city.[67] So many people availed themselves of the opportunity that the document which Sir George Savile, M. P. from Yorkshire, presented to the House of Commons on February 8 bore nearly nine thousand signatures.[68] Enemies of the movement disputed the claim that nine thousand was a majority of Yorkshire freeholders, but the number was large enough to encour-

66 *Wyvill Papers*, p. 9.
67 *Ibid.*, p. 74.	68 *Ibid.*, p. 106.

age Wyvill and his committee to continue their work. Within a short time Middlesex, Hertford, Leeds, Essex, Gloucester, Surrey, Wilts, and Somerset followed the example of Yorkshire; and the cities of York and Westminster had similar organizations.[69] Before the Yorkshire freeholders held their spring meeting, parliament had received thirty-nine separate petitions demanding economy and peace.[70] Most of these appeals came from county associations.

Probably the majority of the men who signed the petitions were naturally conservative, as men are whose fortune lies in land; but an important liberal faction in the associations prevented perfect harmony. The Whig aristocracy of the county were present at the first meeting in York, for they were as anxious for economy in government as were the smaller landowners. Devonshire, Rutland, Rockingham, Effingham, Scarborough, Egremont, and Fitzwilliam wrote a letter to the chairman of the meeting telling him that they approved the suggestions made by the assembly; and they promised to support the movement for economic reform.[71] Before the spring meeting, however, radical influences among the members of the committee were trying to carry the movement beyond the stage of economic reform. The liberals would not be satisfied with lower taxes or even peace with America, desirable as both might be. They insisted upon adding to the reform program changes in parliamentary representation. The liberal group increased in numbers as month after month parliament failed to satisfy the demands of the county petitioners. Although the country gentlemen as a group were interested in a suggestion for increasing the number of county representatives in parlia-

[69] *Ibid.*, pp. 56-108.
[70] *Commons Journals*, XXXVII, 581-724.
[71] *Wyvill Papers*, pp. 44-45.

ment, they knew that any change in representation was
dangerous for one such step would be the preliminary to
others of a more radical character.[72] The liberal phase
of the county movement bothered the administration far
more than the economic. Lord North was so much disturbed that he summoned to Downing Street the noblemen
who had approved the York petition and warned them
against having any further connection with the county
association.[73] The noblemen were beginning to have their
doubts about the movement, anyhow; and at the second
York meeting, the Earl of Effingham was the only one
present of the Whig aristocracy.[74]

The members of the county associations disagreed
among themselves as to the real purpose of their organizations. Many of the attendants at the early meetings
thought they had accomplished their purpose when they
had petitioned parliament: and they took no further
share in the reform movement. The leaders in the county
associations, the active members of the committees, were
extremists; and they had exaggerated ideas of what they
should do. For that reason conservative members of the
associations criticised the way in which the committees
handled association business in the intervals between
general assemblies. For instance, the committees occasionally took the liberty of changing and adding to the
petitions adopted at the regular meetings. The Berkshire
committee went so far as to urge parliament to refuse
supplies until the government had investigated the complaints of the county petitioners. The more conservative
members of the associations, on the other hand, were
aghast at the possibility of leaving the nation without
means of defense. They held a meeting at Reading where

[72] *Lloyd's*, April 17-19, 1780.
[73] Add. MSS., 27918, fs. 1 and 2, pp. 14-21.
[74] *Wyvill Papers*, Introduction, pp. xiv-xv.

they heartily endorsed the petition recommended by the first assembly at Abingdon, but repudiated the work of the committee.[75] Members of a conservative assembly in Chester claimed that they were continuing a meeting previously held in Norwich.[76] They declared that the committee had no legal authority to act, carried a motion approving the original petition, and then adjourned sine die. In this way the conservatives helped to prevent any further activity.[77] The conflict between the two factions in Kent resulted in a second petition to parliament from the conservative group, who emphasized the need of frugality, but disapproved of the committees and even of the associations, which were trying to interfere with the work of parliament and hindered freedom of debate among the members of the House of Commons.[78]

In spite of the reactionary members of the associations, the movement for reform continued. In March, 1780, deputies from thirteen counties, the cities of London, Westminster, and Gloucester, and the towns of Nottingham and Newcastle, met in London, first at St. Albans Tavern and later at the Great Room in King Street, St. James's. Leaders were now resolved to unite the various county associations, in order to obtain more effective results through union. After completing their plans for union, outlining a joint program, and drawing up a memorial which stated their reasons for association, the deputies went home to ask for the approval of their respective groups.[79] From that time on, the conservative element, which was typical of the landed classes, lost its influence in the county association movement. The story of the

[75] *Lloyd's*, Apr. 19-21, 1780.   [76] Probably Northwich in the same county.
[77] *Lloyd's*, Apr. 19-21, 1780.   [78] *Commons Journals*, XXXVII, 761.
[79] *Wyvill Papers*, p. 429. The counties represented were York, Surrey, Middlesex, Sussex, Gloucester, Hertford, Kent, Huntingdon, Dorset, Bucks, Chester, Devon, and Essex.

later work of the associations and their committees belongs rather to the chapter on radical activities than to this which deals with the country gentlemen in their more conservative aspect.

The county associations were successful in arousing the country gentlemen in parliament to a realization of the grave dangers which threatened them if the war with America continued. The repeated demands of the liberals for a broader franchise and a redistribution of seats in the House of Commons made the country gentry fear that they might soon be forced to relinquish their special privileges in representation, unless parliament immediately granted the more conservative requests of the county associations. The union of mercantile classes with the country gentlemen must also have convinced the government that public opinion was against the war. The York committee had recommended that the county associations invite merchants and substantial tradesmen, who were not freeholders, to sign the petitions; and the mercantile classes joined the town and city associations.[80] Most of the petitions deplored the state of trade and manufactures as well as the trials of the landed classes. It was the combination of interests, land, trade, and liberal, that influenced parliament to reorganize the government and end the war.

The country gentlemen demanded from the new cabinet first peace and then economy. The terms of peace did not interest the landholders. They wanted just one thing—relief from their financial burdens; and they were convinced that the desperate state of public and private finance was the result of war. For several years Englishmen had been asking the question: "Can we afford to let the colonies go?" But in 1782 they said: "Can we afford

[80] *Wyvill Papers*, p. 55.

to fight any longer to keep them?" The country gentlemen answered, "No!" In 1775 landholders had been almost unanimous in favor of coercion. In 1778 they began
to doubt the wisdom of that policy. In 1781 they were
flocking to the opposition. Even the placeholders began
to desert the government, for they had interest in land as
well as in office. The country gentlemen were determined
to end the contest with America, because they believed
that whatever the costs of peace, the expenses of war
were more burdensome. First and last, country gentlemen
formed their opinions and made their decisions according to the cash balance; and the country gentlemen were
largely responsible for the resignation of Lord North,
which was followed by peace with the independent states
of America.

CHAPTER VI

ACTIVITIES AND VIEWS OF THE RADICALS.

UNLIKE the majority of merchants and country gentlemen, whose interest in colonial affairs was purely practical, if not mercenary, British radicals were inclined to sympathize with the ideals of the American Revolution. While traders and landed gentry were asking if the Stamp Act was expedient, the radicals inquired if it was just. Liberals in England and America had much in common. In the colonial cry, "Taxation without representation is tyranny," there was something akin to the British complaint of unfair elections and of the unconstitutional influence of the crown in legislation.

Yet with all their idealism, the radicals were not without a certain worldly wisdom and ability to advance their own cause. It is just possible that they would have been less concerned about injustice in America, if they had not found that their support of the colonies reacted favorably upon their own fortunes, and won friends for them in both lands. During the American war, societies of political reformers flourished in England as never before. More frequent elections and a broader suffrage appealed to the normally conservative merchants and country gentlemen who were disgusted with the fact that parliament continued to support the crown in a manifestly unpopular war. But the desire for peace with America was stronger than the wish for a change in the British constitution, and much more effective in attracting new members to the ranks of the reformers. Consequently the radicals redoubled their efforts in behalf of the colonies. The colonists, on their side, were in hearty sympathy with the

British liberal movement, and encouraged their brothers across the Atlantic with letters and gifts of money before offering serious resistance to the British government themselves. John Wilkes was so successful in turning the sympathy of Americans to his own personal advantage that his enthusiasm for the colonial cause appeared to be a pose.

In 1763 Wilkes aroused the hostility of the government by his attack upon the king's speech. Expelled from the House of Commons, he became subject to arrest and was outlawed. The county of Middlesex elected him three times to membership in parliament, and three times he was refused a seat, until in 1774 public opinion forced the government to drop the contest, and Wilkes was finally admitted.[1] In the meantime, all the friends of parliamentary reform rallied about the hero, and temporarily confused the cause and the man. Subjects on the other side of the water saw in Wilkes a champion of liberty, and not only lavished sympathy but emptied their pockets in his behalf. For several years the Sons of Liberty in Boston corresponded with Wilkes, both as individuals and through the secretary of the organization. As early as 1766 one Bostonian named his son after the hero of the Middlesex election controversy;[2] but in 1769 when the Americans were stiffening their resistance to the Townshend Acts, interest in the Wilkes affair was at its height. Believing that liberals in the two countries were united in a common struggle against an arbitrary government, William Palfrey wrote from Boston: "The fate of Wilkes and America must stand or fall together."[3] Thomas Young, another Boston correspondent, appeared confident that parliament would soon yield to the demands of the colonists and their British friends. "Be of good courage," he

---

[1] The most recent *Life of John Wilkes* is by Horace Bleackley.
[2] Add. MSS., 30871, V, 34.   [3] *Ibid.*, p. 114.

wrote to Wilkes, "I hope you will have the satisfaction to see Britain saved as well as France conquered in America."[4] In another letter he assured his London friend that the Americans were watching Middlesex and were disposed to follow her example, but should liberalism in England be defeated, the colonists would continue to resist oppression.[5] Wilkes' friends and admirers were not limited to the Sons of Liberty in Massachusetts.

St. Christopher in the West Indies,[6] South Carolina, Virginia, and Maryland subscribed to the fund for his relief. The gift to Wilkes was the cause of a bitter controversy between the governor and assembly of South Carolina, a controversy which continued for several years. Although the governor refused to sign an appropriation bill, £1500 was nevertheless paid out of the public treasury; and in retaliation the governor refused his assent to all laws until the money should be repaid.[7] The British authorities finally advised the governor to yield to the assembly in this instance, but to refuse such grants in the future.[8] Maryland and Virginia subscribed tobacco for the Wilkes fund; but unfortunately for Wilkes and his debts, the Virginia collector ran off with the donation, and used the proceeds for himself.[9] Welcome financial contributions and flattering letters were the reason for Wilkes' support of the colonial cause, for he had little innate sympathy for American aspirations. He is said to have scoffed at their "pretensions to an independent legislative right

[4] Add. MSS., 30871, V, 176.

[5] Ibid., p. 160.   [6] Ibid., 30870, IV, 133.

[7] Middlesex Journal, Feb. 9, 1770. Journal kept by Hugh Finlay, Brooklyn, 1867, p. 60. Controversial Letters of John Wilkes, Esq., The Rev. John Horne and their Principal Adherents, London, 1771, pp. 157-159.

[8] C.O. 5: 29, f. 66, ff. Lloyd's, Aug. 19-22, 1774.

[9] Kate Mason Rowland, Life and Correspondence of George Mason, New York, 1872, I, 150. Lloyd's, June 29—July 2, 1770.

of internal taxation" until converted by gifts of money and notes of adulation.[10]

Nevertheless, Wilkes' interest in the colonies, real or assumed, encouraged the colonial patriots and influenced the English liberals to regard American demands more favorably. The eyes of the English-speaking world were focussed upon him, because of the position which he held in British politics; and his statements were widely quoted as those of a seer. In replying to a letter from Newcastle-upon-Tyne, thanking him for his zeal in defense of liberty, he wrote: "I consider it as my duty no less strenuously to defend the rights of America than of England, and I feel an equal indignation against the oppressors of our fellow-subjects, whether at home, or on the other side of the Atlantic."[11] A "Patriotic Society in London" expressed the same sentiment in a note to "Mr Adams of the American Congress": "Your cause and ours is one and the same. The present parliament of England, not being duly elected, has no right to make any laws, and consequently the people are not obliged to obey such as may be made by them. Be assured in us you will find every support in our power to give."[12] John Adams and his associates in congress were justified in taking courage from such declarations of interest in their struggles, for dissensions in England served to strengthen their own position; but Americans read into such statements more than their friends intended.

The reasons given by British radicals for denying the authority of parliament in both England and America were quite different from the excuses made by the colonists when they resisted the acts of parliament. British reformers refused obedience to parliament because the

[10] Alexander Stephens, *Memoirs of John Horne Tooke*, London, 1813, I, 178. *Controversial Letters of John Wilkes, Esq.*, pp. 161-169.

[11] *Lloyd's*, Nov. 3-6, 1775.   [12] *Ibid.*, Oct. 11-14, 1776.

House of Commons was not freely elected and did not
adequately represent the British people. Colonial leaders,
on the other hand, opposed parliament for the simple reason that it was not American. They claimed that the colonial assemblies were entitled to make all laws for America,
and that the colonists were, or ought to be, independent of
British legislation. That the Americans should object to
obeying laws of parliament because that body was "foreign to . . . [their] constitution and unacknowledged by
. . . [their] laws" was amazing to the average Englishman.[13] Even the radicals would in general have been
amused at the idea, if the colonists had not been so serious.
However, the associations which British as well as American radicals formed to discuss their needs and work for reform represented all shades of liberal opinion on both
British and colonial problems.

The Supporters of the Bill of Rights were the special
protectors of Wilkes. Their professed object was the preservation of the constitution as established at the Revolution of 1689. The society boasted among its members several men who held seats in the House of Commons, a well
known merchant, a rector, at least two baronets, and a
lord. Meeting at regular intervals in the London Tavern,
they used their influence to reinstate Wilkes, secure freedom of the press, and establish a more liberal form of
government, not only for England, but also for America.[14]
Richard Oliver, a member of the society and a candidate
for parliament in 1770, did not hesitate to make support of
the American claims a leading plank in his platform. The
London livery expressed their approval of that stand by
loud applause, while they hissed the other candidates to
silence.[15] The society itself drew up a "test" for candi-

[13] *Declaration of Independence.*
[14] Stephens, *Memoirs of John Horne Tooke*, contains an account of the
Society of the Supporters of the Bill of Rights.   [15] *Jopson's*, July 16, 1770.

dates to sign, which included a pledge that they would try to restore to America the right of taxation by representatives of her own choice.[16] In 1773 when John Adams of Massachusetts was elected to membership in the society, bonds of sympathy between British and American radicals became stronger.[17]

A second radical organization, the Constitutional Society, grew out of dissensions and personal quarrels among the Supporters of the Bill of Rights. Some of Wilkes' former friends began to fear that he was more interested in having his friends pay his debts than in securing political reform. Disputes which had begun in 1771 made a union of liberal forces for the election of 1773 impossible.[18] Consequently a faction withdrew from the older society, and by 1775 the new organization was well established. On June 7 of that year they voted to raise a subscription for the widows and children of the American victims at Lexington and Concord. They advanced £100 from the "stock purse," and paid the same to the firm of Browne and Collinson on the account of Franklin, who had been receiving other subscriptions for the American cause.[19] When the secretary of the society refused to sign the advertisement for subscriptions, which was to appear in the London papers, John Horne (later Horne-Tooke) accepted the responsibility, and the wrath of the government fell on his head. Two years passed before he was tried on the charge of seditious libel, but the court then declared him guilty, fined him £200, and sentenced him to imprisonment for twelve months. On release from prison, he was obliged to furnish securities for good be-

---

[16] *Lloyd's*, Aug. 24-26, 1774.

[17] *Works of John Adams*, Boston, 1850-1856, II, 325.

[18] *Lloyd's*, June 2-4, 1773. Horace Bleackley, *Life of John Wilkes*, p. 265.

[19] Stephens, *Memoirs of John Horne Tooke*, I, 435. J. B. Daly, *Radical Pioneers of the XVIIIth Century*, London, 1886, p. 141. *Lloyd's*, Apr. 19-21, 1775.

havior for three years.[20] This experience did not deter
Horne from further agitation. On the contrary, in 1780
he was collaborating with Dr. Price in writing a pamphlet
about the policy of the government in war.[21]

In the year 1780, when many Englishmen went over to
the side of opposition, a group of liberals formed another
political organization, the Society for Constitutional Information.[22] The purposes of the new society were similar
to those of other liberal organizations, but its members
were especially active in securing practical measures of
constitutional reform. Major Cartwright, Dr. Brocklesby,
Dr. John Jebb, and Capel Loft were among its founders;
but Major Cartwright was perhaps the best known. Like
John Horne he proved by personal sacrifice the sincerity
of his interest in America. His story is in marked contrast
to that of Wilkes, for it illustrates the unselfish loyalty to
America on the part of a true British patriot.

During the Seven Years' War Cartwright served under
Lord Howe; from 1766 to 1770 he was stationed at Newfoundland, but in 1770 he returned to England. When the
American war opened he was just thirty-six years of age.
He had long cherished a desire for advancement in the
navy and for continued service under Howe whom he considered "the first officer in the world." Furthermore, promotion would make it possible for him to marry. Nevertheless, he refused an offer of a lieutenancy under Lord
Howe because he sympathized with the colonists and
wished to have no part in their coercion. Fearing that he
would be unable to explain his reasons satisfactorily in a
personal interview with the admiral, he wrote as follows:

20 T. B. Howell, *A Collection of State Trials*, XX, 651, ff. A recent work
on this radical clergyman is *John Horne Tooke* by M. C. Yarborough.

21 C. B. R. Kent, *The English Radicals*, London, 1899, p. 89.

22 Kent, p. 86. Daly, Stephens, and even more modern writers seem to con-
fuse the Constitutional Society with the Society for Constitutional Information.

"Thinking as I do on this most unhappy contest between this kingdom and her colonies, it would be a desertion from my principles (which I am sure your Lordship would not approve of) were I to put myself in a situation that might probably cause me to act a hostile part against them." Three days after writing this letter, Cartwright sent Lord Howe a copy of his *American Independence,* in which he defended the colonial claims. He had published the work anonymously lest the knowledge of his beliefs should interfere with his promotion, but he now announced himself as the author.[23] Lord Howe needed no further explanation; and as he was a gentleman with firm convictions of his own, he replied that opinions in politics on such momentous questions were to be as much respected as were opinions on religion.

Although Cartwright thus closed the door to advancement in his chosen profession, he may have found adequate compensation in the approval of his friends. In July, 1776, Nottingham presented him with the freedom of the town, publicly recognizing and commending the manner in which he had asserted his beliefs. Hanging in a place of honor on the wall of Cartwright's dining room was a statement of American radical doctrine, to which Cartwright himself subscribed, the Declaration of Independence.[24] Personally, however, he was too firmly attached to his mother country to accept a position under the American congress. During the remaining years of the war, he trained the militia of Nottingham and stood ready to defend his country against foreign invaders. At the same time he labored incessantly for parliamentary reform, writing pamphlets and organizing the Society for Constitutional Information.

[23] *The Life and Correspondence of Major Cartwright,* edited by his niece, F. D. Cartwright, London, 1826, I, 72-81.
[24] Kent, p. 90.

A fourth radical organization, well known in the period
of the American Revolution, began in the days of the first
Stuart as a sober and conservative society. The Robinhood could trace its history under various names back to
1613, when, as " The Society for Free and Candid Enquiry," it belied its name by prohibiting the discussion
of affairs of state or religion. As to the former, members
agreed: "The taking on us such unwarrantable libertie as
to censure or to call in question the conduct of those whom
the king hath appointed to manage the affaires of his kingdom, is not a fit matter for us to handel."[25] After several
years of meeting in private houses, they decided to adopt
the Essex Head in Essex Street as their headquarters,
where they could have more commodious rooms than private dwellings afforded. At the Essex Head, meetings
were open to anyone wishing to attend, although membership was still elective. After 1747 the society occupied
larger and more convenient quarters at the Robinhood in
Butcher Row, Temple Bar. In the course of one year at the
new quarters, as many as five thousand people are said to
have attended their meetings. As the years passed, the
club grew more liberal. The rules of 1667 declared "That
religion and politics shall be debated in this society, provided decency and good order be observed, both in the
wording the question on those subjects, and in the discussion thereof."[26] By the middle of the eighteenth century
the Robinhood had lost all restraint in its discussion of
political questions. The membership, too, had become
more democratic, and included protestant clergymen, a
Roman Catholic priest, a Jew, surgeons, cabinet-makers,
tailors, a colonial governor, and a vice-consul for the Aus-
trian Netherlands, while in 1764 the presidency was held
by an ordinary baker.

25 *The History of the Robinhood Society*, London, 1764, p. 10.
26 *Ibid.*, p. 55.

Although in the period of the American Revolution, the Robinhood was primarily a tradesmen's society, the members were able to count Oliver Goldsmith among their number, and enjoyed the eloquence of Burke and Barré.[27] Even George III was uncomfortably aware of its existence, for in referring to Governor Johnstone's speech at East India House in November, 1776, the king sarcastically remarked that if the governor and his party had "the desire of keeping up the practice of public speaking," they had better "enter themselves into the famous Society of Robinhood."[28] In the lower room of the society guests were always welcome, but the upper room was reserved for members. Informality apparently characterized the meetings in both quarters; and a bowl of bishop (punch) or other refreshment, for which each man paid a few pence as he entered the room, threatened to arouse more enthusiasm than the orations. In despair of bringing the meeting to order the president once declared: "If you bawl out for porter at the end of the room, for ale at that, for lemonade in one corner, for a mixture of all in another, will not the world say that you come here not in search of truth, but of drink?—Our glory will pass away; our rival, the King's Arms Tavern, will reign in our stead, and be the only nursery for orators and patriots."[29] Members and guests of the Robinhood were, as it happened, less nearly unanimous on the subject of the colonies than were their rivals at the King's Arms. Speeches of a strongly radical and American flavor often resounded through the rooms, but the votes taken at the close of the discussions sometimes disclosed much anti-American opinion.

One winter evening in 1770 a certain Will Chatwell,

27 *Ibid.*, p. 193. *Middlesex Journal*, May 10, 1773.
28 *The Correspondence of King George III with Lord North*, II, 43.
29 *Middlesex Journal*, Jan. 16-18, 1770.

intoxicated by the presence of his audience, or shall we say the ale for which his host was famous, burst into a passionate defense of America. "My opinion is this," he said, "we ought to do justice before we expect obedience. I feel the warmest regard for America. I love the Americans because they love liberty! Liberty has spread like a vine, from this country to the colonies: liberty flourishes in the wilds of America! I honor the plant; I revere the tree; and I would cherish the branches. As to any tumults that may have happened in America, they are the ebullitions of liberty; they are only some breakings-out in the skin of the body politic, which if rudely restrained and improperly checked, may strike inwardly, and endanger the vitals of the constitution."[30] The quality of Will Chatwell's radicalism differed widely from that of Major Cartwright; but there was still less in common between Chatwell's theories and those of the country gentleman or wealthy merchant. If the English squire gave a passing thought to the Americans as he rode to hounds, he pictured a pack of insolent wretches, who by neglecting their duty were raising the tax on English woodland to four shillings in the pound. The merchants and manufacturers felt that their very existence depended upon colonial trade, and hence colonial good-will, but they made no pretense of condoning colonial riots, for tumults would destroy property and indirectly injure commerce. Both merchants and country gentlemen had personal, materialistic reasons for the attitude which each assumed toward colonial affairs. Cartwright was exceptional because his professional success depended upon his taking arms against America, but his opinions of right and wrong caused him to disregard his personal advantage. Chatwell's fortunes, unlike those of merchants, country

[30] *Jopson's*, Jan. 29, 1770.

squires, or army officers, were probably of the day-to-day variety, making it possible for him to indulge his love of liberty without fear of consequences. He had brothers in England and America, men who flourish in times of revolution, for they have everything to gain and nothing to lose.

Orators of the Chatwell type did not always hold the floor at the Robinhood. There were men of anti-American feeling among the speakers as well as in the audience. In June, 1769, the club debated the question: "Do the grievances recited in the Middlesex Petition really exist?" This petition, arising from the trouble over the Wilkes election, not only demanded the cessation of "unjust and unconstitutional practices" in England, but referred to grievances in America, "similar to those of which we complain at home."[31] Most of the speakers on the original question at the Robinhood supported the negative. Because a majority of the audience approved the petition, radicals insinuated that government sympathy at the meeting was due to "ministerial hirelings."[32] The next year, however, at the close of a debate on the American tea act, the audience was clearly pro-government. There were one hundred and twenty-four votes opposing the removal of the colonial tea duty and only fifty-two in favor.[33] The Robinhood furnished an opportunity for friends of America to defend the colonial position; but neither members nor guests were in complete sympathy with colonial claims. The Robinhood Society supported parliament, not America, in the crisis of the Revolution.

The city of London, home of the Supporters of the Bill of Rights, the Robinhood, and other liberal societies, was a center of radicalism. But even among the city livery, the element which in the period of the American Revolution

[31] *Gentleman's Magazine*, June, 1769, p. 291.
[32] *Middlesex Journal*, June 17, 1769.   [33] *Jopson's*, April 16, 1770.

opposed the British administration and favored the colonies met a powerful conservative faction which supported the government. These two groups vied with each other for control in city politics. Commercial interests were strong in London, and the merchants were swayed by the conflicting emotions described in a previous chapter. In 1769, however, a comparatively conservative group of merchants dictated instructions to members of parliament, demanding conciliation of the colonies on the ground that commerce with America was the only profitable trade which England could enjoy "unrivalled by other nations."[34] On the other hand the Middlesex petition of the same year shows the influence of the radicals. That document contained such liberal political ideas that men first hesitated to sign, then questioned the wisdom of presenting it.[35] Because the petition was primarily concerned with British grievances and only secondarily with those of America, the signatures of fifteen hundred and sixty-five freeholders prove little or nothing regarding the interest of London freemen in the colonies. In an address of July, 1769, however, the livery of the city definitely questioned the constitutionality of parliamentary interference in the colonies.[36] By raising the issue of constitutionality, the livery unquestionably alligned themselves with the radicals, for the application of constitutional theory to American problems distinguished the radicals from the organizations of conservative merchants or country gentlemen, who used arguments based upon expediency when urging parliament to make peace with the colonies.

Although the leaders in London municipal politics, the men who were responsible for the petitions to parlia-

[34] *London Magazine*, Feb. 1769, p. 95.
[35] *Gentleman's Magazine*, June, 1769, p. 291.
[36] *Middlesex Journal*, May 30—June 1, 1769.

ment and addresses to the crown, were friendly toward America, it is uncertain how far the livery or the larger body of freemen supported their leaders. In March, 1770, opponents of a remonstrance which dealt with American affairs objected to its being called a ''remonstrance of the livery,'' declaring that it did not represent the livery. They were at least technically correct, because a court of aldermen had passed the measure, and the freemen, not the livery, elected the aldermen.[37] Contemporaries, however, took exception rather to the fact that only five aldermen had been present when the remonstrance was voted upon, and that those five included the most radical among the magistrates: Sawbridge, Trecothick, Stephenson, Beckford, and Townshend. The defense declared, nevertheless, that five members constituted a court for business.[38] If there had not been a strong radical element among the freemen of the city, they would not have chosen radical aldermen to represent them; and if in 1773 the livery had not been friendly toward the colonies, they would hardly have chosen as sheriffs two Americans, Stephen Sayre a native of Long Island, and William Lee, the Virginian.[39] A report that in 1774 the lord mayor and other important city magistrates were contributing to a fund for the Bostonians strengthens the impression that the government of London sympathized with the American colonies.[40]

In the fall of 1774, the election of members of parliament offered a special opportunity for the livery of London to show their opinion on the colonial situation. On

[37] Sir Walter Besant, *London in the Eighteenth Century*, London, 1902, pp. 199-209, for government of London.

[38] *Middlesex Journal*, March 20, 1770.

[39] *Lloyd's*, Nov. 15-17, 1773. In 1775 William Lee, brother of Arthur Lee, was alderman. During the Revolution he was a commissioner from the United States to The Hague, Berlin, and Vienna.

[40] *Ibid.*, Aug. 31—Sept. 2, 1774.

opening the meeting of the livery at the Guildhall, the chairman urged the electors to profit by the example of America, and to resist an arbitrary government in England. He warned his audience that in the near future England might experience injuries similar to those from which America was then suffering. He then asked the candidates for office to sign a paper containing certain promises which they were to fulfill in case of election—promises that pledged the candidate to work for a bill which would restore to Americans the right of freely electing representatives who alone should have the power of taxing the colonies. Four of the candidates, Frederick Bull, Brass Crosby, John Sawbridge, and George Hayley, agreed. Baker refused to subscribe to the test, because he objected rather to the principle of binding the candidate than to the American clauses. More hisses than hands greeted his nomination.[41] But some of the electors boldly declared that they could not see the point of protecting liberty in America, if that meant placing the whole burden of taxation upon Englishmen.[42] The livery were not unanimous on the subject of the colonies, although the majority were inclined to sympathize with America.

The coercive acts of 1774 were unpopular with most influential Londoners, although at that particular moment many merchants were giving up the struggle to keep peace with the colonies. The common council at the Guildhall declared that the coercive acts were "not only contrary to many of the fundamental principles of the English constitution, and most essential right of the subject, but also apparently inconsistent with natural justice and equity."[43] They therefore resolved that the Americans were justified in constitutional opposition. Because the idea of natural justice is peculiarly characteristic of

---

41 *Lloyd's*, Oct. 3-5, 1774.
42 *Ibid.*, Oct. 12-14, 1774. 43 *Ibid.*, Feb. 20-22, 1775.

eighteenth-century radical philosophy, the London livery proved their radical sympathies when they, as well as the Americans, gave parliament's interference with the natural rights of man as an excuse for resistance. The council sent thanks to the Earl of Chatham for his attempt at conciliating the colonies; and a few days later voted to petition parliament against the bill to restrain the trade of New England.[44] The petitioners, who were influenced by injury to their business, opposed the commercial restrictions; but they also criticised the clauses of the bill which gave extreme authority to the governor and council in the colonies. In the seventeenth century, the English had won their freedom from an arbitrary executive; and in the eighteenth century, when they were again fearing an encroachment of the royal prerogative, they eagerly championed the colonies in their struggle with the executive power. Englishmen were, as a rule, much less concerned with the colonial opposition to parliament, than they were with the colonial resistance to the executive which had been going on for three-quarters of a century.[45] The next common hall, or meeting of the livery, also addressed the crown on the subject of America, and declared that the colonists were justified in resisting Great Britain.[46] Disliking the radical tone of the address, the king announced his decision to receive no more addresses from the city except from the body corporate, that is, the whole body of freemen.

According to the lord mayor, the corporation as a whole never met, and hence could take no action.[47] Dis-

44 *Ibid.*, Feb. 13-15, 1775; Feb. 22-24, 1775. The common council consisted of lord mayor, aldermen, and councilmen.

45 It is interesting to note that the *Declaration of Independence*, unlike previous revolutionary statements, makes specific accusations against the crown and refers to parliament only indirectly.

46 *London Magazine*, April, 1775, pp. 208-209.

47 *Lloyd's*, May 3-5, 1775. The freemen met only in their ward motes where they chose their representatives in the city government.

satisfaction with the royal decision resulted in a spirited
meeting of about tweny-five hundred citizens who made
new resolutions against the war and the action of the
ministry.[48] The livery also showed their feeling on the
colonial question when they sent thanks to Lord Effingham for the stand he had taken on military service in
America. Like Major Cartwright, Lord Effingham preferred to sacrifice his military command rather than
consent to bear arms against the Americans.[49] The evidence of popular approval of such examples of self-sacri-
fice, combined with repeated addresses to the king and
renewed instructions to members of parliament, must
have embarrassed the ministry and George III.

During the summer of 1775, the spirit of opposition
thrived in the city. Radical societies and London magistrates seemed to be in league. The rumor spread through
the city that the livery proposed to give two thousand
pounds of the city revenue to the rebels of New England;
but that they were not publishing the fact because of the
prosecution of John Horne.[50] In August the lord mayor
entertained several members of the Society of the Supporters of the Bill of Rights at the Mansion House. Although the reporter stated that "loyal and constitutional"
toasts were drunk, the king may have doubted the utter
loyalty of his subjects, guests of the lord mayor.[51] During
the same month, the lord mayor in his official capacity
found an opportunity to avow publicly the opposition of
the city to governmental policy in America. According
to custom, heralds read the royal proclamation, forbidding
all correspondence between the British people and the
rebellious colonists, at Temple Bar; and the city officers

[48] *Lloyd's*, June 23-26, 1775.
[49] *Ibid.*, July 21-24, 1775. Walpole's *Last Journals*, I, 466.
[50] *Lloyd's*, July 7-10, 1775.
[51] *Ibid.*, Aug. 2-4, 1775.

repeated the proclamation at the Royal Exchange. The lord mayor refused to dignify the occasion by allowing the officers to ride in state and carry the mace. The city did not officially support the proclamation, nor did the mob, for the general hiss at the conclusion of the reading shows that the measure was as unpopular with the common people as with the magistrates.[52] On the other hand a conservative element in the city encouraged the government by petitioning the king on the subject of the "malignant spirit of resistance to law and government" among the Americans; and by expressing the hope that the king would use his constitutional power to subdue the colonists, who were "acting in open defiance of the laws."[53]

When the radical element in the London livery discovered that further activities in behalf of the colonies, including an address to the electors of Great Britain and petitions to parliament and the king, completely failed to affect governmental policy, they abandoned those methods.[54] Though far from acquiescent, London radicals realized that under existing conditions opposition was useless. Nevertheless, the city government continued to demonstrate its liberal tendencies. For example, the common council presented the freedom of the city to Dr. Richard Price, the "Apostle of Liberty," as the French assembly later called him.[55] Of the radical dissenters, friends of America, Price was one of the best known. The American congress even invited him to the United States to assist them with their finances. He declined the in-

[52] Annual Register, XVIII, 149.   [53] Ibid., p. 272.
[54] Lloyd's, Sept. 25-27, 1775; Oct. 23-25, 1775; Mar. 13-15, 1776.
[55] Joseph Priestley, A Discourse on occasion of the Death of Dr. Price, delivered at Hackney on Sunday, May 1, 1781, published in London 1781; and Andrew Kippis, An Address delivered at the Interment of the late Reverend Dr. Richard Price on the twenty-sixth of April, 1781, published in London, 1791, found in Yale Library in Funeral Sermons, vols. XXV and XLVIII. London Magazine, May, 1776, pp. 227-229.

vitation because of advancing age and connections in England; but he considered America "the hope, and likely soon to be the refuge of mankind."[56] His financial writings, though condemned by Adam Smith, attracted widespread attention from a less critical world. Price drew most discouraging pictures of economic conditions in England during the American Revolution; and helped to convince the public that war was the chief cause of their economic ills. Many years passed, however, before the people at large reached this conviction; and in the meantime, from 1776 until about 1780, except for sporadic attempts to hinder the government, London radicals were quiet. On the other hand, the king and his ministers were unable to obtain active support in the city. In 1778 a majority of thirty to one in the common council defeated a motion to present bounties to all men who would enlist in the sea or land service for three years. On the contrary, the council immediately passed a resolution that to give any countenance to the war, while offers of just terms of peace were withheld from America, would reflect dishonor upon the court, and would fail to help the commercial interest of the city.[57] After several mortifying experiences in trying to secure measures of support in the city, George III and his ministers were convinced that such attempts were useless.

London radicals did not renew their active interest in the war until 1780, when the agitation of the county asso-

[56] Francis Wharton, *The Revolutionary Diplomatic Correspondence of the United States,* Washington, 1889, II, 474. By a curious coincidence, when Dr. Price's letter of thanks for the freedom of the city was read to the council, there was also presented a bill for mending the gold box in which the freedom of the city had been presented. The murmur of questions was silenced by the statement that when the box was examined in the council, someone "who had not the love of liberty" had thrust his finger through the bottom. *Lloyd's,* July 22-24, 1776.

[57] *Correspondence of George III with Lord North,* II, 122, note.

ciations stimulated sympathetic activity in the city. Even then the share of the city radicals in the reform program was comparatively slight. But late in December, 1781, alarmed at the apparently strong determination of the king to continue the struggle with the colonies, regardless of public opinion, the lord mayor, aldermen, and livery agreed to a petition presenting practical, economic arguments for making peace with America.[58] Trouble again arose over the manner of receiving the petition. The lord mayor was determined that the king should receive the petition on the throne; and George III was equally determined not to receive the petition except during a levee.[59] The royal decision thus to minimize the importance of the city petition aroused the wrath of the radicals. They used the occasion to reassert their political grievances—unequal representation of the people in parliament and parliamentary corruption; and they also declared that the situation which they deplored was responsible for the war with America and the dismemberment of the British empire. A committee of thirty-six well-known citizens took charge of an active campaign for political reform in the British government. They emphasized the need for more frequent elections and for more equal representation in parliament, and were emphatic in regard to the necessity of immediate peace with America.[60] When in February, 1782, they sent to parliament their petition requesting terms of peace with America, one of many on the same subject, Lord North was already on the point of resign-

[58] *Lloyd's*, Dec. 12-14, 1781.

[59] *Ibid.* According to Lord Stormont, secretary of state for the southern department, the king should receive upon the throne only ''an address properly so called and entitled solely an address.'' *The Correspondence of King George the Third*, V, 308-309.

[60] *Lloyd's*, Jan. 30—Feb. 1, 1782. See in the following pages the story of the county association movement with which this committee was connected.

ing.[61] After long delay the London radicals were permitted to share this popular victory over the crown; but
their reform program was doomed to an early death.

Outside the city radical ideas developed more slowly
than in London itself. London radicals had tried in vain
to establish an extensive system of circular letters in
imitation of the colonial committees of correspondence,
hoping to arouse sympathy for their plans in the counties
and independent boroughs.[62] To be sure, in 1773 the Society of the Supporters of the Bill of Rights in London was
corresponding with similar groups in Northumberland,
Cumberland, and Durham;[63] and by the next year free
debating societies on the plan of the Robinhood were
flourishing in Birmingham, Walford, and Wolverhampton, where women as well as men were at liberty to attend and speak on any subject they thought proper;[64]
but interest in suggestions for reform was desultory.
Strangely enough, the demand for constitutional reform
made little impression until the dissatisfied landholders
instituted the county associations.[65] In these associations
the radicals found an organization through which they
could work for their own ends.

Although the country gentlemen gave to the county
associations prestige, the radicals supplied the permanent
organization and furnished the necessary enthusiasm.
Many of the country gentry who attended the original
assemblies expected first to protest against the extravagance of government and the continuance of an unprofitable war and then to wait for parliament to act. Wyvill,

---

[61] *Lloyd's,* Feb. 25-27, 1782. *Parl. Hist.,* XXII, 1064.

[62] State Papers Domestic, George III, 11; letter from London committee
of correspondence to Craven at Barton Court, Aug. 31, 1775. *Middlesex
Journal,* June 21, 1770.

[63] *York Chronicle,* May 21, 1773.   [64] *Lloyd's,* June 3-6, 1774.

[65] The share of the landed interests in the county associations has been
described in a previous chapter.

the leader of the reform agitation, both in York and in the kingdom at large, was not content to fold his hands while parliament debated. He was determined to arouse the whole country to a realization of the inadequacy of their present form of government, and through the pressure of public opinion to obtain not only peace with America and economy in government, but also more frequent elections of members to the House of Commons and more equal representation of the people in parliament. Wyvill was probably responsible for the committees of correspondence, which developed tendencies much more radical than the original meetings which created them.[66] He was the leading spirit at the meeting of deputies in London in 1780—the meeting that declared "By an unhappy war with America, begotten in the first influence of this despotic system, and nursed with a view of giving completion to it, this fatal influence has been armed with more ample means than it ever enjoyed before for enslaving parliament in the private application of no small part of those monies which have so far exceeded the supplies of former wars, and have been obtained under the pretext of necessary public service."[67]

Wyvill seems to have been temporarily successful, for radical influence was more evident at the second meeting of the York association than it had been at the first. The outcry of the country gentlemen against the expenses of the war was supplemented by a resolution that the American war was not only "impolitic in its tendencies" but "unjust in itself."[68] The committee of the county of Surrey recognized the inconsistency of asserting the political rights of Englishmen while invading American privileges, and protested against the war on the score of justice to

[66] The *Wyvill Papers* furnish an almost complete account of the connection of Wyvill with the county associations.
[67] *Ibid.*, p. 429.   [68] *Ibid.*, p. 163.

America.[69] As the real character and aims of the leaders became evident, the country gentlemen gradually withdrew their support. The second meeting of deputies in London, March, 1781, was much smaller than the one at the close of the preceding year. The representatives from the counties signed the new petition to the House of Commons as individual freeholders, not as deputies from their county associations. Perhaps they had no authority to act otherwise. A wave of conservatism influenced even the corporation of London, for the magistrates forced the county deputies to transfer their meetings from the Guildhall to St. Albans Tavern, and the city committee was abolished.[70]

The old House of Commons, dissolved by royal proclamation in 1780, had given some encouragement to the radicals by accepting John Dunning's famous resolution on the increasing influence of the crown. That body also declared that parliament ought to redress the grievances of which petitioners throughout the country were complaining.[71] But the new house was, for a few months at least, more completely under the control of the ministry. A majority of seventy-seven defeated the motion of Sir George Savile, "representative of Wyvill's congress," as the king called him, to refer the petition of the county deputies to a committee of the whole house. The opposition could not yet control a majority; and in fact, few members of parliament were ever sympathetic toward the radical aims of the county associations. After Lord North resigned and a new ministry came into office, with the intention of ending the war, the majority of the members of the county associations considered their work finished. Wyvill himself wrote that he expected economy in government after the war, and he did not think it wise to

69 *Wyvill Papers*, p. 296.
70 *Ibid.*, pp. 332-334.   71 *Ibid.*, pp. 335-336.

embarrass the ministry by proposing other reforms until they could carry out their own plans. He intended to continue the work for parliamentary reform the next winter, but he then found that enthusiasm for reform was dead. Peace had been the main object of the county associations, and peace was an accomplished fact.[72]

The significance of the views of association members depends upon the extent to which those associations represented the English people and English thought. The associations did not pretend to include all classes of people; but they did to a certain extent represent the thought of the majority of Englishmen at the moment. They were, in some respects at least, more representative of public opinion than was the parliament then in session. Rigby, a government man, denied in the House of Commons that the associations were representative of public opinion, for, he declared, the leaders excluded from the county meetings all who disagreed with them;[73] but Sir Charles Turner, a liberal, declared that the House of Commons failed to represent the people, because it had carried on the American War, "notwithstanding the voice of the people was so much against it."[74] In the opinion of association members, as expressed in speeches and in petitions to parliament, there were three objects to be gained: the reform of parliament, economy in government, and peace with America. The least popular was parliamentary reform, for even the association members themselves disagreed as to the need or wisdom of changes in the British constitution. The history of the associations shows that the influential and privileged classes were opposed to parliamentary reform, for they were satisfied with their own position of superiority and feared the result of change. It is, however, unsafe to infer that the

[72] *Ibid.*, p. 411.
[73] *Ibid.*, p. 478.   [74] *Ibid.*, p. 469.

masses of the people, unrepresented in either the House
of Commons or the county associations, were demanding
the suffrage. They were as yet indifferent to their political position; and in 1780 only a minority of progressive
thinkers believed in more than a very limited extension
of the suffrage. When one considers the other objects of
the associations, economy in government and the cessation of the war with America, the case appears quite
different. By 1781 the country was almost unanimous
on these points; and only the King's Friends still insisted upon prolonging the struggle. The associations
were important because they united various interests, all
temporarily intent upon one object—peace with America.
Merchants, country gentlemen, and radicals agreed that
the results of the war were most unfortunate for England, and that only further misery could result from a
continuation of the conflict. These three classes united
to arouse the nation against the war; and finally forced
the government to abandon its program.

The history of British radicalism in the period of the
American Revolution shows that the reformers in the two
countries were a source of inspiration to each other. They
corresponded with one another and exchanged philo-
sophical ideas, and British radicals wrote pamphlets in
defense of American claims. There was a general understanding and sympathy which linked the progressives in
the two countries. These facts help to explain the simi-
larity in the organization, views, and purposes of the
radical associations in England and America. The aid
to Wilkes, the American offer to Dr. Price, the election
of John Adams to membership in the Society of the Supporters of the Bill of Rights are concrete examples of the
close connection between British and American radicals.
Greater political liberty was a cause common to Americans and Englishmen. Encouragement came from both

sides of the Atlantic, and it is difficult to tell on which side the influence was the more strongly felt.

One can scarcely measure the debt of British radicals to their brothers in America, or *vice versa*. Favoring influences brought success to America first, while French excesses checked the British progress toward parliamentary reform. British radicals, leaders in the years of the American Revolution, continued their activities into the nineteenth century, when their efforts were also partly rewarded. Successful America may have acted as a spur to their efforts, for in 1774 the British cited American resistance as an example for England.[75] In the relation existing between the radicals of the two countries there is a quality of interdependence less tangible and less material than that between British merchant and American customer, but quite as vital. While both merchants and radicals continued their interest in America after the war, the sympathy of British radicals for their friends across the Atlantic is more characteristic of the fundamental friendship and underlying unity of thought which continues to bind together the two great English-speaking nations.

The political aspirations of the British radicals allied them with the American revolutionists; and political theories distinguished the radicals from the merchants and country gentlemen. While the country gentry and merchants criticised the governmental colonial policy for economic reasons, British radicals emphasized political grievances. Aims of individuals varied widely; and opinions regarding the place of the colonies in the empire differed, but characteristic arguments were drawn from "the fundamental principles of the English constitution" and "natural justice."[76] In illustrating their points, the

[75] *Lloyd's*, Oct. 3-5, 1774.

[76] *Ibid.*, Feb. 20-22, 1775. Resolution of the court of common council at the Guildhall, for example.

radicals enumerated instances in which parliament in legislating for the colonies had violated these principles. They criticised, for example, the manner and mode of taxation, the administration of justice, and the power given to administrative officials, as in the case of Massachusetts Bay.

American taxation was one of the subjects of Richard Oliver's speech, following his election to the House of Commons. Oliver, a member of the Society of the Supporters of the Bill of Rights, declared: "The principles of fair government forbid that they [the Americans] should be taxed without representation, as much as that the people of this country should pay taxes to which, or to the continuance of which, they have not consented."[77] The "test" for candidates for parliament, drawn up by the society in 1771, included a promise to "endeavour to restore to America the essential right of taxation by representatives of their own free election, repealing the acts passed in violation of that right since the year 1763, and the universal excise so notoriously incompatible with every principle of British liberty, which has been lately substituted in the colonies instead of the laws of customs."[78] The address of the London livery in 1769 referred to the "unconstitutional regulations and taxations" established in the colonies; while in 1775 the common hall declared that it was an "essential, unalterable principle of liberty, the source and security of all constitutional rights, that no part of the dominion can be taxed without being represented."[79] In all the restatements of the same proposition, one hears the echo from beyond the Atlantic: "Taxation without representation is tyranny."

British radicals also supported American complaints

[77] *Jopson's*, July 16, 1770.   [78] *Lloyd's*, Aug. 24-26, 1770.
[79] *London Magazine*, April, 1775, p. 209.

in regard to administration. In 1769 the London livery
petitioned the king for a removal of specific American
grievances, including the invasion of the right of trial
by jury, the use of general warrants, and the appointment of incompetent civil magistrates.[80] The same petition opposed the plan for the trial of revenue causes by
the civil law judges, who were to be paid from the con-
demnation money. In the seventeenth century Englishmen had won freedom from general warrants, and in the
early eighteenth century the superiority of the common
law courts was secured. Naturally American sympathizers demanded those conditions for the colonists, although the government found other regulations convenient. Incompetent magistrates were the bane of both
England and the colonies, and during the years of the
American Revolution the whole place and pension system
was under attack. The power of the crown rested in part
upon men whose services were rewarded with office. The
result was maladministration in such offices, and an
arbitrary power in the crown. Independence and freedom
seemed to be in danger in both England and America.[81]
The coercive acts of 1775 called forth more opposition on
the score of unconstitutionality; and London radicals
declared that subordination of the colonies in commerce
was all that England should require.[82]

The colonists, in the meantime, were progressing so far
in their demands that only the most radical philosopher
could follow their advance. The less radical merchant
could hardly convince himself that America should be
independent of parliamentary commercial regulations and
so was unwilling to take an extreme position. Consequently the radicals were divided. The extremists, who
hoped to secure parliamentary reform by uniting with

[80] *Jopson's*, July 10, 1769.   [81] *Landmark*, Dec., 1922, pp. 887-890.
[82] *Lloyd's*, Feb. 20-22, 1775. *London Magazine*, April, 1775, pp. 208-209.

the Americans against government, were doomed to disappointment, for England was not yet ready. The help which the radicals could give to America was slight, for they were few in number; but they rendered one distinct service. With the possible exception of the merchants, the radicals were the most wide-awake, the most alert, the most active of all the various British groups concerned with colonial affairs. They advertised conditions; they stirred up others; they engaged in propaganda which convinced the country gentlemen, first, that their substance was being wasted by war, and secondly, that not parliamentary supremacy but royal prerogative was determining their fate. Had it not been for the reformers, England might not have made peace in 1783. The Americans might well believe that their warmest friends were among the radicals. In that group were the most disinterested adherents of the colonial cause. Among the radicals were the only Englishmen who declared that it was not only expedient but right for Great Britain to grant what the colonists demanded.

CHAPTER VII

POLICY OF THE GOVERNMENT.

I. CROWN AND ADMINISTRATIVE OFFICIALS.

WHILE merchants and country gentlemen were destroying all chances of success by disputing with each other about colonial policies, another influence was gradually usurping control of government. The new factor, more subtle and difficult to define than the interests of either commerce or land, was imperialistic. Foreign to the doctrines of Walpole and earlier British statesmen, imperialism developed after the acquisition of territory at the close of the Seven Years' War. The supporters of the peace terms expressed the idea in these words: "Extent of territory and a number of subjects are matters of as much consideration to a state attentive to the sources of real grandeur as the mere advantages of traffic."[1] Imperialists believed that the power and authority of the mother country must be maintained, regardless of the special interests of merchants or landowners. Imperialism in that sense was much more akin to the old Roman idea than to the mercantilist doctrine of "the self-sufficing empire." To the imperialists the supremacy of parliament over the colonies was an end in itself, not merely a means to secure trade for British merchants or lower taxes for the English gentry.

A small but influential group of British officials gradually made of the new theory a creed. This tendency pleased George III; and when occasion permitted, he insisted that his ministers should base colonial policy upon the doctrine

[1] *Parl. Hist.*, XV, 1271-1272.

of imperialism. Even though the king's public speeches might reflect the mind of Grey Cooper or William Eden, confidential advisers of the crown, his private correspondence betrayed the ideas of George III, the man.[2] As early as 1766 his personal wishes had become known to a few observant contemporaries, such as Henry Cruger, the Bristol merchant, who wrote to his father "that the K . . . had empower'd Lord Bute and Lord Strange to say, his private wish was not for a repeal of the Stamp Act, as it would be derogatory to the honour of his crown, and dignity of his Parliament to be compell'd to repeal an act that had been so disrespectfully treated without first exercising their authority by enforcing it."[3] The king was personally in favor of modifying the act, because, as he said, maintaining a part of it "ascertain'd the right of the mother country to tax its colonys"; and because modification would show the colonies that parliament desired to redress any just grievances. According to King George, modification, unlike repeal, would preserve the honor of the country.[4] This suggestion did not appeal to parliament, and the merchants and country gentlemen together were successful in obtaining repeal. The defenders of the Stamp Act, however, were the same men, who at a later date carried into effect a policy of forcing obedience from the colonies. Coercion was a logical part of the new imperialism. From the beginning to the end of the American controversy, the court party consistently advised the use of force; but the ability to dictate colonial policy depended upon a clever manipulation of many factors.

Political antagonisms among the Whigs, as well as

[2] Add. MSS., 34414, f. 337. William Eden furnished a draft of the king's speech, suggesting that Grey Cooper might use it for something more finished.

[3] *Commerce of Rhode Island*, I, 141.

[4] *The Correspondence of King George the Third*, I, 269 and 273.

differing opinions on economic questions, gave the favorite ministers of George III an opportunity to control the government. They were past masters in the art of securing influence. Edmund Burke declared, ''The Power of the Crown, almost dead and rotten as Prerogative, has grown up anew with much more strength, and far less odium, under the name of Influence.''[5] The whole official organization of the eighteenth century contributed to the success of the King's Friends. The business of government was everywhere subordinate to the business of getting jobs.[6] Power and authority in the church, the army, and the state were the privilege of the few. Practically all offices were the gift of patrons, who in turn were dependent upon royal favor. Even the church was not free from the evils of patronage. The clergymen who joined the county association movement did so in the face of the warning that the road to preferment did not lie in that direction.[7] Loyal churchmen supported authority, whether of church or state.

The Anglican organization had its own interests in America; and these were closely allied with the success of government. Since the royal provinces gave the strongest support to the Anglican church, episcopacy had a valid reason for favoring plans which would increase the dependence of all the colonies upon the mother country. The more independent colonies were strongly dissentient in church matters. The following quotation expresses a fairly general Anglican view: ''In respect to the Colonies, it is evident, I think, beyond contradiction, that to secure their obedience no way can be so effectual as a regular establishment of the Church of England, with resident bishops; and an exclusion of dissenters from a share in

[5] *Thoughts on the Cause of the Present Discontent*, London, 1770, p. 12.
[6] Add. MSS., 27918, f. 3, p. 39.   [7] *Wyvill Papers*, p. 354.

the civil government.''[8] Though officials in England recognized the peculiarity of the religious situation in America and the need for toleration, they nevertheless frowned upon special favors or additional powers to dissenters.

For example, the Board of Trade opposed the incorporation of the Presbyterian Church in New York; and Richard Jackson, the legal adviser to the board, objected to the establishment of a new college in Mecklenburg County, North Carolina, because the trustees in that section would be largely Presbyterian.[9] Dissenters were tolerated but not encouraged. In this negative way the home government encouraged episcopacy in the colonies, and episcopacy at home reciprocated by supporting the government. Not only was every country curacy supposed to be a stronghold for the government, but the bishops carried their banner into parliament. In 1766 Cruger wrote to his father in America that nine bishops in the House of Lords ''were for carrying fire and sword to America with this argument, that since you snarl and begin to show your teeth, they ought to be knocked out before you are able to bite.''[10]

Anglican plans for establishing bishops in the colonies heightened hostility in America, and won the sympathy of dissenters in England for their brothers across the Atlantic.[11] Englishmen declared that the Americans were more aggravated by episcopacy than by the Stamp Act.[12]

[8] *The Revolution Vindicated,* Cambridge, 1777, p. 67.

[9] *Acts of the Privy Council of England, Colonial Series,* 1745-1766, § 651; 1766-1783, § 222.

[10] *Commerce of Rhode Island,* I, 141.

[11] Arthur Lyon Cross, *The Anglican Episcopate and the American Colonies,* gives a comprehensive discussion of the question, especially from the colonial point of view. See chapters IX, X, and XI for this period.

[12] *London Magazine,* Sept., 1770, p. 464. Newspaper evidence does not support J. T. Adams' contention that ''the agitation was purely of colonial origin.'' *Revolutionary New England, 1691-1776,* p. 359.

Bishop Secker, Archbishop of Canterbury from 1758 to 1768, was most active in trying to secure the establishment of bishops in the colonies.[13] Opposition was powerful, and feeling ran high on both sides. Bishop Lowth of Oxford, Archbishop of York from 1761 to 1776, declared that "he would vote against the Bill for extending the Toleration Act because the Dissenters would not receive Bishops in America."[14] Bishop Lowth's successor was the Rt. Rev. Dr. Markham, whose loyal sermons drew down the wrath of the opposition in parliament. Most Englishmen believed in his fundamental doctrine, the supremacy of the law; but they differed as to the branch of law which held that position.[15] The radicals, for instance, declared that natural law was supreme, but Markham referred to parliamentary statutes. Since the Anglican bishops believed that the omnipotence of parliament was necessary for the success of their own schemes in America, they and their fellow churchmen took the side of the King's Friends in the colonial controversy.

The newspapers frequently published articles by loyal churchmen who discoursed upon the advantages which both church and state would enjoy if bishops were established in America.[16] Anglicans often mentioned the lack of a strongly established church in the colonies as the principal cause of all the disturbances. Bishop Warburton declared that no government could long subsist without an alliance between church and state. Therefore, in 1774, a correspondent for *Lloyd's* urged parliament before passing the Boston Port Bill to introduce episcopacy into all the colonies.[17] Another correspondent, though quite

[13] *London Magazine*, June, 1769, review of a letter from Bishop Secker to Horatio Walpole. *Ibid.*, Aug., 1770, pp. 410-412; Sept., 1770, pp. 462-464.

[14] Fitzmaurice, *Life of Shelburne*, I, 442.

[15] *Lloyd's*, June 11-13, 1777.

[16] *Ibid.*, Aug. 29-31, 1770; July 24-26, 1771, for example.

[17] *Ibid.*, Mar. 28-30, 1774.

sure that opponents of the measure would eventually become its friends, insisted: "Be those things how they may,
if this appointment of Bishops is essentially necessary
for the joint interest of Great Britain and America, it
is incumbent upon the former as the parent to fix them
immediately among the inhabitants of the latter, as her
offspring."[18] In 1776 one extremist suggested that the
province of Massachusetts Bay be erected into an archie-
piscopal principality, that grants of land and other documents be sealed with the episcopal seal, and that a mitre
and other emblems of episcopal dignity be placed above
the doors of buildings and thus thrust upon the vision of
the Puritans.[19] A study of Anglican opinion shows that
with few exceptions churchmen were imperialists, advising coercion and force in matters of both church and state.
The Anglicans, as we have seen, were prejudiced by the
fact that strong governmental control in America would
tend to further their own interests and selfish aims.

As a professional group, the lawyers of the period,
though almost as unanimous as the churchmen in supporting imperialism, had no special interests in the colonies.
Their opinions, therefore, seem comparatively unbiassed.
When Englishmen took out their law books or studied
colonial charters and precedents, they usually decided
that the colonies had little legal ground for complaint.[20]
Sentiment, business considerations, and radical theory
based on natural rights were the principal grounds for
opposing the measures of government. In 1766 when the
British people were cursing parliament for the Stamp
Act, "all the eminent lawyers (one excepted)" were said

---

[18] *Lloyd's*, Aug. 27-29, 1770.   [19] *Ibid.*, Apr. 8-10, 1776.

[20] Professor Charles McIlwain, *The American Revolution: A Constitutional Interpretation*, finds much to justify the constitutional position taken
by John Adams and his associates; but his arguments have been seriously
questioned. See review of McIlwain's book by E. S. Corwin, *Amer. Hist. Review*, XXIX, 775.

to be convinced that the British parliament had the right to tax America.[21] Blackstone, the great commentator, was frequently quoted on the subject of law in the colonies. Because he classed America among the conquered provinces, he declared that the common law had no authority there. Parliament could control America; but the colonies were bound only by the acts in which they were specifically named.[22]

Lawyers were probably more convinced than were the members of other professions that the supremacy of the British parliament was necessary to maintain the empire. The two chief legal advisers of the crown during the war, Attorney General Thurlow and Solicitor General Wedderburn, agreed with King George that the theory of parliamentary power over the colonies was useless without some practical application. In 1775, in a speech before parliament, Wedderburn declared that interests of more importance than commerce and manufactures were at stake, for the very legislative power of the mother country was involved.[23] The chief dispute between England and America was over the right of parliament to tax the colonies. In the Declaratory Act of 1766 parliament had claimed the right to bind the colonies in all cases whatsoever. In the course of a debate on the Bill for Regulating the Government of Massachusetts Bay, Thurlow went a step further. "To say that we have a right to tax America, and never to exercise that right is ridiculous; and a man must abuse his own understanding very much,

[21] *Jopson's*, Jan. 27, 1766.

[22] Blackstone added in his *Commentaries* "that the rule is generally laid down that acts of parliament contrary to reason are void; but if parliament will positively enact a thing to be done which is unreasonable I know of no power that can control it." Quincy's *Massachusetts Reports*, Boston, 1865, Appendix I, 526, note 26, cites I *Bl. Com.* 91, and comments from the colonial point of view.

[23] *Parl. Hist.*, XVIII, 233.

not to allow that right. To procure the tax by requisition is a most ridiculous absurdity, while the sovereignty remains in this country; and the right of taxing was never in the least given up to the Americans. Their charter is more a matter of legislative power, and whoever looks into it will see that no power whatever was meant to be given them so as to controul the right of taxation from Great Britain.''[24]

Lord Chief Justice Wilmot of the Court of Common Pleas advised the House of Lords to give proof of their opinion that the colonial assemblies did not have equal power with the parliament of Great Britain.[25] Although Wedderburn, Thurlow, and Wilmot were the king's officials and might have been influenced by his opinions, their ideas were not new. Repeatedly through the eighteenth century the crown lawyers had belittled the importance of the colonial assemblies, and had insisted upon the necessity of subordinating them to the king and parliament. George III and his ministers were adapting an accepted theory to their immediate purposes, as the landed interests were also glad to do. The crown officers wished to have power over the colonies for its own sake; the country gentlemen, to obtain revenue. Because they both found that the supremacy of parliament would contribute to the attainment of their own ends, they joined forces just as long as their purposes did not conflict with each other.

Established legal opinion stated that parliament must be supreme, even omnipotent, in practice as well as in theory; though lawyers differed as to the expediency of

---

[24] *Parl. Hist.*, XVII, 1313-1314.

[25] *A Narrative of the Changes in the Ministry, 1765-1767 told by the Duke of Newcastle in a Series of Letters to John White, M.P.*, edited for the Royal Historical Society by Mary Bateson, 2d Camden Series, LIX, 101. This will henceforth be cited as *Newcastle's Letters*.

applying the theory in specific instances. Richard Hey, barrister-at-law of the Middle Temple, explained how parliamentary supremacy could be made to accord with the rights of the people in general. He admitted that the legislature could not be omnipotent as opposed to the whole people; but that the voice of the whole people was mute. Therefore, "those to whom the ordinary powers of legislation in any state are committed must be considered as unconfined in the power of making laws."[26] John Lind is another and perhaps better known English barrister, who supported the rights of parliament as opposed to the colonies so ably that an American has written of his *Answer to the Declaration of the American Congress:* "It is doubtful if any disinterested student of history, any competent judge of reasoning will now deny to this pamphlet the praise of making out a strong case against the historical accuracy and the logical soundness of many parts of the Declaration of Independence."[27]

Lawyers gave their support to the theory of parliamentary supremacy over America, but practical men of affairs, merchants and country gentlemen, lost interest in a theoretical right, when the enforcement of that right destroyed commerce and plunged the country hopelessly into debt. If the interests of land and trade had been identical, the doctrine of "imperium" could never have controlled parliamentary policy. Conflicting opinions in the country, in parliament, and in the cabinet made it possible for the King's Friends to develop in the government a fighting organization under royal direction. Frequent changes in cabinets partly explain the lack of consistency in the treatment of the colonies, before the work

---

[26] Hey, *Observations on the Nature of Civil Liberty and the Principles of Government*, London, 1776, pp. 51, 52, 62.
[27] M. C. Tyler, *Literary History of the American Revolution*, I, 500.

of establishing a personal government under George III was completed.

The ministry of Newcastle and Pitt, which had directed the Seven Years' War, was not only successful but popular. A succession of cabinets followed, each of which seemed to have only one plan of procedure—to reverse the work of its predecessor. During this time, the government was catering but intermittently to the merchants. Only when the interests of the mercantile classes were subordinated to a combination of royal and landed interests was there any firm or consistent treatment of colonial problems. Within these cabinets of brief duration the chancellor of the exchequer was of supreme importance, especially in colonial matters. The demand for revenue from America was of primary concern, and as head or, at least, a very important member of the cabinet, the chancellor of the exchequer largely determined colonial policy. Grenville, who was in office from 1763 to 1765, had no scruples about taxing America. His theory was the generally accepted one: "The Colonies and all British subjects whatever, have an equal share in the general representation of the Commons of Great Britain, and are bound by the consent of the majority of that House."[28] He and his followers continued to uphold the right of parliament to tax America, although in 1765 there had been little discussion of imperial relationships. Men intimately and personally acquainted with the colonies approved the Stamp Act.

Henry McCulloh, who had spent much time in the Carolinas, first as inspector for improving the quit-rents,

---

[28] *The Regulations lately made Concerning the Colonies,* London, 1765, p. 109. Whoever was the author of this pamphlet, which has been variously ascribed, it without doubt expresses Grenville's idea, and may have been written under his guidance. G. L. Beer, *British Colonial Policy, 1754-1765,* New York, 1922, p. 221.

then as secretary for North Carolina, advocated a stamp duty for America, and was probably partly responsible for the measure.[29] William Knox, having been a member of the council of Georgia and provost marshal, was acting as agent for that colony and East Florida in Great Britain in 1765; but was dismissed because he defended the Stamp Act as "the least objectionable mode of taxation."[30] His writings prove conclusively that he believed in the unlimited power of parliament over the colonies according to common law, the colonial charters, and historical precedent. He believed that the colonies should be taxed. Therefore, having discarded as ineffective other possible means of raising money in the colonies, he concluded that taxation by act of parliament was the only practical method. Knox did stipulate, however, that no tax should be levied in the same year in which it was proposed, for he wished to give the colonies an opportunity to agree to the act. He also applied the theory of parliamentary supremacy in such a way that it appealed to the practical merchant and the colonist. For example, he showed that the parliamentary debt act of 1732 had furthered the commercial interests of both, because of the greater facility which it offered in collecting American debts, thus enabling British merchants to give extended credit to the colonists.[31]

The colonial projects of Grenville and his advisers were based upon the assumption that parliament was supreme in colonial affairs. Grenville's application of the theory

[29] McCulloh, *Miscellaneous Representations Relative to our Concerns in America*, edited by W. A. Shaw, reprinted London, 1905, prefatory note. *Grenville Papers*, London, 1852, II, 373-374, note. McCulloh, *A Miscellaneous Essay concerning the Course pursued by Great Britain in the Affairs of her Colonies*, London, 1755, pp. 92-93.

[30] Knox, *The Claim of the Colonies to an Exemption from Internal Taxes*, printed anonymously, London, 1765.

[31] 5 George II, c. 7.

failed to work successfully. In 1767 George III, who heartily disliked Grenville, complained that the latter's conduct had been full of absurdities, since by restraining trade he first deprived the Americans of the means of acquiring wealth, and then proceeded to tax them.[32] Grenville's resignation from office, however, was due to his disagreement with the king on the matter of the regency bill rather than to the trouble brewing in America. Unfortunately, so far as the experiment of raising revenue in the colonies was concerned, the Marquis of Rockingham, successor to Grenville, was weak and inexperienced. The marquis and his party began their administration with an attempt to enforce the Stamp Act; but the exigency of the situation forced them to yield. Neither Rockingham nor any one of his colleagues had a fighting disposition; but in 1766 the combination of mercantile and landed interests was sufficiently influential to control the plans of any government. Although in the case of the Stamp Act repeal his attitude was determined by necessity, he was naturally of a pacific temperament, and in later years opposed every measure intended to coerce the colonies. Yet he failed to sympathize with the American claims to legislative independence. In fact the same government that repealed the Stamp Act passed the Declaratory Act, establishing the right of parliament to bind the colonies in all cases. George III and his friends objected to this distinction between theory and practice. The king was no opportunist on big questions; on the contrary, he held unswervingly to his convictions, even though in so doing he should wreck a nation. In theory the king and Rockingham agreed; in practice they differed widely.

Secretary Conway, who in May, 1766, had been transferred from the northern to the southern department where he had oversight of the colonies, was as peaceable

---

[32] *The Correspondence of King George III*, I, 452.

as Rockingham. His letters to American governors were far from aggressive. He opposed the theory of taxation and hoped to maintain peace by "lenient and persuasive methods."[33] Contemporaries admired his independent attitude later in the war, for he was financially dependent upon the government, having no private fortune and losing his wife's jointure at her death. In 1776 an article in the *London Magazine* contained the following paragraph about him: "Now if we contemplate his very precarious situation in respect of his military emoluments, dependent on the pleasure of the Crown, and the will of its ministers, we stand astonished at an instance of public spirit, of an avowal of public opinion in the days of George the Third, which would have done honour to John Hampden or Andrew Marvel."[34]

Unlike Conway, Burke never denied the power of parliament to tax the colonies. As secretary to the Marquis of Rockingham, he was in full accord with the latter, on the question both of the repeal of the Stamp Act and of the passage of the Declaratory Act. Burke was probably the stronger influence in the partnership, for his was the more decisive character. He believed that parliament should have unlimited power of superintendence as part of its imperial functions. If requisition were made and a colony refused its supply, parliament ought to lay a tax directly upon the province.[35] Burke, however, had such sympathy for the mercantile interests that he was willing ultimately to yield on all points of theory for the sake of maintaining friendly relations with America.

Lord Dartmouth, president of the Board of Trade under the Rockingham ministry, was quite as politic as Burke.

[33] *Parl. Hist.*, XVI, 114-115, 871.

[34] *London Magazine*, Dec., 1776, p. 636.

[35] *Speech on American Taxation, April 19, 1774*, 4th edition, 1783. Election speech at Bristol, *Lloyd's*, Oct. 17-19, 1774.

In January, 1766, he moved the Lords' reply to the king, vaguely pledging their endeavors "to support the King's dignity and the legislative authority of the kingdom over its colonies"; but when the full force of mercantile and landed opinion made itself felt, he advised the repeal of the Stamp Act. In later years although he left the Rockingham party and accepted office under Lord North as secretary of state for the colonies, he never approved of the policy of coercion. Believing absolutely in the right of parliamentary supremacy, he nevertheless was convinced that the government could find a practical solution of colonial difficulties without insisting upon a recognition of that right. It is small wonder that with men of this stamp in the government, a member of the Rockingham administration should have confessed to Henry Cruger that they were embarrassed by lack of royal support.[36]

The refusal of Pitt to join the ministry also troubled Rockingham. In fact, in trying to please everybody—the king, Pitt, the merchants, and the country gentlemen—Rockingham succeeded in pleasing no one, with the possible exception of the merchants. The repeal of the Stamp Act was intended to appease the mercantile classes, and was of course approved by Pitt. The Declaratory Act was supposed to soothe the king and his friends and to prepare the way for future colonial taxation which might relieve a burdened landed class; but it alienated Pitt. Under the circumstances, even with the aid of Grafton, Rockingham could not long maintain a majority.

In the fall of 1766, Pitt himself undertook to form a ministry, with Grafton again coöperating. The Whigs were so disunited that only a combination of factions could hope to survive; yet any coalition seemed to contain so many different opinions and jealousies as to give

[36] *Commerce of Rhode Island*, I, 141.

George III the opportunity that he was seeking, the chance to control government himself. A popular demand, not the personal wishes of the king, brought Pitt to the ministry. In the meantime, while the Whigs quarreled among themselves, George III and his friends were laying the plans which came to fruition only after four years of Whig failures. Had Pitt from first to last been able to keep his grasp of the situation, the Whigs, or at least enough to form a majority, might have kept together.

William Pitt was the popular idol, beloved no less by Englishmen than by Americans, until his acceptance of a peerage somewhat dimmed the luster of his fame. As the Great Commoner he lent the force of his oratorical ability to obtain the repeal of the Stamp Act—ability so great that according to contemporaries "all the arguments of his opponent seemed to be made up of plausibility and imposition, and faded away like artificial lights before the sun."[37] As the Earl of Chatham he accepted office on the fall of Rockingham, but for many reasons this position was a difficult one. In the first place it was impossible to live up to popular expectation. Few men rising to the heights occupied by Pitt during his successes in the Seven Years' War have for a second time won equal renown for public service. The differences in his own party were hard to reconcile; and ill health kept him much of the time a prisoner in his own home. Furthermore, his support in the Commons was endangered by his acceptance of a seat in the upper house. So indignant was the public when the news of the peerage was announced that many people who had treasured his speech relating to the American Stamp Act tossed it to the flames; a tavern keeper who had used the figure of the Great Commoner on his sign turned it

[37] *Jopson's*, Mar. 24, 1766.

upside down; and the bells in several places throughout the country rang muffled, as if in mourning.[38]

When health allowed, the Earl of Chatham contended with these difficulties, and was the exponent of popular rights in the House of Lords as he had previously been in the House of Commons. His views were broad and he was friendly to America and to British mercantile interests. Yet radical ideas were developing so rapidly in the colonies that one is inclined to question whether even the genius of this man, had it remained undiminished, could have found a solution of the imperial problem, satisfactory to both Americans and Britons. He certainly could not please the king, and his views failed to coincide with those of Rockingham and Burke. The latter credited parliament with a general power over the colonies including the right of taxation, though this right might be kept in abeyance. Pitt, on the contrary, said: "It is my opinion, that this kingdom has no right to lay a tax upon the colonies. At the same time, I assert the authority of this kingdom over the colonies to be sovereign and supreme, in every circumstance of government and legislation whatsoever. They are the subjects of this kingdom equally entitled with yourselves to all the natural rights of mankind and the peculiar privileges of Englishmen. . . . Taxation is no part of the governing or legislative power."[39] He did believe in the right of parliament to make laws binding on the colonies, "in all matters touching the general weal of the whole dominion of the imperial crown of Great Britain and beyond the competency of the local representative of a distinct colony."[40] In his eyes legislation for the regulation of trade and navigation was fundamentally important. For this purpose he admitted that external taxes could be levied, thus adopting a dis-

---

[38] *Jopson's*, Mar. 24, 1766.   [39] *Parl. Hist.*, XVI, 99.
[40] *Plan offered to the House of Lords*, printed 1775.

tinction between internal and external taxation, a view untenable and unthinkable in the mind of the king, of his followers, and even of many of the opposition. On these points the Whig party itself could not agree.

When Pitt was in retirement there was no one capable of holding together the loose ends of that party. The Duke of Grafton, his colleague, believed "that the Americans were as liable to be taxed as any man in Great Britain"; but he supported lenient measures, opposed coercion, and considered that in practice taxation was inexpedient.[41] However useful he may have been as the head of a small group of followers, and however necessary to the strength of a Whig ministry, he had little influence in any of the several ministries with which he was connected from 1765 to 1770.[42]

The Earl of Shelburne was Chatham's real representative in the latter's absence; but he failed to keep the various Whig elements united. As president of the Board of Trade in the years immediately following the peace of 1763 he worked enthusiastically over plans for the development of America, failing, however, to obtain the support of his colleagues. In this office, and later as secretary of state, Shelburne remained true to the theory that the value of colonies depended upon their trade with the mother country. Like Chatham he supported the Rockingham administration in securing the repeal of the Stamp Act while opposing the Declaratory Act. In speaking in favor of the repeal of the Stamp Act he emphasized the expediency of the measure and opposed the introduction of constitutional points into the argument.[43] In

---

[41] *London Magazine*, March, 1777, p. 131. *Parl. Hist.*, XVI, 165.

[42] Fitzroy in the preface to *Acts of Privy Council*, V, vii, explains that the duke had had little political experience, and was therefore irresolute at critical moments. The duke tried to include tea with other duties in the act of repeal, but was outvoted in the cabinet.

[43] *Parl. Hist.*, XVI, 155.

1766 he wrote to Governor Bernard of Massachusetts: "Though the Legislature will certainly on all just occasions exercise and enforce its legislative power over the colonies, yet it cannot be doubted but it will exert it with a due regard to the nature of their connection with the mother country."[44] Shelburne, like the rest of the Whigs, was too ready to conciliate the colonists to suit the exponents of the new imperialism.

The theory of "imperium" invaded even the minor offices of government. Maurice Morgann, a clerk in the office of the secretary of state and private secretary to Shelburne, wrote: "I consider the Mutiny Act, and the requisition of a compensation to sufferers as of no other consequence than as the dignity of Great Britain seems staked on their support. The laws of trade and navigation are essential, and must be supported at all risks and with every exertion of power. The other points are doubtful in their principles, and may perhaps be among those rights—to use a language which I do not understand— that are never fit to be exercised, and yet this subtle distinction is the sole ground upon which the repeal of the Stamp Act can be defended, consistently with the Act which affirms the right." Enforcing the act, he thought, might result in general resistance in America with consequent loss of Great Britain's dignity and power. "Some measures, therefore," he added, "it seems ought to be taken of so bold and decisive a nature, as to convince the Americans that the long patience of Great Britain has been so manifestly just and important as to leave no room for jealousies and fears in the minds of the sober and well disposed, and thereby give no pretence for common measures of resistance, and it would be still more desirable if those measures could be directed against a particular Province."[45] This clever argument combining mercan-

---

[44] Fitzmaurice, *Life of Shelburne*, I, 300.   [45] *Ibid.*, p. 318.

tilism and "imperium" did not seem to influence Shelburne, but it may have been more effective with other members of the government. One can only wonder what part the counsels of such subordinate officials played in forming the policy of later administrations.

In 1767 there was at least one member of the cabinet who was distinctly out of place, having no sympathy with the colonial theories of Chatham or Shelburne. This was Charles Townshend, a man of some brilliance but of narrow views. Although like many others he had voted for the Stamp Act and later its repeal, he regretted the latter action. He was ready to defend the principle of the original act, and in practice to insist upon the necessity of a colonial revenue. He refused to recognize any distinction between internal and external taxation.[46] At this time the country gentlemen were again in the ascendant, as the commercial interests had been satisfied; and they demanded a revenue from America. Without asking counsel of his associates, Townshend, as chancellor of the exchequer, rose to the occasion and presented in parliament a measure for taxing the colonies. His death left to others the necessity of dealing with the new American problems raised by the Townshend Acts.

As early as July, 1767, representatives of the Grenvillites, the Rockingham Whigs, and the Bedford Whigs met to attempt a reconciliation and coalition. Letters from Grenville stipulated that Lord Rockingham and his friends "should declare that they would assert and establish the superiority of this country over its colonies; that Mr. Grenville must have satisfaction as to men and measures, and that his friends should have a becoming share of employments."[47] Grenville's demand indicates two significant facts: one, that his following was decidedly

46 *Ibid.*, p. 307.
47 *Newcastle's Letters*, pp. 141 ff.

aggressive in its attitude toward the colonies; the second, that there were too many chronic officeholders for the welfare of Great Britain or her colonies. Hard feeling arose from the implication that Rockingham was willing to abandon the superiority of the mother country; but the break in the party was probably due largely to the fact that the Bedfordites were opposed to having Conway in a civil position, a point upon which Rockingham insisted. Zeal for office, a variety of opinions, lack of a strong leader, and above all absence of constructive measures continued to weaken the ranks of the Whigs. Following the unsuccessful meeting in July, Albemarle wrote to Rockingham: "George Grenville will certainly join Lord Bute, and the court have succeeded to their wish in disuniting a party, that sooner, or later, (connected) [sic] must have drove them all from court."[48] Royal influence was waxing, yet for three years the Whigs worried along in a fruitless attempt to conciliate king, colonies, and conflicting British interests. The question of the retention of the Townshend Acts was the business of chief colonial import before the ministry in those years.

After Townshend's death Lord North became chancellor of the exchequer, a man who from first to last seems to have been but the cat's-paw of the king. After 1770, in the position of prime minister, he uttered the views of the king, forced the royal policies through parliament, and for years repressed whatever private opinions he might have in deference to those of his Majesty, George III. From the point of view of the king, Lord North was indeed a valuable acquisition to the cabinet.

In 1768 Hillsborough, who for the preceding two years had been president of the Board of Trade, became also secretary of state for the colonies. This arrangement removed the colonial business from the pacific Earl of

48 *Newcastle's Letters*, pp. 156-157.

Shelburne into the hands of a man much more likely to carry out the theory of "imperium." "The colonies are our subjects," said Hillsborough; "as such they are bound by our laws, and I trust we shall never use the language of supplication to beg that our subjects will condescendingly yield obedience to our inherent preëminence."[49] He firmly believed in the supreme right of the British legislature, supposing "the right to tax to be included in the general supremacy, and the alteration of charters, and the force necessary to carry either or both into effectual execution to flow consequently from the supreme power of the state over the several component parts of the Britannic empire."[50] He seemed to be wholly lacking in tact or in a desire to conciliate the colonies. His correspondence with the governors must have shown this. At least there was a feeling of relief in America when he left office in 1772. Before that date, however, he had taken his share in strengthening the hand of the imperialists.

So dominant was the spirit of Hillsborough and Lord North in the cabinet that in September, 1768, William Knox, undersecretary of state, wrote to Grenville: "The administration are all, except Lord Shelburne, agreed upon coercive measures. The Chancellor is wholly and absolutely of that opinion."[51] On October 19 Shelburne resigned the seals, not to take office again until the peace ministry of 1782. Chatham himself soon resigned, but his infrequent attendance in town meant that his name alone gave a certain amount of sanction to the ministerial program. The decision of the government to send ships of war to Boston made it necessary for Chatham to withdraw even the nominal support which he had hitherto

[49] Parl. Hist., XVI, 1019.
[50] London Magazine, Nov., 1776, p. 580.
[51] Fitzmaurice, I, 386.

given. Camden, the lord chancellor, did not favor coercion, but he did not assert his opinion vigorously enough to have any influence at this juncture.

For a short time it seemed that the policy of imperialism would be adopted without opposition in Great Britain. At the close of the year 1768, the members of the cabinet were sterner in their attitude toward the colonies than they had been at any previous time. In addition, the country gentlemen were well pleased that another attempt was being made to obtain revenue from America. Although the colonists strenuously objected to the Townshend Acts, mercantile interests in Great Britain did not begin to be seriously affected until 1769. The country gentlemen were less willing to believe that their welfare depended upon commerce than they had been in 1766; and the merchants themselves were only partly convinced of the justice of colonial demands, though they did succeed in tempering the policy of the government in spite of the influence of the king. Nevertheless, the victory in 1770 was with the imperialists. Grafton, Camden, Conway, Granby, and even Lord North disapproved of the retention of the tea-duty.[52] Because it was impracticable as a revenue measure the country gentry were not especially concerned. The merchants and even the directors of the East India Company had asked for its removal. The radicals, of course, had nothing to do with it. The only group in the government that was really pleased with the tea-duty was the one which blindly accepted imperialistic doctrines; and this group by one vote in the cabinet succeeded in maintaining the duty on tea.[53]

Shortly after this royal victory Camden resigned the great seal. The ministerial group was then more unified, and opposition gained an ardent champion. As lord chief

[52] *Middlesex Journal,* July 26, 1770.
[53] *Acts of the Privy Council,* V, vii ff.

justice of the common pleas, Camden had perhaps been the one exception to the statement that all the eminent lawyers believed in the right of the British parliament to tax America.[54] Camden declared that in his opinion there were things which parliament could not do. One of these things was to tax America, for, he said, "Taxation and representation are inseparable; this position is founded on the law of nature."[55] Of him a contemporary wrote: "The natural rights of the Colonists, the privileges and immunities granted by charter, and their representative rights as native subjects of the British empire, are the substrata on which he erects all his arguments, and draws all his conclusions." The critic concluded that he was an able reasoner, but said: he "deals too much in first principles, denied or controverted on the other side; and seems more eager to convince the people of America, though at three thousand miles distance, that they are right, than to persuade his noble auditory that they are wrong."[56] The criticism is probably just, for only practical interests had weight in opposing the schemes of government. Nevertheless, views like those of Camden were not welcome in the ministry.

Even within the cabinet all plans for reconciling the colonies were in vain, for peace must have been based upon terms which George III could not approve. The years 1774 and 1775 saw the fruition of schemes which had long been maturing. In the latter year Grafton resigned, convinced that coercion, of which he heartily disapproved, was the unswerving policy of the government. Lord Dartmouth, who had come over to the King's Friends in 1772, when he entered the cabinet as secretary of state for the colonies, could not bring himself to execute measures which meant war with America. Instead

---

[54] *Ante*, p. 186; *Parl. Hist.*, XVIII, 164.
[55] *Parl. Hist.*, XVI, 178.   [56] *London Magazine*, Aug., 1776, p. 413.

of resigning outright, he accepted the privy seal, given up by Grafton. In the former office he was succeeded by Lord George Germain—a man well qualified to increase colonial discontent.

At this point, when George III was practically his own prime minister, opposition became ineffective. Government was well organized to carry out the designs of the court. The chief ministers from 1763 to 1775 have already been noted, together with their characteristic views. Those who were hostile to imperialism were gradually eliminated. George III did not deliberately remove first one and then another of his enemies from the cabinet. That would not have been feasible even in the eighteenth century. Conditions were favorable for the development of royal power. The country gentry played into the king's hands, for they believed that the colonial policies favored by the imperialists would be of benefit to themselves. At first they approved of the revenue acts and the coercive measures, and helped the King's Friends to defeat the pacific intentions of the merchants. Later, when they had become convinced that peace would serve them better than war, they were unable to prevent the continuation of Lord North's coercive policy. The explanation of his persistence lies partly in the general subservience of administrative officials to the crown, and partly in the popularity of the coercive policy among the members of the government. Though in this period of the American Revolution the official bodies dealing with the colonies, the Board of Trade and Plantations and the Privy Council, were much less influential in colonial affairs than they had been at an earlier time, their acceptance of imperialism gave prestige, at least, to the governmental policy in America. A few ministers, favorites of George III and subject to his domination, rose in importance. In the apathetic state of political life, they in their turn were able to control parliament, and popular opinion was impotent.

In the first sixty years of the eighteenth century, the Board of Trade had been of great importance in determining colonial questions. In 1707 that body had replied to a question of the lord high treasurer: "The greatest part of the business intrusted to our care does regard the administration of the Government, the Laws, Commerce, and the security of His Majesty's Plantations in America."[57] In all these matters the board succeeded in playing a very influential part through its representations and reports to the Privy Council, although it was merely an advisory council with no administrative authority in itself. Established in the interests of trade and plantations, it continued through its years of power to concern itself with both subjects and quite naturally held to the mercantilist theory of the value of colonies. Hence it is not strange that when other theories began to displace mercantilism, the influence of the Board of Trade declined.

Soon after the peace of 1763 the board made a representation to the king in council on the need of surveying the new territory in North America. They advised surveying the territory and settling it as soon as possible "in order that Your Subjects may avail themselves of the advantages which such settlements will produce to the trade, navigation, and manufactures of this kingdom."[58] Because from a military point of view a rapid settling of the west seemed unwise, other branches of the government objected to the plan of the Board of Trade. Although the board was most concerned with commerce, it took other matters into consideration also. In 1766 it complained that the governors in the colonies were too lax in regard to provincial legislation which dealt with ques-

[57] *Calendar of State Papers, Colonial Series,* 1706-1708, § 1192.
[58] *Acts of the Privy Council, Colonial,* 1745-1766, § 537.

tions of the greatest importance, such as commerce and manufactures, the royal prerogative, and the authority of the British legislature.[59] Commerce and manufactures stood first. Until 1770 other branches of the government also considered mercantile affairs of primary importance. But after a contest of four years between the needs of commerce and the rights of parliament, the exponents of "imperium" were victorious.

During those years of conflict the Board of Trade lost much of its power. Although after 1761 it could no longer nominate colonial officers, the creation in 1768 of a separate secretaryship for the colonies was the greatest blow to its importance.[60] The colonial governors were ordered to correspond only with the secretary of state,[61] and not to send duplicates to the board. As head of the board and secretary of state for the colonies, Hillsborough held a commanding position, concentrating in his own hands the larger part of the power once exercised by the board. This body then became merely a council to give advice on matters referred to it, with no initiative of its own in making reports and representations. From 1768 to 1779 Hillsborough and his successors held both offices in the government, first lord or president of the Board of Trade and secretary of state for the colonies. When in 1779 the government returned to the old system, and the board had its own president, quite independent of the colonial department, little business remained for this once honorable body.[62] The only regret caused by its demise in 1782 was

[59] *Acts of the Privy Council, Colonial*, 1766-1783, § 16.

[60] A. H. Basye, *The Lords Commissioners of Trade and Plantations*, pp. 107 and 174.

[61] The board was deprived of its privilege of correspondence by an order in council, August 8, 1766. *Ibid.*, p. 158.

[62] Basye, "Secretary of State for the Colonies," in *American Historical Review*, Oct., 1922, pp. 13 ff. C. M. Andrews, *Guide to the Materials for American History to 1783 in the Public Record Office of Great Britain*, I, 98 ff.

that a number of well-paid places ceased to exist. George III knew how to appreciate the value of these places, worth perhaps one vote in parliament, if the reformers did not; and he as well as the incumbents of such places may have mourned their loss.

Until extinguished in 1782 the board continued to act in matters of detail, collecting and arranging data for the information of officials and parliament; in matters of policy it no longer had any voice. Nevertheless, the members managed to show that on the vital question of parliamentary supremacy they agreed with the majority of Britons. A representation of 1765 speaks with abhorrence of the disrespect shown by Massachusetts Bay and of "the principles tending to a denial of the right of parliament to lay taxes upon your Majesty's subjects in the colonies."[63] The board usually advised the restriction of the powers of colonial legislatures even when they were not actually in conflict with British custom or precedent.[64] When reporting on additional instructions for General Gage, the board referred to the "Act for the better regulating the Government of the Province of Massachusetts Bay in New England," trusting "that this salutary measure will contribute to restore peace and tranquillity within that province and to induce for the future a due obedience to the authority of the supreme legislature."[65] With the members of the board so thoroughly inclined toward at least one phase of imperialistic doctrine, and with their wings effectively clipped on matters of policy, particularly while their business was largely in the hands of one man, the imperialists had nothing to fear from that quarter.

After 1763 the Privy Council as a whole was not con-

[63] *Parl. Hist.*, XVI, 122.
[64] *Acts of the Privy Council, Colonial*, 1766-1783, § 251.
[65] *Ibid.*, § 286.

cerned in the framing of colonial policy. In legal matters, that is, in the review of colonial legislation and in decisions on appeals, in approving appointments to office and other administrative details, and in supervising minor matters, it bore a significant relation to the colonies; but important questions of general colonial control were beginning to be referred to parliament, which after the close of the Seven Years' War assumed increasing authority in America. After considering a report of the Board of Trade on the proceedings in Virginia and Massachusetts in 1765, for example, the Privy Council ordered "That this is a matter of the utmost importance to the kingdom and legislature of Great Britain, and of too high a nature for the determination of Your Majesty in Your Privy Council, and is proper only for the consideration of Parliament, and to that end that it may be advisable for Your Majesty to give directions that the same be laid before Parliament at such time, and in such manner as Your Majesty shall be pleased to direct and appoint."[66] The council did not fail, however, to express an opinion upon the Virginia Resolutions, stating that they contained "an absolute disavowal of the right of the Parliament of Great Britain to impose taxes upon the colonies, and a daring attack upon the constitution of this country."[67] The crown received unhesitating support from the council in attempts to maintain the supremacy of the British parliament over the colonies, even in the question of taxation.

By 1775 the theory of imperialism was thoroughly incorporated in British politics. The Privy Council and the Board of Trade were advising coercion to bring the colonies to submission. Most of the officials who favored conciliation or temporizing had lost their positions, while others more amenable to royal wishes had taken their

---

[66] *Acts of the Privy Council, Colonial,* 1766-1783, § 621.
[67] *Ibid.*

places. Imperialistic policies suited the established church, and were sanctioned by the best legal authorities. Parliament became the tool by means of which the well-advised theory of imperialism could be given practical application. Success depended upon several factors. First, the leaders must embody their ideas in bills which they submitted; and secondly, a majority of the members of parliament must either approve the measures for personal reasons, or be driven to support them by popular enthusiasm in the country. Victory for the imperialists depended upon their ability to control these factors—parliament and public opinion.

CHAPTER VIII

POLICY OF THE GOVERNMENT.

II. INFLUENCE OF THE CROWN ON PUBLIC AND PARLIAMENTARY OPINION.

THE chief credit for organizing the forces of government in parliament is due to Lord North, and more especially to John Robinson, secretary to the Treasury Board, and to Charles Jenkinson, leader of the King's Friends after the retirement of Bute. They also were responsible for whatever measure of popular support the governmental policy received. In different ways and for different reasons each man made himself indispensable to George III.

Lord North's character interests and puzzles one, and when understood arouses sympathy. He was Tory by chance, rather than by conviction. Along with his politics he inherited social position, but he lacked the funds to maintain his rank in comfort. He was dignified, and he enjoyed a certain command of language with some ability to handle figures. Indeed, he was in many ways a most suitable person to represent George III before the House of Commons. But he was weak, indecisive, and distrustful of his own ability. Whether his financial dependence or some mysterious personal influence accounts for his subjection to the king, it is hard to say; but whatever the cause, Lord North remained in office for several unhappy years when he longed to be free.

John Robinson was a man of firmer, more determined character. As secretary to the Treasury Board, and so secretary to Lord North, he supplied the confidence and courage which his superior lacked. Son of a tradesman of Appleby, Westmorland, Robinson had no social standing, but he married wealth. He had inherited enough burgage tenures to carry the election in the borough of Appleby; and this influence in elections was sufficient to give him a certain amount of importance in the eyes of the crown. He had been in parliament since 1764. During the first ten years he sat for the county of Westmorland under the patronage of Sir James Lowther. Disagreements between Lord North and Robinson's patron on the outbreak of the American Revolution made it necessary for him to give up his seat; and after 1774 he represented the government borough of Harwich.[1] From 1770 he served as secretary to the Treasury Board, performing an almost incredible amount of work in that position.

His correspondence was voluminous, for he was in constant communication with the king, Lord North, and major and minor officials of the government, in regard to all sorts of administrative details. Official and unofficial matters passed through his hands, as men confided to him what they hesitated to say directly to the person most concerned. He negotiated with the king for the payment of Lord North's debts, kept the seats in the House of Commons filled with government supporters, managed elections, arranged for presentation of places, and gave advice in regard to loyal addresses and government pamphlets, besides attending to the regular duties of secretary to the board.

Lord North frankly acknowledged his dependence upon his secretary, saying that Robinson certainly earned his "reward" (£5,000); and that if Robinson went out of office, he should go, too, "for he would not do the business

---

[1] *Dict. Nat. Biog.*, vol. XVII; introduction by W. T. Laprade to "Parliamentary Papers of John Robinson, 1774-1784," *Camden Society Publications*, Third Series, XXXIII.

with anyone else."[2] Charles Jenkinson, the third figure in the group, also testified to Robinson's worth. "The idea of your quitting the king's service can never take place," he said. "No one, I am sure, will suffer it. The government could not go on without you."[3] Other members of the government recognized Robinson's importance. Jenkinson wrote to the king: "The Attorney General and Mr. Eden think, that Mr. Robinson has more influence than themselves over Lord North, and that it is necessary therefore to pay court to Him."[4]

Jenkinson himself was an invaluable member of the government. He started political life as secretary to Lord Bute, and for many years led the King's Friends in the House of Commons. During the debate on the Stamp Act, Jenkinson opposed repeal and suggested that the words "explain and amend" should be substituted in the bill for the word "repeal."[5] His experience in office included posts in the Treasury and the Admiralty; and in 1778 he became secretary at war under Lord North.[6] His relations with the king were so peculiarly intimate that he even outlined the king's replies to Lord North;[7] and the king suggested that Robinson correspond with him through Jenkinson.[8] If Robinson was responsible for North's behavior, Jenkinson seems to have directed the relations of both men with the king.[9] The clever arguments of Lord North and the persistent activities of the other two men were necessary to maintain a majority in

---

[2] Hist. MSS. Com. Rep., X, App. VI, p. 31.   [3] Ibid., p. 35.

[4] The Correspondence of King George the Third, IV, 286.

[5] Ibid., I, 275.   [6] Dict. Nat. Biog., vol. X.

[7] The Correspondence of King George the Third, IV, 342.

[8] Hist. MSS. Com. Rep., X, App. VI, p. 24.

[9] Jenkinson, with the advice of Henry McCulloh, is said to have suggested to Bute a stamp tax for America, and to have brought the scheme before Grenville. Grenville Papers, II, 373-374.

parliament and to secure adequate support throughout the country.

Popular support of governmental measures was not as important in the eighteenth century as it would be today in England or in any other democratic country, for the government did not really represent the people. Yet George III realized the growing power of popular opinion, and hoped to lead, instead of follow, the public. To educate the people to believe in the justice of the war with America, crown officials encouraged Samuel Johnson, Adam Ferguson, John Lind, John Shebbeare, and James Macpherson to write in the government's defense.[10] Their articles and those of other government supporters appeared in pamphlet form and also in the newspapers and magazines friendly to governmental measures. This use of the press was necessary, for on the whole, until the year 1775, the British publications were decidedly favorable toward the colonies. Even after the beginning of the war, British newspapers did not hesitate to make trouble for the government by their adverse criticisms. The royal *Gazette* could hardly counteract the effect of the *Middlesex Journal* and other opposition papers. To the very end of the war, however, members of the administration used the press in their attempt to retain control of the government. As late as September 22, 1782, several months after the fall of Lord North, Jenkinson wrote to Robinson on some mysterious business saying that he approved the idea of having a pamphlet written, and wondered if Macpherson would undertake it.[11]

Loyal addresses were another means of deceiving individuals as to the real state of public opinion, though the ministers were not always successful in persuading the towns to present such evidences of their good-will. In

10 See names in *Dict. Nat. Biog.* and chapter I, *ante*, p. 4.
11 *Hist. MSS. Com. Rep.*, X, App. VI, p. 55.

1769 an attempt to obtain a loyal address from the merchants and traders of London failed. What part the government played in the scheme to secure this address is uncertain, but the circumstances are suspicious. One speaker at the mass meeting held for the purpose of preparing an address to the king, said: "It is so hasty and ill-concerted a measure that I am convinced it must be ministerial; and that instead of answering its pretended purpose of a demonstration of respect and attachment to the Th—ne it will furnish a most humiliating proof how little that declared intention is regarded by the public." An address, prepared in advance of the meeting, was presented to the merchants for signing, without opportunity for debate. As a result of such arbitrary methods, a riot ensued, during which the copy of the address disappeared. When order was restored, a committee was named to prepare a new address, and the meeting adjourned to a later date. At the next meeting the merchants carried a resolution which declared that an address was unnecessary, expressed disapproval of the measures taken to secure an address, but nevertheless professed loyalty to the crown.[12] The year 1769, in which the London merchants thus disappointed the government, was decidedly critical for the imperialists, but they were growing more powerful in spite of the merchants.

In 1774 and 1775, when coercion had become a settled policy, George III showed that he was still anxious regarding public opinion. Popular approval of the war would certainly be necessary to raise an army and money to support that army. On February 8, 1775, the king wrote: "The joint Address of the two Houses of Parliament having been carried by such great majorities, to give it the appearance it deserves with the public nothing now remains but its being presented tomorrow with a

---

[12] *London Magazine*, Mar., 1769, pp. 136-138, 147-148, 154-156.

large attendance.''[13] This time the hint alone was sufficient to secure the fulfillment of the king's wish. The
Gazette was able to impress the public with an account of
the support which parliament was giving to governmental
measures. George III and his ministers used all their
knowledge of psychology to keep the people satisfied with
their colonial policy. Nevertheless, in 1775, the government found it difficult to raise troops, and Lord North
complained: ''The cause of Great Britain is not yet
sufficiently popular.''[14]

In 1775 Robinson made a special effort to obtain loyal
addresses from the universities. Oxford, Tory in politics,
readily complied with the first suggestion; but the Whigs
at Cambridge were more reluctant.[15] The Earl of Sandwich, first lord of the Admiralty, wrote to Robinson that
he hoped for the support of Chamberlain and other members who were going down to Cambridge for the purpose
of voting on the question of the address. A canvass showed
that the chancellor's party would oppose the measure;
but that the vice-chancellor would favor it.[16] Friends
of the government finally carried the motion for an address; and the government could then inform the public
that not only a Tory, but also a Whig university approved
the colonial measures. Robinson was often obliged to
answer such perplexing questions as the following from
the Earl of Suffolk: ''The people at Kendal are much
divided in opinion upon American affairs. Dowker wishes
to know whether he is to try to obtain an address from
thence at all hazards.''[17] Failure would only call attention
to a weakness in the government which the king was

13 *Correspondence of George III with Lord North*, I, 227.
14 *The Correspondence of King George the Third*, III, 249.
15 *Correspondence of George III with Lord North*, I, 269.
16 *Hist. MSS. Com. Rep.*, X, App. VI, pp. 11-12.
17 *Ibid.*, p. 12.

anxious to conceal. For that reason the responsibility of deciding whether or not to press the issue in a community where opposition was strong weighed heavily upon the secretary's shoulders. Having decided to test the strength of the government, he usually examined and approved drafts of the addresses before they were submitted to the populace for signing.[18]

Day after day through the autumn months of 1775, thanks to the efforts of John Robinson, the *Gazette* reported loyal addresses from towns throughout the kingdom.[19] Addresses and petitions from those who refused to be intimidated by the American restrictions upon trade helped to counteract the effect of numerous mercantile petitions asking for measures of conciliation. In some cases those who favored the loyal addresses and those who opposed the policy of the government vied with each other to see which would succeed in presenting their petition first.[20] Opponents seldom succeeded in preventing the loyal addresses, but they did keep down the number of signatures. Sir George Yonge, who opposed the address at Devon, said that "His sentiments were known to agree with those of many gentlemen of rank and fortune in the county, and of the freeholders at large, who were absent from the meeting, as well as many of those that were present; and although the meeting was so managed that the address was carried, yet very few could be prevailed upon to sign it."[21] The "management" to which Sir George Yonge referred was probably that of Robinson and his agents, although many of the loyal addresses were unsolicited.

18 *Hist. MSS. Com. Rep.*, X, App. VI, p. 12.

19 Though reported also in *Lloyd's*, they were usually first mentioned in the *Gazette*. Many of the originals are in the Public Record Office, Home Office 55, and in the Guildhall, for which see *Addresses, Remonstrances and Petitions to the Throne*, London, 1865, privately printed.

20 *Lloyd's*, Nov. 10-13, 1775.   21 *Ibid.*, Oct. 30—Nov. 1, 1775.

George III and his ministers tried to keep in close touch with the feeling in the country; and they could not long remain unaware of the growing hostility to measures of the government in 1779. They tried in various ways to stop the rising tide of unpopularity. Having heard of the meeting of freeholders to be held at York on December 30, the king wrote to Lord North: "I cannot conclude without strongly pressing that every measure may be taken to get the friends of Government in Yorkshire to attend the meeting on the 30th at York. Not that I suppose they will be able to stop the violence of the meeting, but it will show that the county is not unanimous in this business; and it may decide whether any contrary Resolution should be taken."[22] While opposition to the government was increasing in York, Bristol seemed to grow more loyal. The conversion of Bristol to governmental policy was a particularly fine feather in the cap of George III, because that trading city had long remained friendly to America. It may or may not have been a coincidence that the mayor of Bristol was knighted very soon after that city had raised a subscription for the support of the government.[23]

Crown officials were eager to secure expressions of popular approval from the country, not only because the people were directly concerned with raising an army and with paying taxes, but also because public opinion was bound to have some influence upon parliament. While the country was at peace and business prospered, the people at large paid little attention to government; but when trade failed, taxes increased, and news of defeat reached England, the British people became politically conscious. At such times they believed that parliament not only failed to represent the people of Great Britain, but that the members ignored the best interests of the country. The public

22 *Correspondence of George III with Lord North*, II, 296.
23 *Lloyd's*, Jan. 21-23, 1778.

then made use of all possible means of influencing parliament.

Today the vote is the most powerful instrument by which individuals can influence the members of parliament; but before 1832 a very small proportion of the British people possessed this effective weapon. Of those who enjoyed the franchise, few were able to use it independently. One man or a small group of men controlled elections in many of the boroughs. In 1783 Dean Tucker estimated that there were two hundred boroughs, cities, or counties where elections were not free.[24] A computation for the year 1793 points to the conclusion that of the five hundred and fifty-eight members of the House of Commons three hundred and seven were returned by patrons; and there is proof that one hundred and fifty-seven were in the control of eighty-four individuals. In view of these facts, Porritt in his *Unreformed House of Commons* states that "It is reasonable to conclude that from 1760 to 1832 nearly one-half of the members of the House of Commons owed their seats to patrons."[25] Porritt also claims that these electoral conditions were at their worst during the first thirty years of the reign of George III. A recent investigator makes a strong case against the independence of even the county members, asserting that according to contemporaries one-half of the county members were relatives of peers, and another fourth owed their seats to two or three members of the House of Lords.[26] All these facts indicate that there were too few independent members to have much influence in parliament.

Nevertheless, in the period of the American Revolution, electors followed the custom of instructing their repre-

[24] Tucker, *Four Letters . . . to the Earl of Shelburne*, Gloucester, 1783, p. 29.

[25] Porritt, I, 310-311.   [26] Laprade, as above, XXXIII, x.

sentatives on matters of special interest during the session. Instructions included both general principles and specific suggestions to guide the representative in his legislative business. When speaking in the House of Commons members sometimes referred to instructions from their constituents, as if these instructions gave weight to their arguments.[27] Candidates for election occasionally signed a "test," promising to follow a certain line of conduct if elected. In some districts candidates voluntarily signed the tests in order to indicate their policies; in others all candidates who had any hope of success were practically compelled to sign. London, Westminster, and the county of Middlesex were most progressive in this matter. In 1775 Catharine Macaulay wrote of a test required of the representatives of London, and advocated that other places follow that example.[28] In 1774 the papers published an "engagement" which John Wilkes and John Glynn were to keep if elected to parliament. During the same election every issue of *Lloyd's* contained numerous announcements by candidates with suggestions regarding the policies which each would follow.[29] At the meetings of the county associations members of parliament frequently presented their views regarding the petitions under discussion. If they did not approve of them they were bold enough to say so, and explained their reasons.[30]

Only the enfranchised could use instructions and tests to influence members of parliament; but anyone could sign a petition. It does not follow that the plea of the unenfranchised cotton spinner was as persuasive as the voice of the country squire. Nevertheless, the petitions of cotton spinners, stocking weavers, silk throwsters, or

[27] *Parl. Hist.*, XVIII, 1007 and 1019.

[28] C. Macaulay, *An Address to the People of England, Scotland, and Ireland on the present important Crisis of Affairs*, Bath, 1775, p. 17.

[29] *Lloyd's*, Oct. 7-10, 1774.   [30] *Ibid.*, Jan. 24-26, 1780.

blanket makers gained a respectful hearing before the
House of Commons. The merchants and manufacturers,
who in 1766 flocked to London to demand from parliament
the repeal of the Stamp Act, did not necessarily have a
vote for any member, although the supposition is that
most of them did. Their private conversations with Lords
and Commoners, in which they described conditions in
the country, had untold influence. Henry Cruger of Bristol wrote of spending three weeks in London, talking
with members of parliament "as it were for my own life";
and he commented on the general ignorance of trade and
the colonies which he discovered.[31] Considering the opportunities for popular control of parliament, attempts
of the ministers to gain support out-of-doors were evidence of good judgment. But the direct means which the
crown employed to obtain a majority in parliament were
more effective.

One method of securing support in parliament was to
convince the members that the measures proposed would
benefit them personally. The country cherished two primary interests in the colonies, trade and revenue; and
for a time parliament seemed to reflect the country.
Trade, however, was only an adopted interest of parliament. The government of England was essentially aristo-
cratic, and land was the basis of aristocracy. The peers
were naturally the great landowners; and between 1761
and 1783 about seventy-one per cent of the total membership of the House of Commons represented landed interests. Over fifty per cent were without doubt owners of
large estates, while the other twenty-one per cent were
evidently younger sons of the aristocracy, holding office
in the army or navy. This twenty-one per cent were certainly members of families belonging to the country
gentry. Eight per cent of the members were in the legal

[31] *Commerce of Rhode Island*, I, 139 ff.

profession, and most of these lawyers belonged to families whose property was in land. Business claimed only nine per cent; and of the business men not quite half were merchants. The others included bankers, East India servants, a mercer, a draper, a fishmonger, a joiner, a sugar refiner, and so forth. Since English law required that members of parliament, with a few exceptions, should have an income from land, these business men had estates in land as well as personal property, and their allegiance was in many cases divided between land and trade.[32] Although new elections changed but slightly most of these percentages, the number of business men increased somewhat. There was a percentage of six and one-half in the parliament elected in 1761, and about nine per cent in the parliament elected in 1780. Since the possessions of about ten per cent of the members are uncertain or completely unknown, only the most general conclusions as to the personal interests of members of parliament can be drawn from a study of the personnel.[33] Nevertheless, the interest in land was so preponderant that it is evident the ministers of the crown could carry through their policies, if they had the confidence of the country gentlemen.

Normally, the government could be certain that the country gentlemen would support a colonial policy which would benefit trade, for the landowners had been brought up to believe that their welfare was involved in whatever affected commerce. Furthermore, there were, according to estimate, about one hundred deputies of cities and great towns, who might be said to represent trade, although they were landholders themselves.[34] Consequently both the

[32] Porritt, I, 169. 9 Anne, c. 5. The title to land qualifying a member to hold a seat was often not bona fide.

[33] Statistics have been compiled from a detailed study of the personnel of the House of Commons, 1761-1783. The interests of about six and one-half per cent are unknown, and of about three and one-half per cent, doubtful, but they were probably landed.   [34] Burgh, *Political Disquisitions*, p. 55.

administration and the opposition used mercantilist arguments to serve their own purposes. Both houses of parliament repeatedly demanded accounts of exports and imports for examination as well as statistics regarding ships built in Amercia for British use, of bullion, and of debts owed to British merchants, and so forth. When the repeal of the Stamp Act was under discussion, one of the most telling questions asked was: "What must become of your own manufacturers here at home, while this contest is carrying on in America?"[35] In 1767 when other taxes on America were levied, an objector said: "If we by taxes increase their expence of living, how shall they save money to purchase from us . . . manufactures and . . . utensils?"[36] Through the succeeding years, such unanswerable questions continued to embarrass the ministers.

Members of the opposition were ready to adopt any line of reasoning that would weaken the position of those in power; but there was always consistent objection to a ministerial policy that disturbed trade. Such men as Alderman Trecothick and Alderman Wooldridge represented the interests not only of a political party, but also of a commercial group of which they were themselves members. When Trecothick referred to the Townshend Acts, his words had more weight than those of a professional politician. He said that all the merchants explained to Townshend the effect the acts would have in America and offered to pay the tax in England, but that the government in spite of their offers resolved to tax the colonies themselves.[37] Edmund Burke's diatribes against a ministry which cut off commerce with America were inspired, no doubt, by the fact that he represented Bristol, the second most important center for American trade in

[35] *Parl. Hist.*, XVI, 110.
[36] *London Magazine*, Nov., 1767, p. 559.
[37] *Parl. Hist.*, XVI, 507.

THE GOVERNMENT 223

the kingdom. When members of the opposition wished to make a particularly effective appeal, they called merchants and traders to the bar of the House of Commons or of the House of Lords to give their actual experiences. During the war, although the government subordinated mercantile interests to those of imperialism, merchants and traders were not forgotten. Members of the opposition annoyed the government with resolutions regarding the large balance due from the colonies to British merchants, the decrease in merchant ships resulting from American captures, the increases in insurance rates, and the high price of American products.[38]

Quite aware of the importance of mercantile strength, having been obliged to yield to it in 1766, the King's Friends followed the lead of the opposition and as far as possible played up to the trading interests. In the early history of the controversy even the royal speeches, when given in public, emphasized the importance of commerce.[39] As the government grew stronger the crown gave less consideration to the wishes of the merchants. In 1770 when the mercantile classes were holding their breath in eager expectation of the relief that the new session of parliament would bring them, George III addressed parliament in a long speech dealing with the distemper among horned cattle. Although he called the attention of the two houses to the situation in America, he made no reference to the scores of petitions which anxious mer-

[38] *Lords Journals*, XXXV, 303.

[39] In 1766 the speech from the throne included the following: ''The many regulations which you have made, for the extending and promoting the trade and manufactures of Great Britain, and for settling the mutual intercourse of my kingdom and plantations, in such a manner as to provide for the improvement of the colonies on a plan of due subordination to the commercial interests of the mother country, are the strongest proofs of your equitable and comprehensive regard to the welfare of all my dominions, an object truly worthy of a British parliament.'' *Parl. Hist.*, XVI, 234.

chants had laid before their sovereign. Contemporary
newspapers resorted to satire. In their reports of the
speech, they confused the horned cattle of which George
III had spoken with the petitioners, and said that the
distemper had first broken out among the London livery.[40]
Petitions and remonstrances distinctly annoyed George
III; but as the right of petition was assured to Englishmen, the king chose to ignore what he could not prevent.

Although the government refused to grant the petitions
of the merchants who opposed duties on tea imported into
America, parliament occasionally passed acts which were
based upon the old mercantilist theories prevailing before 1763. In 1769 and again in 1772 it passed measures
for encouraging the growth and culture of vines and raw
silk in America.[41] Government even explained the partial
repeal of the Townshend Acts as a truly mercantilist
measure. Dr. Shebbeare, a government writer, said in his
Answer to Burke: "When the Americans refused to receive into the colonies the manufactures of glass, paper,
and the other articles, it was discerned by the minister, that
the diminution of sale in these commodities would lessen
the employment of those who worked in producing them.
In order therefore to obviate that evil, the taxes on these
were repealed, that the exportation might no longer be
suspended." Tea was excepted as no British subject was
employed in its culture or preparation.[42]

In 1766, and to a less extent in 1770, the government
yielded to the entreaties of the merchants. After 1774
it assumed the attitude of defending commerce in spite
of the merchants. Because the king had substituted imperialism for mercantilism and wished to forget the merchants who clung to the old theories, it does not follow

that he had no interest in trade. On the contrary, George III believed that the subjection of America was necessary for commerce. In 1779 he was ready to make the following admission: "Whether the laying a Tax was deserving all the Evils that have arisen from it, I should suppose no man could alledge that without being thought more fit for Bedlam than a Seat in the Senate." But he was absolutely opposed to granting independence to America, for he feared that if America gained her independence, the West Indies and Ireland would follow. "Great Britain soon would be a poor Island indeed, for reduced in Her Trade Merchants would retire with their Wealth to Climates more to their Advantage, and Shoals of Manufacturers would leave this Country for the New Empire."[43]

Government supporters insinuated that the members of the opposition were merely pretending to have an interest in trade. In the words of Lord Lyttelton, who was defending the government, "it was no longer a question, whether we should relinquish the right of taxation but whether that commerce, which had carried us triumphantly through the last war, should be subject to the wise and necessary regulations prescribed by the Acts of Navigation, and confirmed by many subsequent acts of Parliament, or at once laid open at the will of the factious Americans who were now struggling for a free and unlimited trade, independent of their mother country, and for powers inconsistent with, and derogatory to the honour and dignity of the imperial crown of England."[44] Hans Stanley, cofferer of his Majesty's household, expressed the same idea when he admitted that the disputes with America would of course stop trade and affect the stock-holders and landed interests, but claimed

[43] *The Correspondence of King George the Third*, IV, 351.
[44] *Parl. Hist.*, XVIII, 36.

at the same time that "unless the supremacy of parliament and the rights of sovereignty were vigorously asserted by Great Britain, the American traffic could not subsist."[45]

When the "Bill for regulating the Government of Massachusetts Bay" was under consideration, William Meredith said that he had never approved of taxing America, "but now that the Americans had not only resisted the act of parliament, but laid violent hands on the merchants' property, it was high time to regulate the course of justice, so that our merchants might trade thither with security."[46] In 1775 when government officials were intent on maintaining the authority of Great Britain over America, they justified their colonial policies to skeptical members of parliament, by saying that those policies would ultimately settle commercial difficulties with America more satisfactorily than yielding to the demands of British merchants and American colonists. From the point of view of the government, those who still petitioned parliament for a redress of colonial grievances were either short-sighted in regard to their own interests, or converts, unconsciously perhaps, to the new economic theory of free trade.

In assuming a mercantilist pose, government officials must have been embarrassed by the opposition of the merchants. Lord North claimed that the arrangements regarding the importation of tea into America, provided in the act of 1773, had been made in the interests of the merchants—that is, for the benefit of the East India Company. On the other hand, Governor Johnstone, one of the directors of the company, insisted that the company had favored repealing the duty, and that only ministerial intrigue had induced the chairman and deputy chairman

---

45 *Parl. Hist.*, XVIII, 186.   46 *Ibid.*, XVII, 1302.

of the company to agree to the government's proposals.[47]
When opposing Lord Chatham's "Provisional Act for
settling Troubles in America," Earl Gower resorted to
mercantilist arguments. He said "that the Act of Navigation would be of no avail, would be no more than a dead
letter, if the laws for establishing the admiralty courts
were repealed."[48] During debates on the bill to restrain
the trade of New England, members of the opposition
accused the ministers of bribing the nation by promises
of spoils from the fisheries from which the New Englanders were to be excluded.[49] In the meantime the public
learned that sloops, frigates, and schooners were being
sent to America to enforce the navigation acts by preventing the colonists from indulging in foreign trade.[50]

In 1775 Acland, a government supporter, suggested
that the Americans were becoming so independent that
their merchants would rival the British in the West Indies
and Europe. Acland advanced the suggestion as an argument for the use of force to subdue the colonies.[51] In the
House of Lords Mansfield uttered the same warning. "If
we do not, my lords," he said, "get the better of America,
America will get the better of us." He then described
the recent increase in American trade and wealth, and
the development of an American navy; and drew a gloomy
picture of the effect of these developments upon British
commerce.[52] By such potent appeals and clever reasoning
many merchants and their friends in parliament were
induced to support the policy of coercion.

More direct and obvious arguments were used to convince the country gentlemen that the American coercive
measures would help the British landholder. Country
gentry, who possessed the real influence in parliament,

[47] Ibid., XVIII, 177-178.   [48] Ibid., XVIII, 208.
[49] Lords Journals, XXXIV, 365-367.   [50] Lloyd's, Feb. 1-3, 1775.
[51] Parl. Hist., XVIII, 732.   [52] Ibid., XVIII, 732.

were violently opposed to an increase in the land tax; and
they were constantly seeking for some means of decreas-
ing expenses, or failing that, some way of shifting the
burden of taxation to other shoulders. They groaned over
the reports of the expenses incurred by the government
in America; and were dismayed at the growth of the national debt. Crown officials, therefore, needed only to
voice the heartfelt resentment of the country gentry themselves in order to gain their support. The country gentlemen in parliament were glad to vote funds for an army
to subdue America, if the colonies would then contribute
to the British exchequer and relieve the British people
of part of their burden.

Pamphlets subsidized by the government made special
appeals to the country gentry on the questions nearest
their hearts, or perhaps one might better say, their pockets. James Macpherson insisted that America should contribute toward her own support; and that if she refused,
the mother country was justified in using compulsion.[53]
Dr. Shebbeare was more bitter in his satirical explanation of the situation. "*They* [the Americans] are to be
exempted from the controul of the legislature, and *you*
obliged to obey it. *They* are to be free from imposts, and
you to be unremittingly *oppressed* for *them*. In fact, they
are to be your *masters*, and you their *slaves*."[54] The country gentry quickly swallowed the bait that was offered.
Promises of revenue from America induced them to support the governmental policy of coercion.

There came a time, however, when both the landed and
the mercantile classes became convinced that neither was
being served by the measures which the government was

---

[53] Macpherson, *The Rights of Great Britain Asserted against the Claims
of America*, Aberdeen, 1776 (seventh edition), published anonymously.

[54] Shebbeare, *An Answer to the printed Speech of Edmund Burke*, London,
1775, printed anonymously.

advocating. They discovered that those measures were based upon the doctrine of power for its own sake, irrespective of the effects upon land and trade; and that Lord North and his colleagues were disregarding the very wishes they were pretending to satisfy. In the later period of royal supremacy, officials paid no attention to petitions, which had been so influential in earlier years. A member of the opposition remarked in the House of Commons that the bill for closing the port of Boston was not to punish the Bostonians but the English merchants, "men who would, in a body, unite in petitioning the House, were they not confident that their petition would be disregarded."[55] In figurative language, Temple Luttrell described commerce as a "dejected suppliant," standing before parliament "in just apprehension from the impending storm . . . Well . . . might she be alarmed, to see a pilot at the helm, as the winds and the billows arise, who rather than part with the game, throws the merchandize overboard . . ."[56] To summarize the attitude of the ministers, one has only to repeat the excuse which in a tactless moment they gave for refusing to consider, at the same time and in the same committee, the merchants' petitions and the American papers. One, they said, concerned an "object of commerce"; the other a "matter of policy."[57] A new era had dawned in British history when ministers tried to separate commercial and colonial policies.

When the country gentlemen, who had been rather easily convinced of the wisdom of coercion, saw the prospects of a revenue from America receding ever farther and farther into the background, they became as dissatisfied with the governmental policy as were the merchants. In the opinion of the government, the main question was no longer one of commerce or revenue, but of the "su-

[55] *London Magazine*, Apr., 1774, p. 172.
[56] *Ibid.*, Sept., 1775, p. 449.   [57] *Ibid.*, June, 1775, p. 290.

preme authority of Great Britain.''[58] Although Lord
North insisted that the idea of taxing America was only
temporarily abandoned, he explained that taxation was a
matter of but secondary consideration when the supremacy of parliament was at stake.[59] These statements
take on new meaning when compared with the private
utterances of George III. Lord North's hearers found
them significant, but failed to understand their full implication until years of unsuccessful warfare in America
and growing burdens in Great Britain had made them
more critical.

Crown officials used methods in holding a parliamentary majority that were more effective than mere argument. Through control of elections, judicious distribution
of places and pensions—in short, by a lavish expenditure
of money—the government gained many votes in parliament. Lack of independent thinking and voting made
parliament notorious in those years. Popular critics complained that the parliament of 1760 always voted with the
treasury bench; that the policy of the House of Commons
changed with the ministry.[60] The same body that passed
the Stamp Act, at the instigation of Grenville, repealed
it at Rockingham's behest, and then, in obedience to
Townshend, voted to levy new taxes upon America.

The parliament of 1768 appeared more consistent, because Lord North was chancellor of the exchequer
throughout its entire history. From the king's point of
view, however, there was need of improvement in that
body. Because of the critical situation in America and
the need of unanimity in government, a new election was
held in 1774. A great effort was made to obtain a strong
majority in favor of the recent colonial measures. The
government enjoyed an advantage over the opposition

---

[58] *Lloyd's*, Jan. 23-25, 1775.   [59] *Parl. Hist.*, XVIII, 940.
[60] *Gentleman's Magazine*, Mar., 1768, p. 115.

because the ministers knew in advance when a dissolution would occur. An unexpected dissolution found the opposition unprepared, while the royal forces were already mobilized for the election campaign. In 1774 George III wrote to Lord North regarding a proposed election: "I trust it will fill the House with more gentlemen of landed property, as the Nabobs, Planters, and other Volunteers are not ready for battle. As soon as you can fix on a proper day for the dissolution, I desire you will write to the Chancellor and Lord President, but not above a week before the measure is to be [put?] into execution."[61]

Ideas of public morality were much more lax than they are today. In the eighteenth century it was a matter of course that seats in the House of Commons should go to the highest bidder. This fact made it fairly easy for the crown to exert an influence in elections. The following may serve as an illustration of a fairly common transaction. On October 5, 1774, Lord North wrote to Cooper, Robinson's colleague in the treasury: "His Lordship [Lord Falmouth] must be told in as polite terms as possible that I hope he will permit me to recommend to three of his six seats in Cornwall. The terms he expects are £2,500 a seat to which I am ready to agree."[62] At the same time Lord North wrote to Robinson, asking him to let Cooper know whether he had promised Masterman £2,500 or £3,000 for each of Lord Edgecumbe's seats.[63]

Elections in Scotland for the sixteen members of the House of Lords also offered an opportunity for ministerial influence. In October, 1774, one of the secretaries of state, according to newspaper reports, sent to each Scottish peer a letter, enclosing an approved list of new members to be voted for in the coming election. The names

61 *Correspondence of George III with Lord North*, I, 201.
62 *Hist. MSS. Com. Rep.*, X, App. VI, p. 6; Laprade, as above, pp. 23-24.
63 *Hist. MSS. Com. Rep.*, X, App. VI, p. 7; Laprade, as above, p. 24.

of the Marquis of Lothian, Earls of Dunmore, Stair, and
Errol were omitted. A letter from the Earl of Stair to
William Bollan, a former agent for Massachusetts, explains in part why the earl's name was not included. "My
conduct in Parliament," he wrote, "in these unhappy
American matters, deserves not the acknowledgements the
late Council of the Province of Massachusetts Bay are
pleased to honour it with; all I can pretend to is a sincere
affection to both countries (whose interests, if rightly understood, are and must ever be the same) with little ability,
and still less power to be of service to either. Great and repeated provocations have drawn down corrections too
precipitate I think, perhaps too harsh, but we must look
forward and hope that through the mediation of men of
temper and disinterested principles conciliatory measures will be fallen on." To quote the editor of *Lloyd's,*
"Sentiments so moderate as the above seemed not to
come up to the ministerial standard; he is therefore left
out of the Court nominations of the 16 Peers to represent
in Parliament the Peerage of Scotland."[64] The chief sin
of the Earl of Stair consisted in presenting a petition on
behalf of Massachusetts. Needless to say, he was not re-
elected. From that time on, during the war, he devoted
himself to writing a series of pamphlets in which he exposed the state of the national finances.[65]

The election of 1774 did not make many changes in
parliament;[66] but the new House of Commons, chosen as
a result of government influence, was rather more sub-
missive to ministerial plans than the former one had been.
The methods which had worked so well in 1774 were used
in the occasional by-elections of following years. In 1775
the Earl of Sandwich wrote to John Robinson in regard
to a candidate for the seat at Huntingdon. The price of the

[64] *Lloyd's,* Oct. 28-31, 1774.   [65] *Dict. Nat. Biog.,* vol. V.
[66] *The Correspondence of King George the Third,* III, 136-137.

seat was to be £2,000 for five years on bond, plus the expenses of election; and the conditions which the candidate
must fill, "the thinking and acting as I do in all American
points, and supporting the present administration in
their whole system."[67] Beginning with November, 1777,
£1,000 a month was taken from the king's privy purse and
put aside for election purposes; for now that the king's
favorites were in office, he was anxious to keep them there,
and to secure for their measures a strong majority in
parliament.[68]

Yet a parliament brought together at so much labor
and cost dared to criticise the government, and in 1780
was making embarrassing demands for economy. Therefore the king wrote to Robinson: "It would be madness
not to call a new Parliament as soon as we have hobbled
through the present session."[69] Consequently an unexpected dissolution took place in September, followed by
a new election, which resulted, temporarily, in a strong
government majority. The success of the election was due
in part to manipulation by the government, but perhaps
even more to the conservative reaction following the Lord
George Gordon riots of that year.[70] Early in the spring
the king had urged his agents to investigate the possibilities of government support in various boroughs. Every
available vote was turned to account. George III even
ordered the houses which he rented at Windsor placed
in the parish rate under the different names of his servants, thus creating six votes which would be given to the
government candidate in a doubtful quarter. Nor was the
king beneath urging his tradesmen to appear for his

---

[67] *Hist. MSS. Com. Rep.*, X, App. VI, p. 11; Laprade, as above, p. 26.

[68] Laprade, as above, pp. 55 ff. Page 57, list of amounts paid for individual
places. *The Correspondence of King George the Third*, V, 461.

[69] *Hist. MSS. Com. Rep.*, X, App. VI, p. 29.

[70] *Correspondence of George III with Lord North*, II, 339.

candidate.[71] However much George III might stress the "dignity of the crown" in the contests with America, there seems to have been nothing to which that dignity refused to stoop when there was a question of gaining the king's own way. Moreover, the purse strings were wide open on such occasions. The general election of 1780 cost the government £50,000, and the results hardly seemed to justify the expenditures.[72]

The government's attempts to control London elections proved fruitless. In 1781 the king wrote to Robinson: "We have so frequently failed in attempts in the City that I am not sanguine in my expectations of success on this occasion, but must think it advisable to encourage Mr. Clarke on this opening should the three opponent candidates stand."[73] Lord North was even less optimistic than his master, and after another failure stated that he was done with London elections; that three or four times he had been led into "idle and foolish expenses there."[74] The simplest way of securing a vote in parliament was to buy a seat from a borough patron; but government funds if judicially used might win an election by other means. For example, when a member from Taunton died, there was a suggestion that premiums be given to the silk and woolen manufacturers to prevent their opposing the government candidate.[75] Ordinarily, however, the government refrained from deliberate bribery, and government candidates received only enough to pay such legitimate expenses as those for "canvasses, polls, and trials before the committees."[76] All such methods were, however, uncertain in their results.

[71] *Hist. MSS. Com. Rep.*, X, App. VI, p. 30.
[72] *The Correspondence of King George the Third*, V, 478.
[73] *Hist. MSS. Com. Rep.*, X, App. VI, p. 43.
[74] *Ibid.*, p. 45.   [75] Laprade, as above, pp. 38-39.
[76] *The Correspondence of King George the Third*, V, 465.

On the whole, a rather more satisfactory means of controlling parliament was to deal out places, pensions, and
contracts to those who would be "grateful." In the
fourteenth century unsuccessful attempts had been made
to exclude officeholders from parliament. Partial results
were obtained in the renewed agitations of the late seventeenth and early eighteenth centuries; and acts passed in
1705 and 1742 debarred the incumbents of certain offices.[77]
Nevertheless, in the period of the American Revolution,
from twenty-five to twenty-eight per cent of the members
of every newly elected parliament held some place of
remuneration or honor under the government. Of the one
hundred and sixty-seven members of the House of Commons who voted in the minority on the repeal of the Stamp
Act in 1766, sixty-one held places, civil or military.[78] There
is no way of knowing how many of the rest hoped to do
so. In 1770, according to a contemporary writer, one
hundred and ninety-two members of the House of Commons held places. Early in that year the majority for the
government was two hundred and sixty-one, the minority
one hundred and eighty-eight. A critic calculated that the
minority made a distinct majority of unplaced members.
"We should be glad," the critic said, "if any person
could inform us, how it comes to pass, that all placemen
are of the same way of thinking, if such places do not
bias their minds."[79] Contemporary opinion against the
system was growing stronger, for in the same year it was
reported that "Several patriotic gentlemen have very
lately engaged in establishing a club on an independent
plan, every member of which declares on admission, his

[77] Porritt, chap. X.

[78] *American Tracts*, II, 3 ff., "A List of the Minority in the House of
Commons who voted against the Bill to repeal the American Stamp Act,"
Paris, 1766. This division must have been on the original resolution, Feb. 21.
The division of March 4 was 250 to 122. *Commons Journals*, XXX, 627.

[79] *Middlesex Journal*, Feb. 19, 1770. *Annual Register*, 1770, p. 72.

resolution neither to accept place, pension, nor any emolument under government, whilst he has a seat in parliament.''[80]

Although Jenkinson said of Lord North that ''One of
his great errors is that he thinks that interest alone without any seasoning is the only motive on which men act,''
the prime minister's lieutenants were expert in giving
the required dash of ''seasoning''; and Lord North soon
learned what was expected of him.[81] The parliament of
1774 had seventy peers holding offices, and one hundred
and seventy commoners with places or contracts from
the government.[82] When the Earl of Carlisle returned
from America, where he had been sent on the second peace
commission, he was made president of the Board of Trade
with a salary of £2,000, double that of previous incumbents, because Lord North feared him.[83] From the point of
view of the government the granting of peerages to commoners was a less satisfactory method of rewarding
loyalty, for the ministry could not afford to lose reliable
men from the House of Commons. By granting offices the
government made sure of certain men whose support
would otherwise have been doubtful. Placeholders were
never entirely independent. On the opening of a session
Lord North was accustomed to call together the placemen
and ask for their support.[84] During the session the ministers kept division lists and made particular note of the
way the placemen cast their votes.[85] The placeholders
usually served the ministers well, and carried important
measures long after many of the independent country

[80] *Middlesex Journal*, Apr. 13, 1770.
[81] *Hist. MSS. Com. Rep.*, X, App. VI, p. 32.
[82] Laprade, as above, pp. 12-17.
[83] Basye in *American Historical Review*, XXII, 336.
[84] *The Correspondence of King George the Third*, IV, 215.
[85] *Ibid.*, III, 71.

gentlemen had ceased to support Lord North and his colleagues.

If those in government employ ventured to break away from their leading strings, they might expect dismissal. To punish a man by dismissing him from office was a more dangerous proceeding than to reward him by a grant of place, and was more apt to incur the wrath of the public. In 1775 the Earl of Suffolk wrote to Robinson in regard to the election in Westmorland County: "There is much dissatisfaction expressed at Sir James Lowther's candidate, but no appearance of opposition. I wish that Lord North would dismiss him from his Lieutenancies, which would be a *coup de grace* to his importance in the two counties."[86] In 1780 these tactics were employed in the case of two noblemen who had been eager for an examination into public expenditure. Immediately after the vote on the question was known, the Marquis of Carmarthen and the Earl of Pembroke received their dismissal from the lieutenancies of the East Riding of York and of Wiltshire, respectively. Dissentient opinion declared: "We cannot entertain a doubt but that the two noble lords . . . suffered this mark of his Majesty's displeasure for their conduct in Parliament."[87] The loss of the lieutenancy of the East Riding was due in part to the connection of the Marquis of Carmarthen, son of the Duke of Leeds, with the landholders' association in Yorkshire.[88] The noblemen who approved the Yorkshire petition received an official warning in the form of a summons to the home of Lord North, 10 Downing Street, where they learned that the York meeting was "improper." They were advised to express their disapproval of the association and to dissuade their friends from attending later

86 *Hist. MSS. Com. Rep.*, X, App. VI, p. 13.
87 *Lords Journals*, XXXVI, 55.
88 Horace Walpole, *Last Journals*, II, 266 and 270.

meetings. The Duke of Northumberland and others agreed, but the Marquis of Carmarthen refused to withdraw his approval of the petition. He of course resigned the "Gold Key," sign of his office of lord chamberlain to the queen. Shortly afterwards, and without warning, a letter from the Earl of Hillsborough notified him of his dismissal from the offices of lord lieutenant and custos rotulorum of the East Riding of Yorkshire. He declared he could not have been more surprised at "commitment to the Tower."[89]

George III himself advised and sanctioned this method of coercing support. In April, 1775, he wrote to Lord North, with characteristically poor grammar: "I consent to Sir Watkin Williams being Lieutenant of Merioneth, if he means to be grateful, otherwise favours granted to persons in opposition is not very political."[90] On March 5, 1779, he advocated the removal of officials who joined the opposition. "I am strongly of opinion," he wrote, "that the general officers who through Parliamentary favour have got governments, on opposing should lose them. This is very different from removing them from their military commissions. In short, Lord North will find me resolved to take every strong measure to keep out a most dangerous faction."[91] In this manner, during the American Revolution, George III and his ministers used the "spoils system" to secure support for governmental policies.

When offices were not given outright to members of

⸱ 89 Add. MSS., 27918, ff. 1 & 2, pp. 14-21. The author of the manuscript used the title, Duke of Leeds, in this connection, but this must have been an error. In 1782 one of the demands of the new administration was the restoration of the late lieutenants of Wilts and the East Riding. *The Correspondence of King George the Third*, V, 422.

90 *Correspondence of George III with Lord North*, I, 245.

91 *Ibid.*

parliament, their good-will could be gained by favors to relatives or friends. Too often a man became governor of a colony simply because he had friends at court, whose services would be of value to the government. Critics complained that the court was interested in America merely because of offices in the colonies which could be used as bribes. In 1769 the rumor spread that the crown was going to create several separate governments in America in order to extend court influence.[92]

Faithful servants of the government demanded and received pensions. In 1782 the Earl of Sandwich wrote to Robinson and Lord North of his disordered finances and need of a pension.[93] Knox, who for many years had served in subordinate positions, also wanted a pension.[94] That was the thing expected; but the government funds were low and the demands heavy. In the previous year Lord North wrote in anxiety to Robinson of the exorbitant demands of Lord S[heffield] and Mr. D[aubeny], who had incurred expenses without his knowledge, but must be paid. He asked Robinson to do it as cheaply as possible, warning him that he would "find it difficult to raise even the lowest sum."[95] According to Lord North only a very small amount was expended on pensions to members of parliament;[96] but the system was bitterly attacked by the public. Pension lists were kept secret and the public may have thought the number greater than it really was. Allowances were sometimes made to a trustee or to a wife, son, or daughter of a member, but the resulting loss of independence was the same.[97]

Contracts for supplying the army with clothing or

[92] *Middlesex Journal*, Aug. 26, 1769.
[93] *Hist. MSS. Com. Rep.*, X, App. VI, p. 52.
[94] *Ibid.*, p. 48. [95] *Ibid.*, p. 41.
[96] *The Correspondence of King George the Third*, V, 469.
[97] *Ibid.*

provisions, if granted to members of parliament, would secure votes for the government. Contracts for rum, or even for sauerkraut, were popularly supposed to make fortunes for the lucky contractors; and the government certainly made bad bargains, unless the ministers expected to be paid by votes. In 1779 the opposition introduced a bill to prevent members of the House of Commons from making any contracts with the government, unless the government had previously advertised and then granted the contract to the lowest bidder.[98] However, the awarding of contracts as government favors continued until after the passage of the Civil List Act in 1782.[99] Another method which the ministers used to secure influence was to give to their friends and supporters advantages in purchasing government bonds. When a certain loan was floated, favorites obtained premiums of from seven to ten per cent.[100]

Even as early as 1775 public opinion was turning against such methods of wholesale bribery. A song of the day illustrates the popular attitude.

> " 'Tis money makes the member vote,
>   And sanctify our ways:
> It makes the patriot turn his coat,
>   And money we must raise.
>
> And a taxing we will go, will go . . ." etc.

Other stanzas complain of taxes at home until nothing is untaxed; of taxes abroad; and of the use of force to compel the payment of these duties. One stanza refers to colonial taxation.

[98] *The Correspondence of King George the Third*, IV, 275.
[99] Laprade, as above, pp. 38-39.
[100] *Correspondence of George III with Lord North*, II, 366.

"Each colony, we will propose,
    Shall raise an ample sum,
Which well applied, under the rose
    May bribe them as at home.

And a taxing we will go, will go . . ." etc.[101]

The people were taxed for funds to bribe members of
parliament to lay heavier taxes on the people, until a
vicious circle was complete. Government methods were so
successful that after 1774 and until the war proved a
failure, imperial policies met little opposition.

Upon one phase of imperialism—the doctrine of parliamentary supremacy—king, officials, and members of
parliament (with a few exceptions) were insistent. In 1774
Governor Johnstone, M.P., the exception which proves
the rule, declared: "It is now clear that the people of
America, actuated with the same firm and resolute spirit
and tinctured with the same enthusiasm which enabled
our ancestors to withstand the unjust claims of the Crown
in the days of Charles the First, are determined to resist the high doctrines of parliamentary supremacy held
forth by this country, which must in its consequences reduce their liberties to a level with the colonies of France
and Spain."[102] Typical radicals made extravagant statements regarding American rights and privileges, but that
story is told in another chapter. For the most part, opposition preferred to take its stand on the ground of expediency. Burke said in his famous speech on conciliation:
"I am not determining a point of law. I am restoring
tranquillity, and the general character and situation of
a people must determine what sort of government is fitted
for them. That point nothing else can or ought to determine." He preferred to ignore the question whether the

[101] *London Magazine*, Aug., 1775, p. 431.   [102] *Lloyd's*, Dec. 16-19, 1774.

mother country was yielding as "a matter of right" or
granting as "a matter of favor."[103] Even Camden severely criticised the inexpediency and lack of sound policy
in the coercive measures, although he also believed that
parliamentary taxation of the colonies was unconstitutional.[104]

The question of constitutionality was a puzzling one.
The Rockingham ministry, by combining the repeal of the
Stamp Act with the passage of the Declaratory Act, appeared to establish a precedent for expediency in dealing
with the colonies, while unequivocally stating the constitutional rights of the mother country. Extreme imperialists insisted on exercising their constitutional rights
regardless of the expediency of particular measures.
Through the years of the American Revolution, imperialists continued to appeal to the practical interests of
the mercantile and landed classes. The chief difference
between the government and the opposition on American
questions was that one stressed theory and the other expediency, each one using the weapon which best suited its
purposes. Lord Mansfield, legal authority for the imperialists, always wished to rule out the question of expediency
and stick to the discussion of right.[105] In 1775 the ministry
really seemed to be going to war for a theory, since Lord
North declared he did not intend to tax America.[106] The
government advised coercion to uphold a theory; the opposition, conciliation for the sake of expediency.

When in 1774 British officials decided that they must
enforce the American acts or surrender all authority over
the colonies, they expressed an opinion long held by
George III. Indeed George III was far more consistent

[103] *Works*, Dublin, 1783, II, 58.
[104] John, Lord Campbell, *Lives of the Lord Chancellors and Keepers of the
Great Seal of England*, Philadelphia, 1848, 2d Series, V, 229.
[105] *Parl. Hist.*, XVI, 171-173.   [106] *Ibid.*, XVIII, 264-265.

than his advisers. He always felt that the repeal of the Stamp Act was a mistake, for he, like Lord Mansfield, believed that the Americans were even then planning their independence.[107] In 1774 the king declared that the colonists had "boldly thrown off the mask" and would be satisfied with "nothing less than a total independence of the British legislature."[108] He spoke of New England as being in rebellion and insisted that blows would be necessary to prove the dependence of the colonies.[109] Believing as he did that independence had long been the object of the rebellious Americans, he was absolutely opposed to temporizing and conciliation. So sure were the King's Friends of this attitude, that they were thrown into consternation by the conciliatory proposition made by the government in February, 1775. But the king agreed to this proposal merely for the sake of causing a rift in the colonies; and he was steadfast in his determination to force obedience from the Americans. He disapproved of suspending the American acts because such a course would suggest that the British government feared the colonies. In November, 1774, even General Gage, who was certainly not inclined to be lenient and who nine months previously had assured his Majesty that the colonies would be meek if Great Britain were resolute, favored suspending the acts to which the colonies objected.[110] George III, however, declared: "We must either master them or totally leave them to themselves and treat them as aliens."[111] He objected to sending commissioners to America to examine into the cause of the rebellion, as the

107 *The Correspondence of King George the Third*, I, 281.
108 *Ibid.*, III, 47.
109 *Correspondence of George III with Lord North*, I, 215.
110 *The Correspondence of King George the Third*, III, 59 and 154.
111 *Correspondence of George III with Lord North*, I, 216.

mother country would thus appear to be more afraid of continuing the disputes than were the colonies.[112]

Royal insistence upon coercion is illustrated by a letter from the king to Lord North in October, 1775. "Every means of distressing America must meet with my concurrence, as it tends to bringing them to feel the necessity of returning to their duty."[113] The private correspondence of the king indicates clearly that George III believed the use of force in America was necessary to preserve the authority of the British government. His public utterances were decidedly less frank and slightly more conciliatory in tone, yet in 1775 the Duke of Grafton resigned on being shown the king's intended speech. George III resembled the Stuarts in believing that the king was always right. In a spirit of complaisancy he wrote to John Robinson in 1776, referring to unpleasant news from France: "The scene may appear gloomy, but I trust with rectitude and resolution a different aspect will be obtained. It has been a very comfortable gift of Divine Providence to me, that when difficulties arise my spirits also increase, for where the cause is just I can never be dismayed."[114] Self-assurance carried the king, and with him many who lacked this quality themselves, rapidly along the road to war and the loss of the thirteen colonies.

Thanks in part to the methods used by government to fill the House of Commons with the King's Friends, and in part to personal convictions among the country gentlemen, the adherents of the royal policy constantly grew in numbers until 1775. For the next three years the government held its own. Then the cabinet gradually lost influence, and was finally forced out of office. In 1774 and 1775 a situation existed which offered to the imperialists

[112] *Correspondence of George III with Lord North,* I, 219.
[113] *Ibid.,* p. 231.   [114] *Hist. MSS. Com. Rep.,* X, App. VI, p. 15.

the very opportunity they needed. Englishmen were indignant at the rebellious attitude of the Americans, and their indignation was reflected in parliament. Even Barré, who usually favored the colonies, supported the bill for closing the port of Boston.[115] Lord North correctly described the feeling in parliament when he wrote to the king: "The disposition of the house independent of any ministerial connection is to maintain the authority of Great Britain over America."[116] To quote Lloyd's: "The House seemed nearly unanimous that the conduct of the Bostonians had been illegal, and deserved punishment, and that this mode was as mild as could with safety be adopted."[117] This unanimity made possible the first fatal step along the path of coercion. The effect of coercion upon the Americans was to crystallize their desire for independence, which in turn tended to strengthen government forces in parliament. Considering the general disapproval of the way in which the colonies were behaving, the clever arguments which government used to convince the merchants and the country gentlemen of the wisdom of coercion, and finally the corrupt means by which the ministers could control votes in parliament, it is no wonder that the opposition was quite helpless. Only twenty-four members voted against the bill for impartial administration of justice, only sixteen against that to prohibit all trade and intercourse with the American colonies, and other measures met correspondingly slight opposition.[118]

As the policy of coercion became fixed, men lost interest in the affairs of government. For years only a few determined members of the opposition rose in the house to

[115] Parl. Hist., XVII, 1169.
[116] The Correspondence of King George the Third, III, 178.
[117] March 23-25, 1774.
[118] Parl. Hist., XVII, 1316; XVIII, 1066.

criticise the ministers. Although in 1770 four hundred
members frequently attended sessions of the House of
Commons, during the war, even when important measures were being discussed, only about one hundred and
fifty were in attendance. In 1782 when hope and interest
revived, the numbers suddenly leaped to nearly four
hundred and fifty.[119] In the House of Lords the use of
proxies had always encouraged inattendance, so the
variation in numbers there is not as noticeable as in the
lower house. Yet when Lord Rockingham and the faithful
Duke of Richmond lost their zeal, it was evident that the
opposition had become hopeless. The ministry was pleased
with this lethargy, and called as little attention to American affairs as possible. While the government could count
on the support of the country gentlemen, the ministers
felt their position was secure.

By 1778, however, the activity of Fox, the new leader
of opposition in the House of Commons, and a growing
suspicion that the government was not making good, began
to threaten the forces of government in parliament. The
failure of Burgoyne's campaign, the entrance of France
into the war, and the increasing burden of taxes, were
undermining the loyalty of all independent men, so far
as their support of the war with America was concerned.
Had Pitt been willing to sacrifice territory in America
by withdrawing the army, he might have organized an
opposition strong enough to force the resignation of Lord
North; but this he refused to do. Pitt died in 1778, and
disputes among the remaining leaders of the opposition
made them too weak to be effective. Commenting on the
differences of opinion among the opposition members in
1780, Shelburne said: "There is no dealing with Mr.
Burke, he is so violently attached to his own opinion that
there is no arguing with him, and has got so much ascend-

[119] Figures are from *Journals* and *Parl. Hist.*

ancy over Lord Rockingham that I protest I see no method of doing anything."[120] The painstaking measures by which George III and his lieutenants had organized the government's forces were also proving their usefulness. All that opposition could do was to expose from time to time the state of the army, the navy, the funds, the weakness of the military plans, and in general the waste of public money. Nevertheless, in 1778, the forces of the government were beginning to disintegrate; and one of the surest signs was the fact that the idea of American independence was becoming more popular in Great Britain, both in parliament and outside.

Men in parliament were now adopting an idea that formerly only such extraordinary theorists as Dean Tucker had held. Members of the opposition, however, could not agree with each other as to the necessity or the advisability of surrendering the colonies. The Duke of Richmond was willing to grant American independence; but Shelburne was strenuously opposed.[121] Men of every faction in the opposition were beginning to fear that the king was striving to establish royal prerogative instead of parliamentary supremacy; and this suspicion made them more ready to end the struggle in America. Those who were willing to continue the war as long as the power of parliament was the stake, withdrew their support when they realized that parliament was merely a mouthpiece and a tool for a few men under the direct control of George III. In the House of Commons James Luttrell said: "To be separated forever from America endangers our liberties and the happiness of every individual in this kingdom much less than giving to the crown the rights and free privileges of subjects who must become more numerous than ourselves."[122] These words

[120] Add. MSS., 27918, f. 2.
[121] *Parl. Hist.*, XIX, 962; 1031-1052.   [122] *Ibid.*, p. 42.

might well bring dismay to the hearts of George III and Lord North, for they struck at the very root of their position. Dunning's famous resolution on the increasing influence of the crown expressed even more boldly the danger threatening parliament.

Although George III was not responsible for the beginning of the American revolt, he prolonged the war by refusing to accept ministers who wanted peace. Even when he began to see the futility of attempts to conquer America, he hesitated to treat with her on terms of independency, while admitting that at some future date it might be well to abandon parts of the continent.[123] He appeared blindly confident of success, although members of parliament were deserting him and even his ministers despaired. In December, 1779, he wrote: "I do believe that America is nearer coming into temper to treat than perhaps at any other period."[124]

Members of parliament were far from sharing the king's optimism. In 1779 even placemen were beginning to attack the ministry. In the spring a motion for the removal of the unpopular Earl of Sandwich was offered in parliament. Speaking in favor of this motion Lord Lyttelton said of himself that "he enjoyed a place under government which ministers were welcome to if they thought it a crime in a man to declare his mind, when the dearest and most vital interests of his country were at stake. Nothing should prevent him from speaking his mind; and, even upon the most sordid motives, he appealed to every lord present, when the fall of stocks, decreased value of landed property, and accumulated new burdens, were taken into account, whether it was worth the while of any lord, or any man of property, to partake of the favours of government, when it was con-

123 *Correspondence of George III with Lord North*, II, 119.
124 *Ibid.*, p. 296.

sidered that what he received as a placeman was no more than what he lost as a landowner or a man of property."[125] His arguments told on the majorities of the government, as one after another placemen as well as independent members joined the opposition.

Lord North, never very stout-hearted, grew depressed many years before his resignation took effect. In the winter of 1777, although the government turned a fair face to the public, Lord North privately confessed to his discouragement. "I am melancholy," he wrote, "notwithstanding our victory. My idea of American affairs is that if our success is as great as the most sanguine politician wishes or believes the best use we can make of it is to get out of the dispute as soon as possible."[126] Conflicting opinions within his cabinet added to North's troubles, for he was unable to make his own decisions and force obedience from others. He showed a tendency to vacillate, causing his ministers to lose confidence in him and in his promises.[127] Public and private credit were so unsound that Lord North distrusted the ability of the government to borrow for even two years.[128] Under those circumstances he begged the king to send for Chatham, but George III declared that he would rather lose his crown than ask assistance of Chatham.[129] As for the opposition, the king said that they were a set of men who would make him a slave for the remainder of his days.[130] There were among the king's ministers men more resolute than Lord North. Wishing to cling to office as long as possible they acted as props to their chief, and with George III shared the responsibility for prolonging the war in America.

[125] *Parl. Hist.*, XX, 455.   [126] Add. MSS., 34414, f. 309.
[127] *The Correspondence of King George the Third*, IV, 160.
[128] *Ibid.*, p. 76.
[129] *Ibid.*, p. 58. In March, 1782, the king actually drew up a draft for resigning his crown. *Ibid.*, V, 425.
[130] *Ibid.*, IV, 61.

William Eden and other subordinates admitted the existence of a "serious emergency," but urged Lord North to continue in office.[131] After a conversation with Lord North, the Earl of Sandwich wrote to John Robinson: "Things are now at the most critical moment; and I think that you should not be an instant from Lord North's side till something decisive is done." And again next day he wrote: "I am convinced that all will go well if you can work him up to decide and act. You have therefore more in your hands at this moment than perhaps anyone in this country ever had before. You are the only person who can give good advice to the person upon whom the fate of the kingdom depends."[132] Robinson must have been equal to the occasion, for the government continued to hold together in spite of growing opposition and the resignations of Earl Gower and Lord Weymouth.[133]

The encouraging results of the election in the fall of 1780 gave a temporary respite to Lord North and his troubles; but worse times followed. During 1780 and 1781 there was talk of negotiating with sections of the opposition, but this talk amounted to nothing. Frankness was missing from the government councils; men distrusted each other. Even Jenkinson threatened to rebel if he had to raise six new regiments; and he wrote Robinson that he believed Lord North wished him to go out of office.[134] The public was well aware of dissension, and as the cabinet continued to carry measures through parliament, marvelled at the phenomenon.[135] George III's fortifications were holding well, but the discontent which began among the placemen in the House of Lords spread to

[131] Add. MSS., 34414, f. 395.
[132] *Hist. MSS. Com. Rep.*, X, App. VI, p. 26.
[133] Basye in *American Historical Review*, XXII, 336.
[134] *Hist. MSS. Com. Rep.*, X, App. VI, p. 41.
[135] *Lloyd's*, Dec. 14-17, 1781.

those in the House of Commons. Rawlinson, convinced that the prosecution of the American war would ruin the mother country, wrote to the Earl of Sandwich that he could no longer vote with the ministry. Unwilling to vote against them, he would either remain absent or vacate his seat.[136] Others with a different sense of honor kept their seats, but began to vote with the opposition. The cabinet reflected the changing face of parliament.

In February of 1782 Lord George Germain (Lord Sackville) resigned. Governor Pownall predicted the resignation at least two months before it occurred, saying: "L . . . G. G. goes out because he abides by his principles and will not give up the Sovereignty."[137] *Lloyd's* reported: "The cabinet wears as many different looks in a week, as the moon does aspects in a month. The retreat of Lord Sackville seemed to imply that the order for carrying on the American war was beginning to cool in the cabinet; and it was generally deemed that his Lordship's retreat was a kind of signal for peace; but we find that the Chancellor, who hitherto has been as strong an advocate for war as Lord Sackville, and who still thinks this country will be ruined by the independence of America retains all his former credit with his Sovereign, as may very clearly be seen by the nomination of his Lordship's brother, the Bishop of Lincoln, to the vacant Deanery of St. Paul's"[138] Yet it was not of Lord North's own free will that he remained at the head of the government.

With the possible exception of John Robinson, George III alone still insisted on continuing the war. He steadfastly refused to listen to Lord North's offers of resignation. As late as February, 1782, he said: "I certainly till drove to the wall will do what I can to save the empire,

---

[136] *Hist. MSS. Com. Rep.*, X, App. VI, p. 46.
[137] Add. MSS., 20733, Almon Correspondence, Nov. 29, 1781.
[138] *Lloyd's*, Feb. 25-27, 1782.

and if I do not succeed, I will at least have the self approbation of having done my duty, and of not letting myself
be a tool in the destruction of the honour of the country.''[139] Lord North was apathetic, those high in office remained away from the House of Commons, and there was
great uneasiness throughout the country. Sir Horace
Mann joined the opposition, saying that although he had
voted for the war, thinking it just and practicable, he
now saw that the object was unattainable and that therefore it was madness to continue.[140] The king was the mad-
man who still urged the prosecution of the war; but at
last even he was obliged to bow to the inevitable. In
March Henry Dundas wrote to Robinson: ''I will fight
your battle while a rag of you remains, but it is a wild
idea to suppose that with a majority of only ten votes
the government of this country in time of war can be
carried on.''[141]

On the twenty-seventh of that month the king announced
to Lord North that he had found it necessary to submit
to a general change of ministers. The bill to enable his
majesty to conclude peace, introduced in March, was
subjected to numerous delays, but finally passed the
House of Commons on May 28. The House of Lords
agreed on June 17, and the king gave his assent on June
19.[142] With what feelings of humiliation and chagrin
George III accepted this shattering of all his hopes and
plans can only be imagined. Perhaps he was comforted
with ''the self approbation of having done [his] . . .
duty.'' The governmental policy of imperialism had failed,
but George III had done his best to make it successful.

[139] *Correspondence of George III with Lord North*, II, 411.

[140] *Parl. Hist.*, XXII, 1075.

[141] *Hist. MSS. Com. Rep.*, X, App. VI, p. 51.

[142] *Commons Journals*, XXXVIII, 814-1064; *Lords Journals*, XXXVI, 529 and 537.

Only those aspects of imperialism which promised material advantages were popular with the British people and with members of parliament. There were few who had the philosophic perception even to conceive, to say nothing of approving, the doctrine of power for its own sake. Selfish interests determined the history of the years 1763 to 1783, and those interests were financial. Out of a combination of various financial interests parliamentary majorities were made. In 1765 the country gentlemen and the government combined a desire for revenue with the theory of the right of taxation. In 1766 merchants and country gentlemen joined forces because the former were touched by the loss of their trade, and the latter, by the rise of poor rates. In 1767, because the desire for revenue again worked well with the theory of parliamentary supremacy expressed in the Declaratory Act of 1766, country gentlemen supported the imperialists. From 1770 until 1779, that ignis fatuus, relief from taxation through American contributions, made majorities for government. In 1780 the country gentlemen looked facts in the face. Lord North feared there would be great opposition to new taxes, "especially [he wrote] if the people compare too nicely the advantages to result from the dependance of America and the evils to be apprehended from these additional burdens."[143] The landed classes cared nothing for theory purchased at the price of financial loss; and from 1779 they grew more and more opposed to continuing the war.

The merchants had failed to influence the government to frame colonial policies upon mercantilist theories only. The court party was unable to secure support for a policy based upon imperialism, because that policy secured no practical advantages for merchants or country gentle-

143 *The Correspondence of King George the Third*, V, 27.

men. Expediency finally overrode theory. The demand for economy closed the war with America, and gave independence to the United States. But the demand for immediate measures of economy brought peace only because many Englishmen had discarded their old ideas regarding the ultimate and permanent value of colonial possessions.

CHAPTER IX

PUBLIC OPINION REGARDING IMPERIAL RELATIONSHIPS AND THE VALUE OF COLONIES.

In the eighteenth century Englishmen were beginning to change their opinions about the value of colonies and the proper relation between a colony and the mother country. Much of the literature of the period is concerned with discussions of these points. Disputes arose between those who clung to the old ideas and those who adopted new ones. There were differences of opinion on these matters even within the group whose interests in the colonies were the same. The speculative philosophers, with nothing to gain or lose, were even more divided. The question of the proper relation between Great Britain and her colonies involved, primarily, the extent to which the parliament of the mother country could legislate for the dependencies.

Opinions in regard to the power of parliament to legislate in colonial affairs ranged from the belief in the absolute omnipotence of that body down to the idea that the colonies were completely independent of its authority. Some men believed that parliament had gained whatever elements of prerogative the British monarch had lost in the sequence of events following the Revolution of 1689. This belief in the prerogative of parliament strengthened the idea that there was no such thing as an unconstitutional act of parliament. Parliament could change the constitution itself. A large group of Englishmen, however, believed that the power of parliament was limited by laws, charters, and customs. A smaller number, comparatively uninfluential in government, derived from existing conditions and contemporaneous colonial demands new theories of imperial relationships. According to the new theories, America should either enjoy direct representation in the imperial parliament, thus entering a closer union with Great Britain, or she should have a parliament of her own and form one of a group of sovereign states, loosely joined for purposes of mutual defense and commerce. Radicals, versed in eighteenth-century philosophy, found colonial demands for freedom from parliamentary interference justified by natural law and the "natural rights of man." Writers on imperial relationships developed one or another of these theories.

The Englishmen who believed in the absolute power of parliament probably outnumbered all others. They included not only those who would stake everything on maintaining parliamentary supremacy for its own sake, but also many who for expediency, that is, to maintain peace and trade relations, would concede in practice what they refused to admit in theory. The idea that colonies were completely subject to the mother country was not new; it had been expressed again and again in the seventeenth and eighteenth centuries. Theorists and empiricists, however, could not meet here on common ground for, as a matter of fact, in the eighteenth century, the colonists had not only asserted a high degree of independence; but on numerous occasions they had successfully resisted the authority of the home government. Therefore, Englishmen who insisted upon the omnipotence of parliament in American affairs were arguing for a purely speculative right which might exist in law, but did not exist in fact.[1]

---

[1] McIlwain, in *The American Revolution*, argues against the right of parliament to control the colonies. His argument is answered by Schuyler in *Parliament and the British Empire*, chaps. I and II.

In 1766 a large majority in parliament acknowledged adherence to this doctrine, the omnipotence of parliament in colonial matters, by passing the Declaratory Act which claimed for parliament the right to bind the colonies "in all cases whatsoever." Extremists who held this view even denied that colonial charters were exempt from parliamentary interference. The anonymous author of a *Letter to a Member of Parliament* declared that body had the power "to crush their existence as a Public."[2] Another contributor to the controversy wrote: "Why this mighty talk about Charters? If Charters are either found inconvenient or abused, a Quo Warranto will revoke them, but most indisputably high treason will forfeit everything."[3]

A fundamental part of the theory of parliamentary absolutism, which kept it from appearing too arbitrary, was the doctrine of virtual representation. By the phrase, virtual representation, Englishmen meant that members of the House of Commons represented not just the interest of the small group which elected them, but the interests of commoners everywhere. Therefore the Americans, though casting no vote for members of the House of Commons, were nevertheless represented. Dr. Samuel Johnson, one of the best known among the exponents of parliamentary omnipotence, said it was an absurdity that the colonists should "not be included, like millions of their fellow subjects, in the general system of representation."[4]

2 London, 1765, p. 21; review in *Gentleman's Magazine*, Dec., 1765, pp. 578-579.

3 *Lloyd's*, Oct. 28-30, 1765.

4 "The Patriot Addressed to the Electors of Great Britain," 1774, *Works*, N. Y., 1811, p. 140. In his dictionary Dr. Johnson defined pension as "generally understood to mean pay given to a state hireling for treason to his country." Opponents later attacked him for accepting a pension from Bute in 1762, although Burke said that the pension was given for literary merit, not for political opinions. *Dict. Nat. Biog.*, vol. X; *Jopson's*, Apr. 2, 1770.

Unfortunately for the life of this theory, there was an increasing number of Englishmen who did not think that it should be applied even to Great Britain, much less to the colonies. Dr. Johnson might declare, "All government is ultimately and essentially absolute";[5] but he failed to convince British, as well as American, liberals. A new political era was dawning, in which there would be no place for the ideas of Dr. Johnson or his convert, John Wesley, the founder of Methodism.

Unlike the majority of dissenters, Wesley was a strong supporter of the government in its colonial policy during the American Revolution. He denied that the origin of power was in the people. He based his contention on the following argument: "If this be so, then it belongs to every individual of the human species; consequently not to freeholders alone, but to all men; not to men only, but to women also; nor only to adult men and women . . ., but to those who have lived eighteen or twenty years. . . . But none did ever maintain this nor probably ever will."[6] Since power did not originate with the people, Wesley said they could claim no more than superior authority was pleased to concede to them. In regard to representation, he explained that he personally was no more represented in parliament than were the Americans, but that he did not for that reason consider himself a slave.

Inasmuch as it was one of the ancient rights of Englishmen, claimed by the Americans, to be taxed only by their representatives, the question of whether or not the Americans were represented in parliament was intimately connected with the more practical matter of taxing the colonists by act of parliament. Believers in the omnipotence of parliament and the virtual representation of the colonists in the British parliament saw no objection to the

5 "Taxation no Tyranny," 1775, *Works*, p. 155.
6 "The Origin of Power," 1772, *Works*, New York, 1839.

Stamp Act or the Townshend Acts. In fact many men failed to see how there could be any governing power without the right of taxation. Applying this idea to the empire, one man said: "In every Empire a supreme legislative authority over the whole must exist somewhere, with an adequate power to controul and bind all and every part of which it consists; otherwise it would be an Empire without government, without laws, and without power." Moreover, "the right of levying supplies on the people for the necessary purposes of government is a right inherent in the Constitution, and inseparable from it: a right so essential to Government that it could not subsist without it."[7]

In England land held as freehold was entitled to representation. That is, every forty-shilling freeholder enjoyed the privilege of voting for a member of the House of Commons. But in America, according to some contemporaries, there were no freeholds in the English sense of the word. A writer for the *London Magazine* declared: "The whole course of chancery proves that their estates are only commercial chattels, subject to the disposition of the last will of the owner, and chargeable with all the debts of the deceased proprietor."[8] Parliament, according to that theory, was justified in taxing so-called freeholders in America, whether they were represented literally, virtually, or not at all. Even the king, according to James Macpherson, could not grant exemption from parliamentary taxation.[9]

Historically and logically, according to English Whigs at least, parliamentary supremacy over the colonies as

[7] *Civil Liberty Asserted and the Rights of the Subject Defended against the Anarchical Principles of the Reverend Dr. Price,* London, 1776, pp. 46 and 94.

[8] Feb., 1766, pp. 78-79.

[9] *The Rights of Great Britain Asserted Against the Claims of America,* Aberdeen, 1776, published anonymously.

over England resulted from the Revolution of 1689. Americans, on the contrary, denied that the Revolution of 1689 had affected royal control over America. American radicals insisted that the colonies were dependent upon the crown alone. Englishmen were alarmed at the evidences of royal influence at home, they feared the increase of power abroad, and earnestly pointed out the dangers and fallacies in the American contention.[10] Parliamentary supremacy, unless parliament were utterly degraded, was a safeguard against autocracy.

There are many and varied expressions of the right of parliament to tax the Americans. "Anti-Sejanus," for example, wrote: "The right of taxation over the colonies is a point which none but a republican leveller, or the wildest visionary in politics would dare to dispute."[11] Another writer, basing his argument on historical grounds, said: "There is no principle in our constitution, neither was it ever the ancient practice . . . that any part of the community had a right to tax themselves to defray the national expence of the government."[12] Even Junius, as severely as he attacked the ministry in his *Letters,* declared that taxation was "inseparable in theory from the condition of colonists."[13] So far as pure theory was concerned, the government had the support of a large section of public opinion, although during the years of the American Revolution, the British in increasing numbers declared the government program inexpedient.

Indeed, absolute supremacy of parliament over the colonies was a popular belief; but when men began to analyze the theory they were inclined to modify it. One of the most commonly accepted limitations on the power of

---

[10] Add. MSS., 27916, p. 11.
[11] *London Magazine,* Feb., 1766, p. 78.
[12] *Ibid.,* Jan., 1771, p. 42.
[13] *Letters of Junius,* London, 1876, II, 102-103.

parliament was that imposed by colonial charters. This was the only restriction which John Lind was willing to admit. In general, with keen shafts of satire, combined with clear logic, Lind mercilessly tore down the fabric of theory built up by the colonists and their British sympathizers.[14] He stood firmly for the historic rights of parliament, contending that no new theory had been evolved in recent policy. Like Grenville he refused to see any distinction between internal and external taxation. He left little ground for the complaints from the colonies and the opposition in parliament that the acts of parliament were unconstitutional, for he reminded his readers that parliament could change the constitution at will. Aside from restrictions included in the original charters, Lind believed parliament had complete control over all conquered or acquired territory.[15]

Eminent among those who asserted a limited power of parliament over the colonies was Thomas Pownall, a colonial governor of much experience. An essential part of his theory was the distinction between internal and external taxation. The former, he said, was not included among the rights of parliament over the colonies. On the other hand, he declared that to exempt the colonies from taxation by parliament was just as impossible as for that body to exempt the colonies from subjection to the king. Unlike Lind, Pownall thought that the constitutional rights of parliament could be definitely defined. The colonial claim to entire freedom from its authority, he said, was of recent growth, put forward by men "ignorant of the constitution of Great Britain, and of their own best

[14] Although Lind's three sisters each received a pension of £50 a year because of his work, that fact could have had no effect upon his earliest writing, where his own views are clearly given.

[15] Lind, *Remarks on the Principal Acts of the Thirteenth Parliament*, London, 1775, p. 47.

liberty as derived from it."[16] England's first express departure from her constitutional position, he explained, occurred when an internal tax was laid upon the colonies; America's came when "they not only in doctrine, but by deed, denied the right which Great Britain hath, of imposing external taxes."[17] Pownall believed that a clear announcement of the reciprocal rights of colonies and mother country might settle the quarrel and establish peace. His sane and practical suggestions apparently had no weight with government. There is no evidence that government authorities paid any attention to his astute analysis of the colonial situation in *The Administration of the Colonies*. He himself apparently felt that his advice was slighted, for in 1775 before the House of Commons he declared that he would never again give an opinion regarding America in that house, as those he had given in the past had been disregarded.[18] His doctrines were essentially those of the mercantile classes. He doubtless had their interests in mind, for he continually, while the possibility existed, looked forward to the time when the colonies should be considered "essential parts of one organized whole, the commercial dominion of Great Britain."[19]

Believers in compromise asserted that America ought to contribute to the imperial treasury even though parliament's power of taxation were limited. In spite of the difficulties experienced in the past in securing financial aid from the colonies, Burke, Shelburne, Effingham, and Abingdon still believed the government ought to try the

[16] *Administration of the Colonies*, London, 1766 (3d edition), Appendix, Section III, p. 11.

[17] *Ibid.*, London, 1774 (5th edition), "wherein a line of government between the supreme jurisdiction of Great Britain and the rights of the colonies is drawn," part II, p. 78.

[18] *London Magazine*, March, 1775, p. 112.

[19] *Administration of the Colonies*, (3d edition), p. 202.

method of obtaining supplies through requisitions. Parliament might still reserve authority to require payment if the colonies refused. Burke, for example, said: "I consider the power of taxing in parliament as an instrument of empire, and not as a means of supply."[20] Lord Effingham expressed a similar idea in the House of Lords when he said that parliament should have the power to tax only in case any particular province should refuse grants in proportion to the others, or if they should violate the privileges granted in their charters.[21]

The Earl of Chatham was one of a small group who believed the power of taxing was excluded from the legislative power of parliament. To be sure, he said, "I assert the authority of this kingdom over the colonies to be sovereign and supreme, in every circumstance of government and legislation whatsoever"; but, he continued, "Taxation is no part of the governing or legislative power."[22] In advising the repeal of the Stamp Act, he declared: "We may bind their trade, confine their manufactures, and exercise every power whatsoever, except that of taking their money out of their pockets without their consent!"[23] These varying opinions about the rights of parliament over America made it impossible for government officials to please the British, to say nothing of the American, public, with their colonial policies.

In the emergency of colonial revolt, a few contemporaries advised that Great Britain forget the past, ignore both theory and fact, and build up, as it were from new materials, an empire in which America would hold a place

[20] Edmund Burke, *Speech of April 19, 1774* (4th edition), p. 93. See also Shelburne's plan in *Observations on Civil Liberty* by Richard Price, and Earl of Abingdon's *Thoughts on the Letter of Edmund Burke to the Sheriffs of Bristol*, Oxford, 1777 (6th edition).

[21] *London Magazine*, Sept., 1775, p. 457.

[22] *Ibid.*, Oct., 1766, p. 507.   [23] *Ibid.*, p. 512.

suited to the importance which she had recently acquired.[24]
One suggested solution of the problem was to allow Americans to sit in an imperial parliament in Great Britain.
This was not a new idea; but under the stress of the
American Revolution Englishmen gave more attention
to this possibility than ever before. When the colonists
might perhaps have accepted the suggestion, the British
were not ready; when Great Britain might have made
some such concession, America would no longer be satisfied with anything less than complete independence. In
1766 various writers made serious suggestions for American representation, and the newspapers even reported that
parliament was considering such a scheme.[25] The Chatham
Papers contain a proposal for postponing the Stamp Act
for three years, during which time the colonists were to
elect members to parliament. Then the new parliament
was to reconsider the whole matter of the Stamp Act.[26]
Macpherson wrote: "If they complain of being taxed
without having the privilege of sending members to
Parliament, let them be represented, Nay more: Let their
Representation increase in proportion to the revenue they
shall furnish."[27]

Although Soame Jenyns sarcastically remarked that
"the sudden importation of so much eloquence at once
would greatly endanger the safety and government of
this country," and that "in the end it would be cheaper
for us to pay their army than their orators," such men

[24] R. G. Adams, *Political Ideas of the American Revolution*, treats the
ideas of imperial organization in an interesting but purely speculative way.

[25] *An Account of a Late Conference on the Occurrences in America*, attributed to Joshua Steele, London, 1766; *Hist. MSS. Com. Rep.*, XIV, 10, p.
51; *Jones' Coventry and Warwick Ledger*, Aug. and Sept., 1765; *Gentleman's
Magazine*, Feb., 1766, "The History of a Private Convention."

[26] Chatham Papers, 97.

[27] *The Rights of Great Britain Asserted against the Claims of America*,
Aberdeen, 1776, p. 96.

as the Earl of Chatham and Adam Smith were willing to consider the scheme.[28] Chatham's idea was evolved after several years of controversy. He knew that America could be conciliated only by large concessions.[29] Adam Smith's suggestion was intended to disrupt the colonial union. He proposed that "to each colony, which should detach itself from the general confederacy, Great Britain should allow such a number of representatives as suited the proportion of what it contributed to the public revenue of the empire, in consequence of its being subjected to the same taxes."[30] An anonymous writer of 1774 advocated a similar arrangement for colonial representation, with the stipulation that the colonies should be taxed in the same mode and proportion as British subjects in the mother country. "This," said the writer, "would remove their fears, and thus might the whole of the British and American British subjects be very honourably, safely and wisely represented, in one central Parliament at Westminster, which would clearly and manifestly operate to the great strength and glory of the British Empire."[31] The author of *A Letter to Dr. Tucker* worked out a rather elaborate plan for an imperial organization to take the place of the temporary scheme of administration. The fundamental feature of his plan was the representation of the colonial assemblies at Westminster. Each assembly would send one member to sit for seven years. Parliament then, in case one colony threatened the welfare of another, might discipline the obstreperous province by suspending her in-

---

[28] Soame Jenyns, "The Objections to the Taxation of our American Colonies by the Legislature of Great Britain, Briefly Considered," 1765, *Works*, pp. 339-340.

[29] W. L. Grant, "The Colonial Policy of Chatham," *Bulletin of the Departments of History and Political and Economic Science in Queen's University*, Kingston, Ontario, No. 1, Oct., 1911.

[30] Adam Smith, *Wealth of Nations*, London, 1887, II, 135.

[31] *Lloyd's*, Feb. 9-11, 1774.

stitutions. No local privileges or peculiarities were to be
allowed in America, but by a vote of parliament one common constitution would be applied to all.[32] William Knox
advised allowing the colonies to send representatives to
parliament, not because parliament was lacking in authority to tax, but because the colonies were growing in importance. He made it clear that he still believed parliament
was "absolute and compleat" over subjects of the realm.[33]

These rather vague suggestions for an imperial parliament included the old idea of a sovereign body in the
mother country; but the conception of colonies sharing
in the work of legislating for the empire was new. If Englishmen had accepted any such plan, they would have been
obliged to abandon the fundamental concept of colonies.
British officials were too conservative to make such radical changes in colonial government. For many years after
the American Revolution precedent was a determining
factor in shaping colonial policies. While George III was
his own prime minister, the government was too intent
on working out imperialistic policies to consider other
possibilities.

Radicals suggested that a federation might settle the
mooted question of relations between Great Britain and
America. Such a federation would give to each part of the
empire the greatest independence consistent with union.
As William Adam explained, it would mean a union of interests. According to Adam's plan, even a nominal dependence of the colonies upon the British parliament
might be abandoned. The prerogative of declaring war
and making peace should, however, reside in the king. In
all other respects the American Congress should have all

[32] *A Letter to Dr. Tucker on His Proposal of Separation between Great
Britain and Her American Colonies*, London, 1774, pp. 12-14.

[33] *The Present State of the Nation*, attributed to William Knox, London,
1768, pp. 80-81.

the powers assumed during the revolution. For consultation on matters affecting both countries there should be a council appointed by the king, resident in America, and another, also appointed by the king, resident in Great Britain. Furthermore, natives of one country should be considered as natives of the other while the two countries should enjoy mutual free trade.[34]

Granville Sharp, Richard Price, and Major Cartwright also worked out, more or less independently, plans for a British imperial federation. Sharp considered it absurd for England to legislate for America. He advocated a union in which America, Ireland, and other parts of the empire should be equal.[35] Price's main idea can be found concisely expressed in one paragraph from his tract, *Observations on the Nature of Civil Liberty.* "An Empire," he wrote, "is a collection of states or communities united by some common bond or tye. If these states have each of them free constitutions of government and with respect to taxation and internal legislation, are independent of the other states, but united by compacts, or alliances, or subjection to a Great Council, or to one monarch entrusted with the supreme executive power: In these circumstances, the Empire will be an Empire of Freemen."[36] One significant feature of these schemes is that they assume a contract between equals. As Cartwright suggested, the contract would be a treaty for a league of friendship, which, in the case of America, would follow the recognition of the independence of that country. Cartwright's

[34] *An Examination into the Conduct of the present Administration*, London, 1778.

[35] *Gentleman's Magazine*, Jan., 1775, p. 38. Sharp proved his friendship for America by resigning his office in the ordnance rather than execute orders for the war. F. D. Cartwright, *Life and Correspondence of Major Cartwright*, I, 58-59. Prince Hoare, *Memoires of Granville Sharp, Esq.*, London, 1828.

[36] Price, p. 28.

plan, however, provided for fifteen independent states of
each of which the king should be head, as he was the head
of Great Britain.[37] In that case America would not be
united.

Boerhadem, writing in the *Gentleman's Magazine*, also
suggested a federation—a union among the various parts
of the empire similar to that among the provinces of the
Dutch commonwealth.[38] Adherents of the federation
scheme foresaw advantages in an alliance with America,
even though that country were not dependent upon Great
Britain, "Both countries to be leagued together under one
Sovereign, each People retaining their distinct Rights,
and neither, as a People subordinate to the other."[39]
William Pulteney thought the chief advantage in such a
union would be found in time of war, for it would prevent
America from uniting with the enemy.[40]

Many of these advocates of a new imperial relationship
had one characteristic in common. They abandoned the
historical argument, and appealed to natural rights, the
groundwork for the claims of British and American radicals. Abandoning logic drawn from charters, statutes, and
precedents, Cartwright asked how Americans could be
bound by laws, in the making of which they had had no
share. He distinctly stated that arguments for colonial
independence should rest upon America's right to independence as "a principle taken for granted."[41] The belief

[37] *American Independence the Interest and Glory of Great Britain,*
London, 1775, pp. 62 ff. In 1922 at the meeting of the American Historical
Association, Professor Schuyler of Columbia University read a stimulating
paper on Cartwright and other English radical philosophers.

[38] Boerhadem, "A few Thoughts on American Affairs," *Gentleman's
Magazine,* Feb., 1775, pp. 69-71.

[39] *Occasional Letters Upon Taxation,* London, 1780, p. 13.

[40] Pulteney, *Consideration on the Present State of Public Affairs,* London,
1779.

[41] *Postscript to American Independence,* p. 8.

in natural rights was far from being as prevalent in Great Britain as in America, yet it did occasionally find expression in the magazines, and even in parliament. In May, 1774, a writer for the *London Magazine* said: "To reason about charters . . . is ridiculous, as if men had no right of a higher nature than royal grants and charters, rights superior to, and independent of them."[42] In the House of Commons Temple Luttrell declared: "Acts of parliament, or other diplomatic titles, may be produced to shew a formal, and perhaps uncontested assumption of power at some given period of time, but will not countervail the primeval and indefeasible rights of mankind, whenever such rights shall be asserted by a clear major part of the community. . . . All persons," he said, "have natural rights—a free people have legal rights, independent of parliamentary edicts, and of which no form of government whatever can deprive them."[43] With the same meaning, but with slightly different wording, a writer for the *London Magazine* said: "The idea of liberty in the abstract is the same in one continent as another."[44] During the American Revolution, a radical paper called *The Crisis* frequently published articles developing the theory of natural rights.

As we have seen, British and American philosophers who claimed for the colonies absolute or limited independence of parliament drew their arguments from various sources: from the charters granted to the colonies in their early history, from the British constitution, or from the doctrine of natural rights. The first point had limited application. Of the colonies that orginally had charters, several had lost them through accepted legal procedure. Of the charters that remained intact, the Pennsylvania document definitely acknowledged the authority of parlia-

42 May, 1774, p. 243.
43 *London Magazine*, Nov., 1775, p. 559.   44 *Ibid.*, Feb., 1766, p. 80.

ment and demanded of the colony obedience to parliamentary legislation and parliamentary taxation; and even the Maryland grant, which contained the broadest powers of the proprietary charters, and the charters granted to Connecticut and Rhode Island, stipulated that laws made for the colony should not be repugnant to English laws. Parliamentary authority was either stated or implied in the colonial charters, although they were issued before the Revolution of 1689, when parliament assumed many attributes of the royal prerogative.

Arguments drawn from the theory of the British constitution were weak, for even Blackstone, the acknowledged legal authority of the period, defended the omnipotence of parliament. Although men might declare that custom had established certain things which parliament should not do, there was no power above parliament and that sovereign body could in effect change the constitution. Great Britain had no supreme court with authority to declare acts of parliament unconstitutional and therefore null and void. In the eighteenth century the only logical and practical means of redress for grievances against parliament was revolution, if that body remained obdurate. The unconstitutionality of an act of parliament was difficult to prove, since from one point of view parliament from its very nature could not pass an unconstitutional measure. Yet there was a small number of Englishmen who tried to justify phases of the colonial claims by references to the British constitution. They declared that the power of parliament over the colonies was limited, and in so doing intimated, if they did not actually assert, that the legislature of Great Britain was acting unconstitutionally when it overstepped those limits. William Pultney, elder brother of Governor Johnstone, made such an implication when he wrote: ''From the view that I have taken of the subject, I think it must appear to every man who will permit himself to judge without prejudice, that the objection of the Americans to their being taxed by this country was not an unreasonable caprice, but of a most serious and important nature; and that the British Parliament, being neither elected by them, nor imposing at the same moment on themselves and their constituents, the taxes they were to vote on America, had not those constitutional checks, to prevent an abuse of that dangerous power, which is in truth the essence of the British Constitution."[45] In 1769 the petitions of both Bristol and Middlesex referred to the "unconstitutional" practices of the government in dealing with the colonies.[46] Yet the idea that there was a supreme law which parliament or any legislative body could not violate was much more common in America than in England. That doctrine was worked out in the constitutions of the individual American states and later in the federal constitution. In the meantime, theories of natural rights offered the most satisfactory justification for limiting the power of parliament.

If one accepted the doctrine of natural rights, at once the problem of colonial privileges versus parliamentary authority became simple. One no longer perplexed one's mind with the conflicting legal opinions of the day or the confusing mass of historical evidence relating to the colonial position. One considered liberty and independence as rights to which the laws of nature entitled human beings. No arguments were necessary. Historical fact could neither prove nor disprove the laws of nature; and men who accepted the philosophy of natural rights found it a

[45] *Thoughts on the Present State of Affairs with America and the Means of Conciliation*, London, 1778, printed anonymously but attributed to Pultney, p. 42.

[46] *Middlesex Journal*, Nov. 22, 1769. *Gentleman's Magazine*, June, 1769, pp. 289-291.

convenient starting point for revolution. That particular philosophy found an important place in the revolutionary documents of the colonies and in the writings of radical sympathizers in England.

In all this discussion of constitutional theory, one wanders far afield from what Englishmen in the eighteenth century would have called practical politics. While some of the philosophers with heads above the clouds were speculating on the rights of the Americans, other men with their feet upon the ground were considering the most practical treatment of the colonies. The crucial test for every suggestion was its practicability and its advantage to Great Britain. The majority of Englishmen took the subordination of colonies to the authority of parliament for granted; but whether in practice England ought to struggle to maintain a loosening hold or renounce all authority was another question. Changing ideas in regard to the practical value of colonies helped to answer this.

Before the middle of the eighteenth century men valued colonies almost exclusively for the commercial advantages to be derived from them. The following is a typical mercantilist explanation of the value of colonial possessions. "Great Britain and Ireland (for I wish to consider them as united in interest and connection with the colonies) stand in pretty much the same relation to the colonies as a manufacturing farmer's house and garden in the village, does to his adjacent farm." The mercantilist went on to explain that the garden was sufficient to supply the farmer and his family with many necessaries and delicacies, while he could bring from his farm materials for manufacturing and bulky materials for market. It would make no difference to whom he sold the materials he did not need. "His chief care is that his own teams are the carriers, that the money his products are sold for is brought back to him, and that his servants do not lay out their wages at other shops than his.''[47] To assure these conditions the mercantilists favored the old navigation laws.

During the American Revolution mercantilists realized that colonial contentment was essential for trade development; but they were so engrossed with the necessity for a monopoly of colonial trade, that they were inclined to abandon America if monopoly were lost. Parliamentary regulation of trade seemed necessary if the colonies were to be a paying proposition. That is, mercantilists were inclined to advise either one of two extremes in dealing with the colonies: maintain them in due commercial subjection or give them independence. There was, however, an increasing number of people in Great Britain who no longer held the pure mercantilist theory.

Although the government continued to quote mercantilist theories it really abandoned the mercantilists when it first proposed to tax the colonists. In one of his famous speeches on taxation, Edmund Burke pointed to the inconsistency of the government. ''Whether you were right or wrong in establishing the Colonies on the principles of commercial monopoly, rather than on that of revenue, is at this day a problem of mere speculation. You cannot have both by the same authority.''[48] Other mercantilists were not slow to declare that it was contrary to the whole idea of colonies to expect revenue from them. ''Thus it signifies nothing whether Great Britain has a right to tax her colonies or not.''[49] Those who continued to think

[47] *The Present State of the Nation,* London, 1768 (2d edition), attributed to William Knox, p. 78.

[48] Edmund Burke, *A History of American Taxation from the Year 1763 to the End of Last Session,* London, 1775, p. 39.

[49] *The Present State of Great Britain and North America with Regard to Agriculture, Population, Trade, and Manufactures,* London, 1770, attributed to John Mitchell, p. 360.

that subordinate colonies were essential for the commercial prosperity of Great Britain advocated reform in administration, in currency, and in fact in everything that could make the colonies more contented without depriving the mother country of her advantage in trade.

As mercantilist ideas were modified, suggestions for relaxing restrictions on colonial trade were made. Some writers believed that the colonists should have equal privileges with other British subjects. One writer realized the alarm the East India Company would feel at this proposal, but said: "And yet, whatever minister shall arise and direct his administration upon this infallible principle of national policy, will augment the national wealth, increase the revenue, enrich the British manufacturer, give bread to the labourer, and spread universal cheerfulness over the whole face of this happy land."[50] A more serious assault upon the mercantilist principle was the suggestion that Great Britain legalize colonial trade with the Spanish West Indies.[51] Even in 1766 there were those who had the temerity to proclaim that absolute freedom of trade would be beneficial.[52]

Adam Smith was the great exponent of the theory of free trade, but he was frank to say that he considered the adoption of his principles a mere Utopia, for he realized that it would take years to convince men of the logic of his teaching. He pointed out that Great Britain's treatment of her colonies had been more liberal than that of other European countries. Furthermore, inasmuch as America was a new country, in need of a large supply of manufactures, the British mercantilist policy had not as yet been disadvantageous for the colonies. For the mother country, however, the dangers of the mercantilist system were

50 *Gentleman's Magazine*, Feb., 1766, Letter from T. T-d, p. 71.
51 *Lloyd's*, March 11-13, 1765.
52 *Gentleman's Magazine*, Feb., 1766, p. 67.

great, as her trade was forced into unnatural channels. "The expectation of a rupture with the colonies," he wrote, "accordingly had struck the people of Great Britain with more terror than they ever felt for a Spanish Armada or a French invasion. . . . Some moderate and gradual relaxation of the laws which give to Great Britain the exclusive trade to the colonies, till it is rendered in a great measure free, seems to be the only expedient which can enable her or even force her to withdraw some part of her capital from this overgrown employment, and to turn it, though with less profit, towards other employment."[53] According to Adam Smith, the monopoly of colonial trade threatened the mother country more than America. His famous work, the *Wealth of Nations,* was published at a significant moment in American and British history—in 1776, the year in which the colonies decided they must be free.

Matthew Robinson-Morris and Adam Ferguson, though representing opposing political parties, nevertheless agreed that a monopoly of colonial trade was no longer indispensable. Robinson-Morris advised enlarging the trade of both Ireland and America.[54] Significant of the attitude of government and country gentlemen is a quotation from a pamphlet by Ferguson, printed at government expense: "We are arrived at an age of experience, in which all parties might see the expedience of exchanging restrictions in trade for compensations in revenue."[55] Pownall in the later years of the war also advocated free commerce, free ports, and a free sea, with a council of commerce for all Europe and North America, and an

[53] *Wealth of Nations,* London, 1887, II, 116-117.

[54] *Considerations on the Measures carrying on with Respect to the British Colonies in North America,* London, 1774, p. 54.

[55] *Remarks on a Pamphlet lately published by Dr. Price,* London, 1776, p. 54.

international court of justice. Pownall, like a few other advanced thinkers, believed that the desire for a monopoly of trade was no longer sufficient reason for keeping the colonies. Yet he declared that a friendly alliance would further the commercial and other practical interests of all the countries concerned.[56] A few men believed that the advantages to be gained from union with America were great enough to justify a connection on any political terms. But when the prospects of revenue failed, expenses increased, and merchants saw that a peaceful, independent America was worth more to them than a hostile, subject country, the idea of American independence rapidly gained favor.

Among the British advocates of American independence, forerunners of the nineteenth-century politicians who worked for a "Little England," was Josiah Tucker. Tucker was a fanatic, but the constant reiteration of his precepts may have made some impression upon his contemporaries. To discredit the value of colonies was an integral part of his commercial doctrine. As early as 1764 he wrote *The Case of Going to War for the Sake of Trade,* in which he attacked the extraordinary influence of the merchants in affairs of government. So great was the popular enthusiasm over British successes in the war with France that his theories were unacceptable. Several years later this early tract was reprinted in a volume with several others. Having then experienced difficulties with America, a larger part of the reading public was prepared to consider, if not to accept, his suggestions. Tucker was so sure that Great Britain would profit from freedom of trade that he had no hesitation in declaring that separa-

---

[56] Pownall, *A Memorial . . . to the Sovereigns of Europe,* London, 1780. *A Translation of the Memorial into Common Sense and Intelligible English,* London, 1781, attributed to E. Jennings. See review in *Gentleman's Magazine,* Jan., 1781, pp. 31-33.

tion from the colonies would be to her advantage. He contended that colonial trade had never been as valuable as men thought. Trade with America would inevitably continue, as that country was commercially dependent upon Great Britain. Tucker believed that all countries should produce those things for which they were best suited, and that for those products they could always find a ready sale at a satisfactory price.[57] "It is freedom," he wrote, "and not confinement or monopoly which increases trade."[58] He consistently opposed war with the colonies, and advised granting them their independence without a struggle. It was during the disturbances over the Stamp Act that he first announced this policy. According to his own explanation, a merchant suggested that he write *A letter from a merchant in London to his nephew in America concerning the late and present disturbances in the colonies*. The merchant was so astonished at the dean's proposals for settling all colonial difficulties that the original conclusion of the tract was changed. Tucker's fourth tract, however, was written to show his own earnest convictions.[59] He never believed that the colonies could effect a permanent union among themselves. On the contrary, he expected that they might seek a reunion with Great Britain. This the mother country must strive to prevent, because of the great financial burden imposed by colonial possessions. For the same reason he opposed all plans for imperial union or federation, fearing that Great Britain would have the heaviest responsibility. Unlike Adam Smith, who looked with equanimity upon the possibility of the removal of the capital or seat of empire to America

[57] *Cui Bono*, Gloucester, 1781.

[58] *An Humble Address and Earnest Appeal*, Gloucester, 1775, p. 74.

[59] *Gentleman's Magazine*, Jan. and Feb., 1774; book reviews, pp. 29-30, 78-80. Tucker, *Four Tracts together with Two Sermons on Political and Commercial Subjects*, Gloucester, 1774.

in future years,[60] Tucker thought that this danger was another reason for avoiding all political connections with the new country.[61]

Utilitarians also decided that colonies were of little value. Whatever Bentham's views may have been when he assisted John Lind to prepare his first work on the colonies, by 1793 when he wrote to the French National Convention a pamphlet entitled, *Emancipate Your Colonies*, his opinions were firmly fixed.[62] Utility was the universal test to apply to colonies, and the events of the American Revolution convinced many Englishmen that there was nothing to be gained from colonial relationship. Even as early as 1766 *Lloyd's* printed the following: "It is neither wise nor prudent in any nation that consists of an island like Utopia, whose chief strength is in ships

[60] Adam Smith, *Wealth of Nations*, London, 1887, II, 138.

[61] *An Humble Address and Earnest Appeal*, pp. 40-41. Compare satirical verses by Soame Jenyns in "The American Coachman," *Works*, Dublin, 1791, I, 169-170.

First stanza:
> "Crowned be the man with lasting praise,
>   Who first contriv'd the pin
> From vicious steeds to loose a chaise,
>   And save the necks within."

Last stanzas:
> "Hungry at last and blind, and lame,
>   Bleeding at nose and eyes;
> By sufferings growing mighty tame
>   And by experience wise;
>
> With bellies full of liberty,
>   But void of oats and hay
> They both sneak back, their folly see
>   And run no more away.
>
> Let all who view th' instructive scene,
>   And patronize the plan,
> Give thanks to Gloucester's honest Dean,
>   For Tucker, thou'rt the man."

[62] Jeremy Bentham, *Works*, part I, Edinburgh, 1838, preface, p. xiv.

and sailors, to plant Colonies on a Continent.'' Of what use can it be, the article continued, for the mother country to be drained of men and money to get possessions for the off-scouring of other nations, who would at the earliest possible moment declare their independence?[63] While only a few men developed these ideas into an elaborate philosophy, the general public became skeptical about the desirability of keeping their colonial possessions.

As far as theory was concerned, the majority of Englishmen believed that the colonies should by right be completely subordinated to the authority of the British parliament. In practice they were usually willing to concede as much of this authority as suited their individual interests. Others defended a limited dependence upon parliament, as outlined by laws, by customs, and by charters, because correct in theory. A few doctrinaires or extreme radicals attempted to uphold the sovereignty of America on the score of natural rights. All theories, however, counted for little when they conflicted with individual interests. Temporarily at the beginning of the war, passions blinded many men to everything except their rights. In later years many of these same men may have looked back with misgiving as did Edward Gibbon when he wrote in his *Memoirs*: ''I took my seat at the beginning of the memorable contest between Great Britain and America, and supported with many a sincere and silent vote, the rights, though not perhaps the interest, of the mother country.''[64] ''Upon the whole,'' he said, ''I find it much easier to defend the justice than the policy of our measures; but there are certain cases where whatever is repugnant to sound policy ceases to be just.''[65]

Changing opinions about the value of colonies, combined with ideas of what was expedient under the cir-

[63] *Lloyd's*, Jan. 27-29, 1766.
[64] Gibbon, London, 1891, p. 166.   [65] *Ibid.*, p. 400.

cumstances, prepared Englishmen for the loss of America
in 1783. Coercion failed. The colonies would not agree to
conciliation on any terms that could answer the purpose
of pure mercantilists, the landed interests, or the government. Englishmen became apathetic in regard to the few
advantages to be derived from colonies, and ever more
sensitive to the inconveniences and even disasters that
resulted from their possession. From 1778 the European
war very nearly eclipsed all interest in American affairs.
In 1776 controversial writings about America practically
ceased. In the years that followed there was only an occasional pamphlet concerning the colonies, except those
which dealt with the subject of the national debt or heavy
taxes resulting from the war with America. After 1778
magazines and newspapers devoted appreciatively less
space to American news. In 1783 when peace was finally
concluded the British people were more united in their attitude toward America than they had been at any time in
the preceding twenty years. They felt a sense of relief—
relief from the burdens of the war, from the ordinary
expenses of maintaining the colonies even in times of
peace, and from the continuous controversy that for many
years past had destroyed all possibility of imperial harmony.

BIBLIOGRAPHICAL NOTE

FOR a study of public opinion in the period of the American Revolution the number of sources is so overwhelming that any account of these sources seems superficial. The material is almost inexhaustible; but there are nevertheless certain collections of manuscripts, printed documents, pamphlets, magazines, newspapers, and contemporary works of other kinds which in retrospect seem to have contributed most liberally to my knowledge of the period.

GUIDES

C. M. Andrews' *Guide to the Materials for American History to 1783 in the Public Record Office of Great Britain* and C. M. Andrews' and F. G. Davenport's *Guide to the Manuscript Materials for the History of the United States to 1783 in the British Museum, in Minor London Archives, and in the Libraries of Oxford and Cambridge* were of the greatest assistance in locating manuscripts.

MANUSCRIPTS

Of the papers in the Public Record Office the following were most serviceable: Colonial Office Papers 5, Chatham Papers, Admiralty Papers 1 and 2, and the State Papers Domestic of the Reign of George III, including the Entry Books and the Naval Papers. The Additional Manuscripts in the British Museum proved most valuable, although the King's Manuscripts and the Egerton Manuscripts were also helpful. In general the manuscript material served to verify or correct opinions based on the printed material of the period. Occasionally I was able to find information which was lacking in any contemporary printed sources. This was especially true in connection with the study of colonial impressment.

PRINTED OFFICIAL DOCUMENTS

Of the printed official documents the following have been most useful: *Acts of the Privy Council of England, Colonial Series; Calendar of Home Office Papers of the Reign of George III; Calendar of State Papers, Colonial Series; Statutes at Large;* Howell's *A Collection of State Trials; Journals of the House of Commons; Journals of the House of Lords;* and *The Parliamentary History of England.* These publications contributed information for all sections of this work, but especially for the chapters dealing with the opinions of government officials. Volume 62, Part II of the 1878 *Parliamentary Papers* contains a list of the members of the House of Commons with the places from which they were returned. I used this list as a basis for my study of the personnel of the House of Commons during the years of the American Revolution. The *Historical Manuscripts Commission Reports* include material which would not otherwise be easily available to the student, and they are invaluable although the brevity of the abstracts is sometimes tantalizing. I have frequently referred to the reports of the Abergavenny Manuscripts X, 6 and the Dartmouth Manuscripts XIV, 10.

PRINTED CORRESPONDENCE AND MEMOIRS

The printed correspondence and memoirs are indispensable for the study of opinions. The *Commerce of Rhode Island* (IX and X of the seventh series of Massachusetts Historical Society Collections) contains correspondence of Henry Cruger, a typical British merchant. For the chapter on the radicals, *The Life and Correspondence of Major Cartwright* (ed. F. D. Cartwright, London, 1826), Prince Hoare's *Memoirs of Granville Sharp* (London, 1828), the "Political Papers Collected by the Rev. Christopher Wyvill, Chairman of the Late Committee of Association in the County of York" in *Excerpta Antiqua; or a Collection of Original Manuscripts* (York, 1797), and *The Controversial Letters of John Wilkes, Esq., The Rev. John Horne, and their Principal Adherents* (London, 1771) have been valuable. By observing the same events through the eyes of several individuals one may come nearer to the truth than would be possible by depending upon the vision and judgment of only one individual. A comparison of the following has helped to shed light on a variety of matters: *The Journal and Letters of Samuel Curwen* (Boston, 1864), *Diary and Letters of Thomas Hutchinson* (Boston, 1884), *The Letters of Horace Walpole* (London, 1857), Walpole's *Memoirs of George III* (London, 1894), *Last Journals of Horace Walpole* (New York, 1900), Edward Gibbon's *Memoirs and a Selection from his Letters* (London, 1781), *The Grenville Papers* (London, 1852), *The Letters of Junius* (London, 1876), *A Narrative of the Changes in the Ministry 1765-1767, Told by the Duke of Newcastle in a Series of Letters to John White, M. P.* (edited for the Royal Historical Society by Mary Bateson, London, 1898), and the *Parliamentary Papers of John Robinson, 1774-1784* (edited by William Thomas Laprade for the Royal Historical Society, London, 1922). *The Correspondence of King George the Third from 1760 to December, 1783* (arranged and edited by the Honorable Sir John Fortescue, London, 1928) has added materially to our knowledge of the opinions and activities of the court during the American Revolution. Before the publication of this valuable work, I depended quite largely upon W. B. Donne's edition of *The Correspondence of King George the Third with Lord North from 1768 to 1783* (London, 1867).

PAMPHLETS

Of the one hundred and thirty odd pamphlets which I used for this study it is possible to mention here only those which were most important. The library of Yale University is fortunate in possessing a large number of pamphlets including the Wagner Collection, the College Pamphlets, and miscellaneous tracts. I have been able to locate at the Widener Library at Harvard and at the New York Public Library a few valuable pamphlets for this period which I could not find at Yale. Others are to be found only in the British Museum.

The pamphlets which give information about the opinions and activities of the mercantile classes in the period after 1763 are fewer than one might expect. The majority of the mercantilist pamphlets belong to an earlier date. However, *Considerations on the Trade and Finances of this Kingdom, and on the Measures of*

Administration with Respect to those great National Objects since the Conclusion of the Peace, ascribed to Thomas Whately (London, 1769) and George Heathcote's *A Letter to the Right Honourable the Lord Mayor, the Worshipful Aldermen, and Common Council* (London, 1762) present the views of the mercantilists. Henry McCulloh's *Miscellaneous Representations Relative to our Concerns in America* (reprinted London, 1905), especially the prefatory note, McCulloh's *Miscellaneous Essay concerning the Course pursued by Great Britain in the Affairs of her Colonies* (London, 1755), and William Knox's *The Claim of the Colonies to Exemption from Internal Taxes* (London, 1765) not only show the attitude of minor officials toward the stamp duty, but also help one to understand conditions in the eighteenth century. Pamphlets which deal with the financial situation during the later years of the Revolution include William Eden's *Four Letters to the Earl of Carlisle* (London, 1779) and *Fifth Letter to the Earl of Carlisle* (London, 1780), John Horne's (Horne Tooke's) *Facts Addressed to the Landholders, Stockholders, Merchants, Farmers, Manufacturers, Tradesmen, Proprietors of Every Description, and Generally to All the Subjects of Great Britain and Ireland* (London, 1780), and an anonymous tract entitled *A Letter to the Noblemen, Gentlemen, etc., who have addressed his Majesty on the Subject of the American Rebellion* (London, 1776).

For the study of the problems of the country gentlemen Charles Smith's *Three Tracts on the Corn Trade and Corn Laws, A New Edition with Additions from the Marginal Manuscripts of Mr. Catherwood* (London, 1804) are very suggestive. Many phases of agricultural conditions are described by Arthur Young in the following pamphlets: *The Expediency of a Free Exportation of Corn* (London, 1770), *The Farmer's Letters to the People of England* (London, 1767), *Farmer's Tour through the East of England* (London, 1771), *Political Arithmetic containing Observations on the Present State of Great Britain; and the Principles of her Policy in the Encouragement of Agriculture* (London, 1774) and Part II of the same work (London, 1779), *A Six Months Tour through the North of England* (London, 1770), and *A Six Weeks Tour through the Southern Counties of England and*

Wales (London, 1768). A rare pamphlet by Nathaniel Kent, *Hints to Gentlemen of Landed Property* (London, 1775) and Josiah Tucker's *Reflections on the Present Low Price of Coarse Wools, its Immediate Causes and its Probable Remedies* (London, 1782) explain some of the difficulties which the landed classes faced in this period. Nicholas Barbon's *A Discourse of Trade* (London, 1690, reprint Johns Hopkins Univ. Press, 1905) and Jeremy Bentham's *Defence of Usury* (Philadelphia, 1796 and in *Works,* Edinburgh, 1838) are helpful in obtaining an understanding of the methods of reckoning land values. Financial conditions were influential in forming the opinions of the landed classes and pamphlets by Richard Price, Matthew Robinson-Morris and John Dalrymple were widely read by their contemporaries. Price wrote *Observations on the Nature of Civil Liberty* (London, 1778) and *Additional Observations on the Nature and Value of Civil Liberty* (London, 1777). The works of Robinson-Morris include *Considerations on the Measures Carrying on with Respect to the British Colonies in North America* (London, 1774), *A Further Examination of our Present American Measures and of the Reasons and the Principles on Which they are founded* (Bath, 1776, pub. anon.), and *Peace the Best Policy or Reflections upon the Appearance of a Foreign War, the Present State of Affairs at Home and the Commission for Granting Pardons in America* (London, 1777). To John Dalrymple is attributed *The Address of the People of Great Britain to the Inhabitants of America* (London, 1775). Leonard Smelt's *An Account of Some Particulars Relative to the Meeting held at York on Thursday the 30th December, 1779* (London, 1780), originally printed anonymously under the title *An Account of Some Particulars which Passed at the Meeting Held at York . . .,* and an anonymous pamphlet, *The Yorkshire Question, or Petition, or Address* (London, 1780) explain features of this famous county meeting which are not clear in Wyvill's account. One of the most ardent champions of the country gentlemen was Soame Jenyns. His collected works were published in Dublin, 1791.

Occasionally a pamphlet adds to one's knowledge of political conditions in the eighteenth century. For instance, Catherine

Macaulay's *An Address to the People of England, Scotland, and Ireland on the present important Crisis of Affairs* (Bath, 1775) explains the "test" as a means of controlling a member of parliament; and John Horne's *Facts Addressed to the Landholders* . . ., previously cited, indicates the popular objections to the practices of government. Many of Edmund Burke's speeches in opposition to governmental measures were published separately, but they are also included in the collection of his works published at Dublin in 1783. The pamphlets written by government sympathizers present various aspects of the orthodox official view. The collected works of Samuel Johnson, a rabid opponent of American ideas, were published in New York, 1811. Many of his writings were originally published in pamphlet form. Other pro-government pamphlets are attributed as follows: James Macpherson, *The Rights of Great Britain Asserted against the Claims of America: Being an Answer to the Declaration of the General Congress* (Aberdeen, 1776) ; John Lind, *Remarks on the Principal Acts of the Thirteenth Parliament of Great Britain* (London, 1775), *Three Letters to Dr. Price containing Remarks on his Observations on the Nature of Civil Liberty, the Principles of Government, and the Justice and Policy of the War with America* (London, 1776), and *An Answer to the Declaration of the American Congress* (London, 1776) ; John Shebbeare, *An Answer to the Printed Speech of Edmund Burke, Esq., Spoken in the House of Commons, April 19, 1774* (London, 1775) ; Ambrose Serle, *Americans against Liberty or an Essay on the Nature and Principles of True Freedom* (London, 1776). An excellent supplement to Serle's printed pamphlet is his manuscript Diary describing, with characteristic comments, his residence in New York, May 6, 1776, to July 22, 1778. This manuscript is now in the Huntington Library.

The pamphlet literature of the period is especially valuable in a study of contemporary theories, although the pamphlets are so frequently propagandist in tone that they may be misleading. There are usually pamphlets on both sides of important public questions; and hardly a phase of imperial relationships is left untouched by the pamphleteers. In addition to the pamphlets and collected works referred to in other connections I made use of the following: John Wesley, *The Origin of Power* (first pub. 1772, in *Works*, N. Y., 1839); Willoughby Bertie, 4th Earl of Abingdon, *Thoughts on the Letter of Edmund Burke to the Sheriffs of Bristol* (Oxford, 1777); [Joshua Steele], *An Account of a Late Conference on the Occurrences in America* (London, 1766); *A Letter to Dr. Tucker on His Proposal of Separation between Great Britain and Her American Colonies* (London, 1774); William Knox, *The Present State of the Nation;* William Adam, *An Examination into the Conduct of the Present Administration from the Year 1774 to the Year 1778 and a Plan of Accommodation with America* (London, 1778); *Occasional Letters Upon Taxation; Upon the Means of Raising the Supplies within the Year, to Answer the Expences of a Necessary War* (London, 1780); William Pulteney, *Thoughts on the Present State of Affairs with America and the Means of Conciliation* (London, 1778); John Mitchell, *The Present State of Great Britain and North America with Regard to Agriculture, Population, Trade and Manufactures* (London, 1770); Adam Ferguson, *Remarks on a Pamphlet lately published by Dr. Price, intitled Observations on the Nature of Civil Liberty, the Principles of Government and the Justice and Policy of the War with America, etc., in a Letter from a Gentleman in the Country to a Member of Parliament* (London, 1776); Thomas Pownall, *A Memorial Most Humbly Addressed to the Sovereigns of Europe on the Present State of Affairs between the Old and New World* (London, 1780); E. Jennings, *A Translation of the Memorial into Common Sense and Intelligible English* (London, 1781). Josiah Tucker was responsible for the following tracts: *The Case of Going to War for the Sake of Procuring, Enlarging, or Securing of Trade, Considered in a New Light Being a Fragment of a greater Work* (London, 1763); *Cui Bono? or an Inquiry what Benefits can arise either to the English or the American, the French, Spaniards or Dutch, from the Greatest Victories or Successes, in the Present War? Being a Series of Letters Addressed to Monsieur Necker, Late Controller General of the Finances of France* (Gloucester, 1781); *Four Letters on Important National Subjects Addressed to the Right Honourable the Earl of Shelburne, His Majesty's First Lord Commissioner of the Treasury* (Gloucester, 1783) ; *Four Tracts together with Two Sermons, on Political and Commercial Subjects* (Gloucester, 1774) ; *An Humble Address and Earnest Appeal to Those Respectable Personages in Great Britain and Ireland, who by their Great and Permanent Interest in Landed Property, Their Liberal Education, Elevated Rank, and Enlarged Views, are the Ablest to Judge, and the Fittest to Decide whether a Connection with or a Separation from the Continental Colonies of America be Most for the National Advantage and the Lasting Benefit of These Kingdoms* (Gloucester, 1775) ; *A Treatise Concerning Civil Government in Three Parts* (London, 1781).

OTHER CONTEMPORARY PUBLICATIONS

There are other contemporary works, which are too long to be classed with the pamphlets. The following were useful because of their statistics and because of their comments upon trade: A. Anderson, *An Historical and Chronological Deduction of the Origin of Commerce, Revised, Corrected, and Continued to the Year 1789 by Mr. Coombe* (Dublin, 1790) ; Anthony Brough, *A View of the Importance of the Trade between Great Britain and Russia* (London, 1789) ; J. Burgh, *Political Disquisitions or An Enquiry into Public Errors, Defects and Abuses* (Philadelphia, 1775) ; William Playfair, *The Commercial and Political Atlas; representing by means of stained copper-plate charts, the Exports, Imports, and General Trade of England; The National Debt, and Other Public Accounts with Observations and Remarks* (London, 1786) ; Malachy Postlethwayt, *The Universal Dictionary of Trade and Commerce with large Additions and Improvements* (London, 1774) ; John, Lord Sheffield, *Observations on the Commerce of the American States* (London, 1784). Adam Smith's *An Inquiry into the Nature and the Causes of the Wealth of Nations* (London, 1887) by its criticisms elucidates the contemporary mercantilist theories and by its illustrations contributes to a clearer understanding of the economic conditions of the period. For a clear and comprehensive analysis of the administrative problems in America, there is no better contemporary work than

Thomas Pownall's *The Administration of the Colonies* (3rd edition, London, 1766; 5th edition, London, 1774). *The History of the Robinhood Society* (London, 1764) is a quaint account of an interesting radical organization. John Cartwright, leader of the parliamentary reformers, was the author of *American Independence the Interest and Glory of Great Britain* (London, 1775), published anonymously and of *The Legislative Rights of the Commonalty Vindicated; or Take Your Choice* (London, 1777).

NEWSPAPERS AND MAGAZINES

Through the newspapers and magazines of the period one may perhaps come nearer to the people than through any other medium. Newspaper reports are not always correct; one cannot depend upon an isolated statement of fact; one needs to verify newspaper accounts by reference to other sources. Nevertheless, the general impressions which one receives by turning page after page of contemporary news sheets are, I believe, much more reliable than most comments on public opinion by prejudiced observers of the day. *Lloyd's Evening Post and British Chronicle* is a rich source for the activities and opinions of the mercantile classes. I also found valuable supplementary material in *Jones' Coventry and Warwick Ledger, Jopson's Coventry Mercury or the Weekly Country Journal*, the *Middlesex Journal,* and the *York Chronicle.* The provincial papers are disappointing, because they make almost no attempt to represent local opinion. The reports of correspondents for the London papers are more satisfactory in that respect.

The *Annual Register* gives the important news of the period in a convenient summary; but the *Gentleman's Magazine* and the *London Magazine* are much more useful in a study of opinion. Of all the magazines of the period I found that these two portrayed most clearly the views of various classes of the English people in regard to the disputes with the colonies. For the brief essays, for the accounts of events, for the book reviews, and for the reports of parliamentary debates the magazines are valuable.

INDEX

Abingdon, Earl of, see Bertie.

Acland, John Dyke (M.P.), government supporter, 227.

Adam, William, proposes federation, 266-267.

Adams, John, of Boston, Massachusetts, receives letter from British radicals, 155; elected member of Supporters of the Bill of Rights, 157.

Adams, Samuel, 2, 35.

Addresses, see Petitions.

Admiralty, vice-admiralty courts in America, 52; instructions regarding impressment in America, 90; grants letters of marque and reprisal, 110.

Africa, effect of American war on British trade. with, 111.

Almon, John, publisher, 6; *Prior Documents*, 7.

America, see Colonies and United States.

Anglicans, authority in church, 183; interest of, in colonies, 183; plans for establishing bishops in America, 184; favor omnipotence of parliament, 185.

Annual Register, 7.

Army, supplies for, furnishes business for mercantile classes, 103; contracts for supplying, 107; attitude of country gentlemen toward, 132; regiments supported at private expense, 143; power in, 183.

Baker, candidate for parliament, 166.

Bank, Ayr, 68.

Bank of England, founding of, 67; stops discount business, 69; London merchants raise subscription for, 69.

Barré, Colonel Isaac, on apathy of country gentlemen, 141; speaks at Robinhood, 161; supports bill for closing port of Boston, 245.

Barrel staves, imported by West Indies, 24; rise in price of, imported into Great Britain from America, 39.

Beaver, imported from America, 23.

Beckford, William, London alderman, 165.

Beeswax, imported from America, 23.

Bentham, Jeremy, on utility of colonies, 278.

Bertie, Willoughby (fourth Earl of Abingdon), favors requisitions from colonies, 262.

Birmingham, manufacture of iron in, 22; unemployment in (1765), 37; emigration of laborers from, 37; employment in, after repeal of Stamp Act, 47; increase in business in, 63; decrease in business in, 77; merchants and manufacturers petition parliament, 85, 87; method of securing loyal petition in, 88; increase of exports from, 108; business boom in, with prospect of peace, 113.

Blankets, for American trade, 22; contracts for, for army, 107.

Boerhadem, on federation, 268.

Bollan, William, former agent for Massachusetts, 232.

shend Acts, 51; complaints of, by country gentlemen, 123-125; land tax as source of revenue, 124; poor rates and church tithes, 125; attitude of landowners toward American, 128; rising poor rates (1766), 129; reduction of land tax, 130; increase in land tax, 133.

Tea, tax on imports of, into colonies, 51; colonies refuse to import, 64; East India, Act, 73-74; tax on, retained (1770), 131; tax on, approved by imperialists, 202.

Test, drawn up by Supporters of Bill of Rights, 156; for London candidates for parliament, 166, 178; as a means of controlling parliament, 219.

Thrale, Henry, member of parliament from Southwark, 58.

Thurlow, Edward, attorney general, on parliamentary power over the colonies, 187.

Thynne, Thomas (third Viscount Weymouth), resigns office, 250.

Tobacco, imported from America, 19, 23; fluctuation in price of, 29; speculation in, during war, 106; subscribed by Maryland and Virginia to Wilkes' fund, 154.

Tooke, see Horne-Tooke.

Townshend, Charles, chancellor of the exchequer, proposes new plan to tax America, 51, 130; referred to by Burke, 132; on taxation, 199.

Townshend, London alderman, 165.

Townshend Acts, passage of, 51; colonists demand repeal of, 52; effects of, on merchants and manufacturers, 130-131; failure of, as revenue measure, repealed except tax on tea, 131.

Trade, balance of (1768), 53.

Trade, Board of, representations of, showing mercantile influence, 31;

opposes incorporation of Presbyterians in New York and college in North Carolina, 184; business of, 205 ff.; on parliamentary supremacy, 207.

Treaty of 1763, 32.

Trecothick, Barlow, London merchant, on use of credit, 29; chairman of merchants' committee (1765-1766), 41; sheriff of London, plans banquet to celebrate repeal of Stamp Act, 45; London alderman, 165; on the Townshend Acts, 222.

Trowbridge, petitions parliament, 87.

Tucker, Dean Josiah, on colonies as a disadvantage to Great Britain, 138, 276-278.

Turner, Sir Charles (M.P.), quoted, 175.

Unemployment, of cotton spinners, 2; following non-importation, 22; (1765-1766), 37, 129-130; (1774), 77; during the war, 96.

United States, trade with, 114; attitude of mercantilists toward peace with, 114-115; friendship of British merchants for, 116.

Universal Magazine, 5.

Virginia, subscribes to Wilkes' fund, 154.

Wakefield, sends address of thanks to Rockingham, 46.

Warburton, William, Bishop of Gloucester, 185.

Watson-Wentworth, Charles (second Marquis of Rockingham), prime minister, 39; retires from ministry, 46; received in York, 46; opposed to coercion, 192; policy of ministry of, 242; loses zeal, 246.

Wedderburn, Alexander, solicitor general, quoted, 187.